Revisiting India-East Asia Connections

Problems and Prospects

Revisiting India-East Asia Connections

Problems and Prospects

Edited by

SANDEEP KAUR

KNOWLEDGE WORLD

KW Publishers Pvt Ltd

New Delhi

ISBN 978-93-91490-43-0 Hardback
ISBN 978-93-91490-44-7 ebook

Published in India by Kalpana Shukla

KNOWLEDGE WORLD
KW Publishers Pvt Ltd
4676/21, First Floor, Ansari Road
Daryaganj, New Delhi 110002
Phone: +91 11 43528107
Marketing: kw@kwpub.in
Editorial: production@kwpub.in
Website: www.kwpub.in

Printed and Bound in India

Contents

PART II
Evaluating Role of China in India-East Asia Connections

PART III
Measuring Value Chain and Trade Relations in India-East Asia

PART IV
Building Economic Relations in India-East Asia

Foreword

India's economy has been getting integrated with the rest of the world especially since 1991. This integration has been almost entirely through trade in commodities, services, capital and in the movement of natural persons or migration. There is now a growing literature that has attempted to posit a positive correlation of sorts between this increased economic integration and the performance of the economy defined in terms of the increased rate of growth which for some time has broken the historical growth rate barrier of 3 per cent. Despite this, there are two aspects of India's trade that has come in for some discussion and debate. First is whether India has diversified her trade away from her conventional markets abroad read as developed countries and the second one is whether she has been able to change the composition of this trade away from low technology labour-intensive manufactured products and primary commodities to high technology and capital intensive manufactured products. One instrument which India has used in effecting perceptible changes in both the direction and composition of her especially exports is entering into Free Trade Agreements of various sorts with countries in the South East and East Asian regions as these countries have large and growing markets and some complementariness with India that increased integration with these countries is likely to change India's export composition to something more desirable and at the same time opens up the enormous possibility of India inserting herself into the growing global value chain for high technology and medium high technology products such as electronics and automotive products. With more than one-third of the world trade taking place through these global value chains, countries like India must have higher participation rates in GVCs than what was historically recorded. Despite all these policies of increasingly looking East for both markets and technology, India's exports of commodities, services, capital and movement of natural persons is increasing with the traditional markets in the developed world. At the very same time, the emergence of China as the world's factory and the increased technological capability of certain East Asian countries such as Korea and Taiwan, and entrepôt cities like Singapore has meant that India's trade with these countries too have shown a significant increase in more recent times. At the last count, India has signed 42 FTA's and some of the most comprehensive ones have been with that signed with the ASEAN group of countries. There is now a raging debate in the country about the beneficial effects of these agreements in improving our trade deficit in the current account of our Balance of Payments. Another aspect that has come in into discussion is the beneficial effects of our trade with China with constant complaints of cheap Chinese imports to the country, very often allegedly of the dumping variety decimating the country's already small manufacturing sector. This has frustrated even some of the more desirable policies such as our Make in India programme and making our country much more import-dependent on China. The case of mobile phone manufacturing is an important illustration of this line of thinking. Given the considerable opposing views on this subject, often coloured by ideological predilections, the reader in both the academic and policy communities deserve a collection of papers that seeks to unravel these contentious propositions on the positive or otherwise aspects of India's increased integration with South East and East Asian economies. In my considered view that search more or less ends with Sandeep Kaur's Revisiting India-East Asia Connections: Problems and Prospects. The 15 carefully selected papers divided into four sections takes the reader through an informed excursion of sorts that too most often through an unclouded pair of lenses. The papers are evidence-based and state-of-the-art analytical tools in some cases at least to arrive at meaningful conclusions. I have no hesitation in considering this compilation as an important contribution to three sets of economic literature: (i) impact of FTA's on India's trade performance; (ii) impact of India's insertion into GVCs on her trade performance; and (iii) impact of growing trade with China on India's economic performance. The potential reader is likely to profit immensely by dipping into the 15 chapters of this fine collection.

Sunil Mani, Ph.D
Director and RBI Professor
Centre for Development Studies
Trivandrum, Kerala
May 25, 2021

Acknowledgements

This volume carries the revised papers that were presented at an National Conference on "Revisiting India East Connections: Problems and Prospects" organised by me in the Department of Economic Studies, Central University of Punjab, Bathinda on March 7-8, 2019. This conference was organised with the objective of empowering policymakers and other stakeholders in India and East Asia on rethinking the connections between their regions that could bring enormous gains.

I am grateful to the Indian Council of World Affairs for providing the financial support to organise this conference. I would like to thank Hon'ble Vice-Chancellor Prof. Raghavendra P. Tiwari for his endless support for bringing out this volume and Ex-Vice Chancellor Prof. R.K. Kohli for cooperation in organising the conference. This conference could not possible without the guidance of esteemed dignitaries of Central University of Punjab including Prof. Ramakrishna Wusirika. Dean Academic Affairs, Prof. P. Rama Rao, Ex-Dean Incharge Academic, Prof. V.K. Garg, Dean Student Welfare, Prof. S.K. Bawa, Ex-Director, IQAC and Prof. Anjana Munshi, Dean Research.

I feel privileged to thank Prof. Lakhwinder Singh, for delivering the Keynote address and constant guiding and supporting for the conference and making the event successful. I also thank to Prof Raja Ram Panda, Lok Sabha for delivering the presidential address and Prof. D.K. Madaan for delivering the Valedictory address in the conference.

I would also like to record my thanks to all the participants at the conference for contributing to the conference. I would like to thank to my all students who make this event successful.

Dr. Sandeep Kaur
Associate Professor & HoD
Department of Economic Studies
School of Social Sciences, Central University of Punjab
Bathinda 151001

List of Abbreviations

ASEAN	Association of Southeast Asian Nations
AOA	Agreement of Agriculture
ACP	Africa, Caribbean, and Pacific
AIFTA	Asian-India Free Trade Area
AIA	ASEAN Investment Area
AIG	ASEAN Investment Guarantee
ASI	Annual Survey of Industries
ADF	Augmented Dickey-Fuller
AOA	Agreement of Agriculture
CBI	Confederation of British Industry
CCA	Commercial Cooperation Agreement
CCP	Common Commercial Policy
CEO	Chief Executive Officer
CIM	Minister of Commerce and Industry
CAGR	Compound Annual Growth Rate
CPI	Consumer Price Index
DIPP	Department of Industrial Policy and Promotion
DISP	Defence International Security Partnership
DVA	Domestic Value Added
EEA	European Economic Area
EEC	European Economic Community
EFD	Economic and Financial Dialogue
EEPIA	European Federation of Pharmaceuticals Industries and Association
EII	Export Intensity Index
FDI	Foreign Direct Investment

FII	Foreign Institutional Investment
FTA	Free Trade Agreement
FVA	Foreign Value Added
GVA	Gross Value Added
GVCs	Gross Value Chains
GATT	General Agreement on Tariffs and Trade
GDP	Gross Domestic Product
GOI	Government of India
GPA	Government Procurement Agreement
GSP	Generalised System of Preference
GST	Goods and Service Tax HDI Human Development Index
ICSSR	Indian Council of Social Science Research
III	Import Intensity Index IDI Import Dependency Index
IIT	Intra-Industry Trade
ILO	International Labour Organisation
IMF	International Monetary Fund
IMRB	Indian Market Research Bureau
IPR	Intellectual Property Rights
IT	Information Technology
IUKFP	India-UK Financial Partnership
JETCO	Joint Economic and Trade Committee
JAS	Japan Agricultural Cooperatives
KEI	Knowledge Economy Index
MOU	Memorandum of Understanding
MSR	Maritime Silk Route
MNEs	Multinational Enterprises
NASSCOM	National Association of Software and Services Companies
NAFTA	North American Free Trade Agreement
NCU	National Co-operative Unit
NEM	Non-Equity Mode

NSG	Nuclear Suppliers Group
NIC	National Industrial Classification
OECD	Organisation of Economic Co-operation and Development
OPEC	Organisation of Petroleum Export Countries
OFDI	Outward Foreign Direct Investment
OBOR	One Belt, One Road
PPP	Purchasing Power Parity
PTA	Preferential Trade Agreements
PWC	Price Waterhouse Coopers
PACs	Primary Agricultural Credit Societies
PCU	Prefectural Co-operative Units
PDC	Purely Double Counted
RCEP	Regional Comprehensive Partnership Agreement
RBI	Reserve Bank of India
RCA	Revealed Comparative Advantage
RCEP	Regional Comprehensive Economic Partnership
ROO	Rules of Origin
RoW	Rest of the world
RVA	Return Value Added
SAARC	South Asian Association for Regional Cooperation
SSA	Sub-Saharan Africa
SIA	Sustainability Impact Assessment
SMEs	Small and Medium Enterprises
SPS	Sanitary and Phyto-Sanitary
SREB	Silk Route Economic Belt
TBT	Technical Barriers to Trade
TC	Trade Creation
TCI	Trade Complementarily Index
TCS	Tata Consultancy Services
TII	Trade Intensity Index
TD	Trade Diversion
TPPA	Trans-Pacific Partnership Agreement

UKIBC	UK-India Business Council
UKIERI	United Kingdom India Education Research Initiative
UKTI	UK Trade and Investment
UNCTAD	United Nations Conference on Trade and Development
VIIT	Vertical Intra-Industry Trade
WEF	World Economic Forum
WITS	World Integrated Trade Solution
WTO	World Trade Organisation

About the Contributors

Prof. Rajaram Panda is Lok Sabha Research Fellow, Parliament of India, with tenure for two years. He is a thorough academic with rich experience in teaching, research and writing. Dr. Panda is a professional researcher, a prolific writer, commentator of international standing. An M. Phil and Ph.D from JNU in International Studies, some familiarity in Japanese, Dr. Panda has worked with some of the most influential organisations. He completed his stint as Senior Fellow with the Institute for Defense Studies and Analyses (IDSA), a think tank of the Govt. of India. Prior to this, he had a long stint with The Japan Foundation, Indian Council of World Affairs, ICSSR, Jawaharlal Nehru University etc. He also worked as a journalist with the Eenadu Group and headed the Foreign Affairs department of the group. Dr. Panda has received several honours and awards. He is a recipient of Orissa Govt. Merit Scholarship for Higher Studies, Japan Foundation President's Cool Effort Award, Asahi Shimbun Foundation Fellowship, South Korean Govt. Scholarship and The Japan Foundation Fellowship. He also held the ICCR India Chair Professor at Reitaku University, Japan, for two years (2016-2018). He has been invited to present papers, deliver lectures in various countries particularly in the Asia-Pacific region. He is recognised as an expert on Asia-Pacific Affairs. Apart from research and publications in print media he maintains a rich presence in the electronic media, the Web and participates in TV debates. His field of special interest is Japan and broadly on the Asia-Pacific region, security affairs, foreign policy and economic issues, with micro-focus on the East Asia. Dr. Panda is widely travelled: Japan (12 times), Australia (twice), New Zealand (once), Singapore (once), Sri Lanka (once), Bhutan (once),

France (once), Myanmar (once), South Korea (twice), the Philippines (once), Vietnam (five times), Brunei (once) and Brazil (once). He has authored two books (sole-authored), co-edited 6, over, 147 research papers in professional journals, contributed chapters to 21 books, and countless numbers of web commentaries and newspapers. Currently, Dr. Panda is the Executive member of the India Council of World Affairs, New Delhi.

Prof. Davinder Kumar Madaan is Professor of Economics & Head, School of Social Sciences, Punjabi University, Patiala, India. He has experience of more than 28 years in research/teaching, and 12 years in Academic Administration. He worked on various academic and administrative positions at Punjabi University, Lovely Professional University, Phagwara, Government of Madhya Pradesh, and Ministry of External Affairs' Project on 'South and Central Asia' at CRRID, Chandigarh. His area of research is International Economic relations, particularly South Asia; and development economics. His publications include 4 books and 90 research papers/ articles. He presented research papers in 108 International/National Conferences. Five Ph.D and 8 M.Phil students were awarded degrees under his guidance. He completed 3 research projects including The World Bank's minor project on "India and Her Neighbours", and The Asia Foundation's project on "Understanding Non-Tariff Trade Barriers between India and Pakistan". Currently, he is doing a major project on "Trade Relations among BIMSTEC Countries". He visited China, Indonesia, Thailand, Pakistan, Bangladesh, Nepal and Sri Lanka for academic purposes. He was elected as Secretary, Indian Economic Association (IEA) for the tenure 2017-20. He is also Honorary Secretary, Patiala Branch of the Indian Institute of Public Administration (IIPA) for the tenure 2015-19. He acted as Chairperson/Key Speaker/Rapporteur in many International/ National Conferences. He also served as EXPERT in Selection Committee/Ph.D.Viva-Voce/Paper Setting/Evaluation/Presentation in the leading universities of India and abroad.

Dr. Reena Marwah (M.Phil, Delhi University; Ph.D, Himachal University, India, International Business) is Associate Professor, Jesus and Mary College, Delhi University. She was an ICSSR Senior Fellow, MHRD, Govt. of India, affiliated with the Centre for the Study of Developing Societies, New Delhi from June 2017 to May, 2019, during which her study was on Reimagining India-Thailand Relations. She has also been on deputation as Senior Academic Consultant, ICSSR, Ministry of Human Resource Development, Govt. of India for three years (2012-2015) and continued, on behalf of ICSSR to coordinate/lead the India-Europe Research Platform (EqUIP) till July 2017. She is a permanent faculty member of Jesus and Mary College, Delhi University, India as Associate Professor and has been teaching Indian economy, macroeconomics and politics of globalisation. She is the recipient of several prestigious fellowships including the McNamara fellowship of the World Bank, 1999-2000 and the Asia fellowship of the Asian Scholarship Foundation 2002-03, during which she undertook research in Thailand and Nepal. She is also a Senior Fellow of the Institute of National Security Studies Sri Lanka (*INSSSL).* During her teaching and research experience, she has worked closely with several think tanks, international donors, embassies, ministries of the Government of India and research councils in Asia. Among her research interests are international relations issues of China, Philippines, Thailand and India, and development issues of gender, globalisation and poverty in South and South East Asia. In addition to several chapters and articles published in books/journals, she is co-author/co-editor of 15 books and monographs including Contemporary India: Economy, Society and Polity (Pinnacle 2009, 2011), co-edited volumes including Economic and Environmental Sustainability of the Asian Region (Routledge 2010), Emerging China: Prospects for partnership in Asia (Routledge 2011), On China by India: From a Civilisation to a Nation State (Cambria Press, USA); Transforming South Asia: Imperatives for Action, (Knowledge World, India) 2014; The Global Rise of Asian Transformation, (Palgrave Macmillan) 2014. Her latest authored books are: Reimagining India-Thailand Relations:

A Multilateral and Bilateral Perspective (2020) (World Scientific, Singapore) and China's Economic Footprint in South and Southeast Asia: A Futuristic Perspective (2021) (World Scientific, Singapore). She is the founding editor of Millennial Asia, a biannual journal on Asian Studies of the Association of Asia Scholars, published by Sage Publications.

Dr. Sunetra Ghatak is currently with the National Institute of Public Finance and Policy (NIPFP), New Delhi, India as a Research Fellow. Before that, she served at many leading think-tanks in Delhi, like Research and Information System for Developing Countries (RIS), National Centre for Agricultural Economics and Policy Research (NCAP), Institute for Studies in Industrial Development (ISID). She holds a Ph.D in Economics from Jawaharlal Nehru University, New Delhi. She is a Consultant at Baseline, West Bengal, an organisation that deals with social sector data and was Joint Editor of Centre for Development and Human Rights Bulletin of Centre for Development and Human Rights (CDHR), New Delhi. She has ten years of experience in the field of socio-economic and development research. She has contributed several research papers on development economics in various prominent national and international journals. Her specialisations include labour, health, gender and trade-related issues.

Prof. Ayub Mehar is 'Executive Director' of the Economic and Financial Policy Research Center in Iqra University Karachi (Pakistan). He has been serving as 'Economic Advisor' of the Economic Cooperation Organisation (ECO) Chamber of Commerce for 3 years and also 'Director General' in the Federation of Pakistan Chambers of Commerce and Industry (FPCCI) for 7 years. Development Financing, Macroeconomic Policies, International Trade and Finance are areas of his interest. He proactively completed several policy research studies on strategic issues including, 'Infrastructure Development by Liberalizing Economic Policies: The Straight Path of Economic Prosperity',

'Financial Cooperation in South Asia: Recent Development and Challenges', and 'FDI, Infrastructure Development and CPEC: Is There a Connection?' In recognition of his expertise, the Technology Policy and Assessment Center at Georgia Institute of Technology acknowledged his membership in the distinguished panel of international experts for Indicators of Technology-based Competitiveness, which is a project of the US National Science Foundation, United States Government.

Dr. Rajesh Kumar is an Associate Professor of Political Science and Head of the School of Social Sciences, Guru Nanak Dev University, Amritsar. He has done his M.A. & M.Phil. in Political Science from Guru Nanak Dev University, Amritsar. He was awarded his Doctoral Degree in International Relations, from School of International Studies, Jawahar Lal Nehru University, New Delhi, in the year 2000. He holds a teaching experience of 21 years and 6 months. He specialises in India's Foreign Policy, South Asian Politics and International Relations. He has published a number of articles on India's foreign relations, including "U.S. and South Asia in the New Millennium", *Pakistan Horizon*, Vol. 53, No. 1, January 2000, Karachi, Pakistan; "Indo-U.S. Nuclear Cooperation and Confrontation (1980-2005)" *Punjab Journal of Politics*, Vol. 29, No. 1, 2005; "Dynamics of Indo-U.S. Nuclear Deal and its Strategic Implications" *Punjab Journal of Politics*, Vol. 34, No. 1, 2010; Indo-U.S. Strategic Partnership on High trajectory", *World Focus*, Vol. 35, No. 12, 2014; "India and Climate Change: UN Framework", *World Focus*, Vol. 36, No. 10, 2015; "India China Relations: Avoiding Strategic Arms Race", *World Focus*, Vol. 38, No. 11, 2017. He is the author of the book "Indo-US Politico Strategic Relations", 2007. He has made contributions in edited volumes published by Palgrave, Macmillan, Singapore and B.E.P, New York. He has filled in chapters for many books on International relations and Foreign Policy of India. He has attended International Workshop on 'Defense Technology and Cooperative Security in South-Asia' (September 20-29, 1998, Shanghai, China), organised by the R.C.S.S., Colombo, Sri Lanka. He has also attended the Conference of the

Alumni of the RCSS Summer Workshop on 'South Asia Facing the New Millennium' (September 21-23, 1999) in Colombo, Sri Lanka. He has been a Life member of the Indian Political Science Association for over 17 years and a member of the International Political Science Association for about 2 years. He is a life member of NAPSIPAG, JNU, New Delhi.

Dr. Kulwinder Singh is an Assistant Professor at the University Business School of Panjab University, Chandigarh, India. His research areas are International Economics and Development Economics. Dr. Singh has about 15 papers published in renowned journals like *Foreign Trade Review*, *Economic and Political Weekly* (EPW) and *Indian Journal of Economics and Development*. He had attended several national and international conferences. He has successfully submitted a research project entitled 'Punjab State Electricity Consumer Survey' to Punjab State Electricity Regulatory Commission, Chandigarh. Moreover, he owns lifetime membership in the Indian Economic Association, Indian Accounting Association, Indian Society of Labour Economics and Society of Economics and Development.

Dr. Ajay Ranga is Associate Professor (Law) and Senator University Institute of Legal Studies (UILS), Panjab University, Chandigarh. He has about sixty-five research papers have been presented in different international, national and regional seminar/conference. He has been published thirty research papers in different research journals of national and international repute with high impact factor. One book *Crime Escalation and Slum Development* has been published with an International Publisher by him.

Dr. Rajiv Kumar is Assistant Professor at Smt. Aruna Asaf Ali Govt. PG. College Kalka, Panchkula Haryana. He has Teaching experience of more than 10 years. He has taught in Department of Evening studies - MDRC from 2011-17. His research area are Human

Resource Management, Banking & Finance and International Business Economics. Dr. Kumar has 17 Publications in various National and International journals, and books. He has presented more than 30 paper National and international seminars and conferences. Presently, Dr. Rajiv is working on the Research Orientations in Colleges of India and Branding of Human resources through educational institutions.

Dr. Surinder Kumar Singla is Assistant Professor & HOD in the Department of Economics at the DAV College, Bathinda (Punjab). He has more than ten years of teaching and research experience. He has to his credit more than two dozen of research papers published in various journals of national and international repute. He also authored two books. He has successfully completed one research project funded by the Indian Council of Social Science Research, New Delhi. He has supervised two Ph.D and eight M.Phil students. Moreover, he is a lifetime member of the Indian Economic Association.

Dr. Shubham Karmakar is a Ph.D scholar at the School of International Studies, University of Trento (Italy). He holds MAs in Chinese from Jawaharlal Nehru University (India) and in Applied Linguistics from the University of Limerick (Ireland) funded by Government of Ireland Scholarship. He also has a Postgraduate Diploma in Sino-American Relations from Johns Hopkins University (Nanjing campus) jointly funded by JHU and NJCG scholarships. He has received awards such as the 'Young Sinologist' award from China's Ministry of Tourism and Culture (2019) and a Junior Research Fellowship (India). Dr. Shubham worked as an Assistant Professor at the Department of Chinese Studies at Doon University, teaching BA and MA courses on Chinese language and culture. He has also taught Chinese at Marry Immaculate College (Ireland). He has published articles and book chapters on topics ranging from Applied Linguistics to International Relations. His current research focuses on China's soft power, foreign policy and media discourse.

Dr. Sandeep Kaur is Associate Professor and Head in the Department of Economic Studies at the Central University of Punjab, Bathinda, India. She owns eclectic research and teaching experience essentially in the fields of International Economics, Environmental Degradation, and Political Economy. Dr. Kaur has about 30 papers published in renowned journals both at the national and international levels. Besides this she is a real cosmopolitan: she got Indo-Canadian Shastri Travel Grant, 2012 and attended many international conferences at Denmark, Canada, and Bangladesh. She successfully completed about four research projects on current emerging issues on thermal power generation, tourism services, regional trade blocks and land acquisition for developmental projects. Moreover, she owns lifetime membership in the Indian Association for Research in National Income and Wealth.

Manpreet Kaur is a research scholar, pursuing Ph.D from the Central University of Punjab, Bathinda India.

Harpreet Singh is an Assistant Professor in Guru Kashi College, Punjabi University Patiala, India. He is pursuing Ph.D from Guru Nanak Dev University Amritsar, India. His research interests include the rural economy and innovation.

Manpreet Singh is working as Lecturer of Economics at Kendriya Vidyalaya No. 1, Srinagar, J&K. His research interests are in the areas of International Economics, Money and Banking, and Agriculture Economics. He has three years of teaching and research experience. He pursuing his Ph.D from Punjab School of Economics, Guru Nanak Dev University, Amritsar. He has presented 10 research papers in various National level conferences/Seminars and 4 papers published (2 in journals and 2 in edited books).

Prof. Paramjit Nanda is working as Professor in the Punjab School of Economics at Guru Nanak Dev University, Amritsar. She is former head of the Punjab School of Economics. Her research interests are in the areas of International Economics, Money and Banking. She has 36 years of teaching and research experience. She has authored about 90 research papers, which has been published in books and journals of national and international repute. She has authored two books and completed two research projects. She has participated and presented the papers in about 100 national/international conferences/seminars. She has guided about 50 M.Sc./M.B.E. students for research projects and eight students for Ph.D. She is a life member of about ten academic associations relating to economics, labour, agriculture, political, regional development and international trade etc. She was awarded many times by Rotary Club, Amritsar for her excellence in teaching and research.

Divya Vaid is Ph.D Research Scholar in the Department of Economics, Panjab University, Chandigarh. Her research interests are in the areas of International Trade and Banking. She has three and half years of teaching experience. She pursued her B.A., M.A. Eco. from GNDU affiliated college and M.Phil. (Eco.) from Department of Economics, Panjab University, Chandigarh. She has published research papers in an international journal. Currently, she is working as an assistant professor economics at Chandigarh University Mohali.

Dr. Meenu is working as an Assistant Professor in the Department of Economics, Panjab University, Chandigarh. Her research interests are in the areas of International Trade, Environment Economics and economic development. She has been teaching since 2007 and her specialisation includes Quantitative Techniques, Indian Economy and Environment Economics. She pursued her B.Sc. (Hons.) Economics, M.Sc. (Hons.) Economics and Ph.D (Eco.) from Punjab School of Economics, Guru Nanak Dev University, Amritsar. She has published research papers in journals/chapters in a book of national and international repute and a book. She has supervised 03 M.Phil. students and presently, she is supervising four Ph.D students of Panjab University.

Dr. Vishal Sarin has obtained Ph.D degree in economics from Punjabi University, Patiala, Punjab, India. Currently working as a Professor in the Department of Economics at Mittal School of Business (ACBSP accreditation by the USA, and the 2nd ranked in the Management field in India) with Lovely Professional University (LPU) since September 2007. He has published more than 20 research papers in coveted journals including ABDC Ranking and SCOPUS listed journals, presented papers in 20 conferences, published 4 books, resource person in 8 FDPs on data analysis and research methodology. His area of specialisation includes Trade Specialisation and Competitiveness, Trade Analytics, Trade and Financial Integration. Dr. Sarin is also holding one copyright on 'Talent Management Index'. Dr. Sarin is a part of EGEA Green Economy Project co-funded by ERASMUS+ Programme of the European Union.

Dr. Naveen Sood is an Associate Professor in the Post Graduation Department of Economics at DAV College Jalandhar, Punjab. Prof Sood has about 26 papers published in renowned journals both at the national and international levels. Besides this, he has presented about 34 research papers in international and national conferences/seminars. He has also been appointed by the Punjab Public Service Commission, Patiala as evaluator of the Punjab Civil Services Examinations. He also owns a lifetime membership of the Indian Economic Association. Presently, he is pursuing his Ph.D from Lovely Professional University, Phagwara. Moreover, he has also attended 12 workshops/FDP.

Dr. Kuldeep Singh is working as an Assistant Professor in the Department of Post Graduate Studies, Panjabi University Regional Centre, Bathinda. His research interests are in the areas of Economics of growth and development, Agriculture economics and international economics. He has eight plus years of regular teaching experience. His specialisation includes Economics of growth and development, Public Economics and Quantitative Methods. He pursued his B.Sc. (Hons.) Eco., M.Sc. (Hons.) Eco. and Ph.D (Eco.) from Punjab School of

Economics, Guru Nanak Dev University, Amritsar. He has published research papers in journals of national and international repute. Presently, He is supervising four Ph.D students of Punjabi University Patiala.

Jaskiran Kaur is a Junior Research Fellow in the Department of Post Graduate Studies, Punjabi University Regional Centre, Bathinda. Her research interest is in the field of Development Economics and International Economics. She pursued her B.Sc. (Hons.) Economics from Punjabi University Patiala, M.Sc. (Hons.) Economics from Guru Nanak Dev University and is now pursuing Ph.D from Punjabi University Patiala.

Dr. Baldev Singh Shergill teaches Economics to undergraduate students at Punjabi University Guru Kashi College in Talwandi Sabo, Punjab. His research interests include rural studies, microeconomic field work based studies, knowledge economy and development economics related issues and livelihood issues of the poor and vulnerable of the region where he lives. He has published research papers and articles in reputed academic journals and edited books.

Swarnjeet Kaur is a research scholar, pursuing Ph.D from Guru Nanak Dev University Amritsar, India.

Dr. Swati Mehta is an Assistant Professor in the Punjab School of Economics at the Guru Nanak Dev University, Amritsar, India. Her area of research includes economics of innovation and technical change, technology spillover, economic development and the Indian manufacturing sector. Dr. Mehta has published papers in renowned journals both at national and international levels. She has also presented her research work in many conferences in India and abroad.

Dr. Suresh Kumar is an Associate Professor in the Post Graduate Department of Economics at Doaba College, Jalandhar. He is having twenty three years of research and teaching experience in the field of Banking, International Economics and Development Economics. He has about twenty research papers published in various renowned journals at the national and international levels. He has also successfully completed a 'UGC-Sponsored' Minor research Project on the title "Consolidation in the Indian Banking Industry through Mergers and Acquisitions: Issues and Evidences: Post-Reform Scenario". He has also attended about fifteen workshops/Faculty Development Programmes/ Refresher Courses in the field of Economics and Econometrics.

List of Tables and Figures

TABLES

Figures

Inaugural Remarks

Rajaram Panda

It gives me immense pleasure to make some inaugural remarks on the occasion of the National Conference titled "Revisiting India-East Asia Connections" "Problems and Prospects" organised by the Department of Economics, Central University of Punjab, Bathinda. In particular, I wish to express my thanks to Dr. Sandeep Kaur to reach out to me to share some of my thoughts on this very important aspect of India's increasing engagement with the larger Asia.

Having been researching on the various dimensions of India's engagements with South East and East Asia or what is being described in academic parlance the Indo-Pacific region for over four decades and having acquired some familiarity with the past and the present, I would like to make some observations on broadly three dimensions: Cultural and civilisational, political and economic, and defence and security/ strategic vis-à-vis the region.

First, cultural and civilisation: India's present engagement with the countries in the region is not recent. It goes back to centuries. The spiritual connect through Buddhism that spread throughout the region found greater acceptance. At the same time, trade and commerce flourished when Indian traders and merchants travelled on long voyages to countries such as Indonesia, Malaysia, Thailand, the Indo-China states of Vietnam, Laos and Cambodia and others, carrying with them spices and other materials and bringing back with them products from the region on return. These traders carried with them Buddhist monks who prayed for their safety and also took along India's spiritual tradition with them to the countries they travelled. Unlike the European powers who too engaged with trade and commerce with the countries of the region but had the hidden agenda of domination and colonisation, Indian traders many of whom decided to settle there were assimilated themselves with the local regional culture and with the people and became a part of them. One can find many Hindu and Buddhist temples even today in many of the countries in the region, which explains the rich historical tradition India has with the region. For example, one can see the remnants of Hindu and Buddhist relics in the Cham region in Vietnam and similar things in other Southeast Asian countries. Another example is the Boita Bandana on the Kartik Purnima day is celebrated every year in Odisha signifying the sea voyages of merchants from the state and praying for their safe journey. The Bali Jatra in Indonesia is equally popular. Similar examples are aplenty. This historical and civilisational connect is immensely contributing to the present day relationships of India with the region.

Second, political and economic: In view of the deep understanding between India and the countries in the region at the political level, and because of mutual trust, India has shared common viewpoints with all the countries in the region though some of the countries in the region have different forms of government. There are high level political visits on a regular basis which have contributed to deepen mutual trust and understanding. At the economic level, since India abandoned the centrally planned economy and import substitution economic policy approach and opted for market economy with a focus on export-oriented growth after the liberalisation policy in the early 1990s, the complementarities between the economies have created a win-win situation for both sides. The earlier Look East Policy gave way to Act East Policy, implying thereby that India wanted to give a greater thrust to its foreign economic policy with a view to integrate with the economies of the region and the world. This was initially done by signing several Free Trade Agreements. Some of these have not worked to India's interests and India is thinking to review and renegotiate some of them. It was in view of this, India opted out of the mega trade pact, the Regional Comprehensive Economic Pact (RCEP). The crucial consideration is that India's trade deficit with 11 of the 15 RCEP nations has ballooned to some $105 billion, with China alone accounting for some $54 billion. The Modi government is strategizing to protect the domestic industries and wants to negotiate greater market access to the RCEP countries on a reciprocal basis. The option is not closed but remains open, though China is eyeing on the big Indian market where it can dump its products. As it transpires, RCEP minus India is going to remain a lame duck pact. Notwithstanding this, India shall continue to engage with the individual countries of the RCEP grouping on a bilateral basis and wait till its concerns are addressed before it takes a decision on the RCEP.

Third, Security/Strategic: This third dimension is critical to not only India and the region but has greater salience beyond the Indo-Pacific region. China's aggressive posture and expansionist behaviour is a matter of concern to the smaller countries of the region. It has territorial disputes with several countries, including with India. Its military modernisation continues to surge. The South China Sea is the latest flashpoint. Believed to be endowed with rich resources, China claims more than 90 per cent of this oceanic space, disregarding the claims by some other countries of the ASEAN bloc. Vietnam, Brunei, Taiwan, the Philippines, Malaysia, etc have claims to the areas of the South China Sea which fall in their exclusive economic zones. Vietnam has taken a tough stance to fight with China if the former's advance is seen as detrimental to its national interests. Vietnam has a reliable friend in India and invited India's ONGC to be involved in drilling oil in the areas it claims its own.

The Philippines went to the International Court at The Hague for arbitration and obtained a verdict in June 2016 in its favour. The court said China's historical claims were invalid. China disdainfully rejected the court's ruling knowing well that the court lacked enforcing authority to its ruling. Since then, China has been trying to break Asean unity by enticing the Philippines and negotiating bilaterally. Therefore, if India's economic interests are affected by any Chinese action, the Indian Navy shall have the legitimate reason to intervene to protect India's national interest.

The presence of the Indian Navy in the Indian Ocean is crucial for maintaining order. What India, Vietnam and other ASEAN members want is to conduct trade in accordance with rules-based order, freedom of navigation and overflight and in accordance with the UN Law of the Sea, all of which China seems determined to violate with impunity. The strategic importance of the South China Sea is so huge that the economic interests of several countries shall be adversely affected as trillions of dollars worth of cargo transit through this strategic oceanic space. If any single nation tries to take control of this global common, there shall be always a situation where there shall be scope for conflict. Maintaining order in sea, therefore, is of extreme importance. India has greater strategic convergence of interests with most of the countries in the region. There are several other considerations as well.

These are some of the points I flagged which the day-long conference shall deliberate. I am sure the deliberations shall be useful and the recommendations that come out of the conference shall be of use to the policy makers and other stakeholders.

Valedictory Address

Davinder Kumar Madaan

The theme chosen for this Conference i.e. *Revisiting India-East Asia Connections: Problems and Prospects* is very important in the present scenario. East Asia is the eastern sub-region of Asia,includes China, Hong Kong, Macau, Taiwan, Japan, Mongolia, North Korea, and South Korea. East Asia has a significant share in the world output and trade. East Asians comprise around 1.6 billion people, making up about 22 per cent of the global population and 24 per cent of the global GDP. The East Asia Summit (EAS), established on 14 December 2005, has 18 member countries from East Asian, Southeast Asian, and South Asian regions, based on the ASEAN (Association of South-East Asian Nations) Plus 8 mechanism including Australia, China, India, Japan, New Zealand, South Korea, USA and Russia.

Here, it is important to know about ASEAN. ASEAN was established on 8th August 1967 with the signing of the Bangkok Declaration by five member countries, namely, Indonesia, Malaysia, Philippines, Singapore, and Thailand. Five more members joined it later, namely, Brunei Darussalam (January 1984), Viet Nam (July 1995), Laos, PDR (July 1997), Myanmar (July 1997), and Cambodia (April 1999). They constitute 8.6 per cent of the world population, 3.4 per cent of world GDP, 6.9 per cent of world trade and 3 per cent of world area during 2017. Their per capita income was US$ 4274 in 2017. ASEAN Free Trade Area (AFTA) became fully operational w.e.f. 1st January 2010 among the ASEAN-6 original members. The ASEAN-10 proposed to establish ASEAN Economic Community by 2025.

In 2017, the USA was the single largest economy in the world, accounting for 24 per cent of world GDP/Production and 11.7 per cent of world trade with only 4.3 per cent of the world population. Its per capita income was US$ 58270 during this period. After USA, China was the 2nd largest economy in the world in terms of GDP. Its per capita income was US$ 8690 during 2017 as compared to US$ 350 in 1991. China accounted for 18.4 per cent of the world population and 12.1 per cent in the world trade with 15.2 per cent of world GDP. Japan follows with 6 per cent of world GDP and 4 per cent of world trade with only 1.7 per cent of the world population with its per capita income as US$ 38,550 in 2017.

India is a lower middle income economy of the world with a per capita income of US$ 1800 only in 2017. It accounted for 17.8 per cent (1.32 bn) of the world population (7.44 bn) and 3.2 per cent of the world GDP during 2017. Its share in world trade was 2.1 per cent during this period. India was the 6th largest economy of the world in terms of the size of GDP (US$ 2600 bn) during 2017 after Germany and UK. The per capita, GNI of India was US$ 350 in 1991. In the past, the Indian economy grew at 0.8 per cent during 1900-1950, 3.5 per cent during 1950-80, and 5.6 per cent during 1981-90 (World Bank). India adopted economic reforms consisting of liberalisation, privatisation and globalisation in July 1991. As a result, the economic growth rate increased appreciably. Presently, India is the fastest growing major economy in the world with an annual average GDP growth during 2014-19 higher than the growth achieved since economic reforms began in 1991. Indian economy is estimated to achieve a growth of 7.2 per cent in 2017-18. The overall average annual growth rate of India (real GDP at 2004-05 prices) was 6.6 per cent during 1991-2017. India is emerging as an important player in the world economy as reflected in World Bank's Ease of Doing Business 2019 Report, which improves India's ranking 77th as compared to 142 in 2015.

The North East India comprises the eight states of Arunachal Pradesh, Assam, Manipur, Meghalaya, Mizoram, Nagaland, Tripura and Sikkim. It has 1643 km the long international border with Myanmar, a member of ASEAN countries, in the East. This makes the North-East a prospective hub of international trade and commerce with ASEAN.

The North-East India is often described as the Gateway to South-East Asia.

The North East India is mostly hilly; it has plains on both sides of the river Brahmaputra and the Himalayan range around it. It is endowed with forest wealth, and ideally suited to produce a whole range of plantation crops, spices, fruits and vegetables and flowers and herbs. It managed to achieve this distinction of emerging as a hub of organic spices, particularly ginger and turmeric cultivation in Meghalaya and Manipur; and black pepper in Arunachal Pradesh. Further, 9 per cent of the country's rubber production comes from this region. 5,000-10,000 tonnes of coffee are produced in the North-East, largely in Mizoram and Nagaland. 55 per cent of the country's tea production is in this region. The four Agri Export Zones in the region are pineapples (Tripura), ginger (Sikkim), orchids and cherry pepper (Sikkim) and fresh and processed ginger (Assam).

Assam provides huge potential in sectors like hydrocarbons, oil and natural gas, limestone, bamboo, handicrafts and tea. Assam tea is well known for its distinctive quality. Manipur has huge potential in sectors like power, agro-based industries, etc. IT and ITES, agro processing, floriculture and bamboo are some areas that offer huge opportunities to investors in Mizoram. The state also grows fine quality of grapes, which can be utilised for large-scale wine production. *The North-East surely is a region waiting to happen.*

Despite these great advantages, the North-East has not grown at par with the rest of the country, and the region's potential has not been tapped properly. *With necessary infrastructure development within the region, and the building of connecting links between North-East India, and South-East Asia, the economic potential of the region can be suitably exploited.*

India has been actively engaged with the regional groupings of the developing countries like ASEAN, Bay of Bengal Initiative for Multi-Sectoral, Technical and Economic Cooperation (BIMSTEC), etc. as a part of her 'Act East Policy'. The ASEAN-10, established on 8th August 1967 was meant to accelerate the economic progress of the South-East Asian region. The important milestone between India and ASEAN was achieved on 13th August 2009, when ASEAN-India Free Trade

Agreement (AIFTA) was signed. India-ASEAN trade and investment relations have been growing steadily, with ASEAN being India's fourth largest trading partner. India's trade with ASEAN has increased to US$ 70 billion (Exports: 30 bn) in 2016-17. FDI inflows into India from ASEAN between April 2000 to May 2016 was about US$ 49.40 billion, while FDI outflows from India to ASEAN countries, from April 2007 to March 2015, as per data maintained by DEA, was about US$ 38.672 billion. The ASEAN-India Agreement on Trade in Service and Investments was enforced on 1 July 2015.

On the other hand, BIMSTEC-7 including India was formed on 6th June 1997 in Bangkok after initiation on the process of sub-regional cooperation among South and South East Asian nations. BIMSTEC constitutes a bridge between South and South East Asia around the Bay of Bengal. All small neighbouring countries are purely guided by economic interests rather than by political interests under BIMSTEC. The BIMSTEC Free Trade Area Framework Agreement (FTA) was signed in 2004 by member countries. The huge complementarity arising out of India's Act East Policy, give rise to immense opportunities for India and BIMSTEC countries to develop their trade and investment relations, using the North-East as a primary focal point. India wants the BIMSTEC FTA should be done quickly, especially when the SAARC is in stagnation due to Pakistan's political interests, and BIMSTEC is minus Pakistan.

India currently is working with ASEAN on multiple connectivity projects, through land, water, and air.

Land connectivity between ASEAN and India is through India-*Myanmar-Thailand Trilateral Highway*. It *connects from Moreh in India to Mae Sot in Thailand*. In 2012, it was decided to further extend the Trilateral Highway to Cambodia and Vietnam. But over the years, this initiative has stalled due to the lack of institutional and financial support from all three countries. However, the India, Myanmar, and Thailand Motor Vehicles Agreement (IMT MVA) is in the final stage. On realisation, this will become the first-ever cross border facilitation agreement between South and Southeast Asia, thus allowing free movement of cargo, passenger, and personal vehicles along the roads linking these three countries.

Railway link between New Delhi to Hanoi (Vietnam) is under consideration. Further, Mekong-India Economic Corridor (MIEC) involves the integration of four Mekong countries – Vietnam, Myanmar, Thailand, and Cambodia, for connecting Ho Chi Minh City, Dawei, Bangkok, and Phnom Penh with Chennai (South and Southeast Asia).

Water connectivity between ASEAN and India has been initiated through the Kaladan Multi-Modal Transit Transport Project (KMMTTP), funded by the Indian government in 2008. The KMMTTP connects Kolkata to Sittwe (Myanmar) by sea and Paletwa (Myanmar) by the river. A road is also planned to connect Paletwa to Zorinpui on the India-Myanmar border, which is behind schedule. The major part of this initiative has been constructed but currently. *ASEAN and India are exploring the signing of an ASEAN-India Maritime Transport Cooperation Agreement.* Since ports and waterways are responsible for the flow of the merchandise trade between ASEAN and India, investment in quality infrastructure is essential for better connectivity, trade growth, and maximum utility of resources. *The Introduction of the "Sagar Mala" project by Prime Minister Narendra Modi, whereby India plans to invest in port infrastructure for improved integration and connectivity through the sea, is an encouraging step in this direction.*

For Air connectivity, some ASEAN countries have direct flights to India, but there is sufficient scope for improvement. India in the past has announced a Line of Credit of $1 billion to encourage such connectivity projects between India and ASEAN.

Summing Up

With the uncertain environment in the West, many Asian countries are realizing the importance of connecting with each other as their combined market size is half of that of the world. Proposed Regional Comprehensive Economic Partnership (RCEP), a pact between the ASEAN (including Thailand), India, China, Japan, Australia and New Zealand, which is expected to be signed in the near future. The RCEP is viewed as an alternative to the Trans-Pacific Partnership (TPP), a proposed trade agreement that includes several Asian and American nations but excludes China and India. Therefore, the role of East Asia, ASEAN and BIMSTEC are very much important for building broader economic cooperation. The complementarities between Asian countries are obvious from the fact that the share of intra-regional trade was more than half of their global trade. Studies have shown that broader regional integration in Asia has the potential of generating billions of dollars of new output and put Asia on the fastest growth path.

Exploring opportunities through connectivity projects will not only check existing insurgencies, but also help India's northeastern states to develop their economic potential and integrate with mainland India. India needs to pursue its "Act East" Policy, and continue its efforts to engage with ASEAN and BIMSTEC through the gateway of North-East.

I hope the present conference would be suggesting some follow-up actions to be taken by the government for Regional Connectivity, Trade and Growth of India and East Asia.

Thank you.

Introduction

Sandeep Kaur

Two key pillars of India's present foreign policy i.e. 'Neighbourhood First' and 'Act East' have strong geo-strategic and geo-economic relevance in the modern capitalism. 'Act East Policy' initiated in 1992 under the umbrella of 'Look East Policy' was merely an economic agenda earlier, but later on it has gained in terms of political, strategic and cultural ties. The Indian government has launched 'Act East Policy' in 2014 with the inclusion of other Indo-Pacific countries, which have strong strategic and economic relevance. No doubt, the policy has raised tremendous opportunities as connections of India with East Asia lie in trade, transport, digital and people-to-people, which are yet to be explored. 'Act East Policy' has been focussing on the extended neighbourhood in the Asia-Pacific region. India's neighbourhood approach is a crucial factor in the Act East policy, which will help to reshape the connections with various countries of Asia.

China, one of the strong nation in East Asia is playing a major role with other countries through investment and openness, On the other side USA is withdrawing itself from globalisation. Both are major trade partners of India. So, the policy can be used as balancing the power of China. This policy's objective is also to counter the growing Chinese influence in the Northeast region for the successful implementation of the policy. This policy would also eventually provide enhanced connectivity to the states of the North Eastern region. To create connectivity for trading corridors with Myanmar and Thailand, India has initiated many connectivity projects like the Trilateral Highway Project with Myanmar and Thailand, the Kaladan Project with Myanmar, and the development of the Sittwe port in Myanmar, etc. These will have a direct impact on the development of India's North-Eastern states. So the present theme is required to rebuild and rethink in the prospects of building connections of India with Asia in new directions.

Many infrastructure projects like Sagarmala Project, China- Pakistan Economic Corridor, Belt and Road Initiative, Lalkadan Multi-Modal Project and many more can also build connections. India has lack of infrastructure investment to build these connections. In this regard, what role various Asian giants in building infrastructure connections can play? is required to understand.

The breakdown of the EU and USA's move towards protectionism has made many countries to realise the fact that there is a need to strengthen the economic and political relations with other economies as well. ASEAN's role in regional integration cannot be denied, which can be a successful example for revisiting SAARC and Bay of Bengal Initiative for Multi-Sectoral Technical and Economic Cooperation (BIMSTEC) for India. Also, Bangladesh, Bhutan, India and Nepal (BBIN) initiative, which signed a historic Motor Vehicle Agreement (MVA) in 2015, is another connection for regional integration. Rejuvenation of these various initiatives through 'East Asia Policy' is another approach for using connections effectively.

India's trade to GDP ratio is nearly 25 per cent. But in terms of merchandise trade, it is just 1.7 per cent of global merchandise exports. Due to relatively less competitiveness in the manufacturing sector, Indian merchandise exports are not enough as compared with other Asian giants. India has already made free trade agreements with ASEAN, Japan and Korea. India's trade with Asian countries is more than 50 per cent (IBEF, 2013). Trade agreements usually affect goods not services. On the other side, Global Value Chain (GVC) is an important aspect in the present globalised era. It provides opportunities for industrial upgrading. As the name implies it shows and explains "exports of goods and services are incorporated imported inputs and included foreign and domestically produced value added in this global chain". According to UNCTAD (2013), East and South East Asian countries are at the top position in the list of GVC participation. In this regard, trade connectivity in various emerging aspects of globalisation can be explored through this policy.

To make a contribution in the pool of mounting discourse on the matter, a conference on *Revisiting India-East Asia Connections: Problems and Prospects sponsored by the Indian council of world affairs has been organised on 7-8 March, 2019 in the Central University of Punjab, Bathinda.* The conference's main endeavour is to reinvigorate the geostrategic and geo-economic connections of India with Asia so that the 'Act East Policy' would be worked out effectively. The conference has invited papers on the main theme of '*Revisiting India-East Asia Connections: Problems and Prospects*' from across the world So, this edited book is the collection of the selected papers presented in this conference and aims to explain these various connections, by collecting the most recent theoretical and empirical research on the problems and prospects of India- East Asia relations. It covers a number of important aspects that advance theoretical and empirical research on this issue and provides policy makers with valuable insights about how important connections could be encouraged in India- East Asia. The book is divided into the following four parts:

Part I: Building Diaspora and Infrastructure and Connections in India-East Asia Relations

Part II: Evaluating Role of China in India-East Asia Connections

Part III: Measuring Trade and Value Chain Relations in India-East Asia

Part IV Building Economic Relations in India-East Asia

Each part is further divided into various chapters. The first part comprises of three chapters under its theme. The first chapter entitled *Indian Diaspora in Thailand: Cementing Historical and Cultural Relations* written by *Reena Marwah* explains the historical, cultural and religious ties of the Indians with the Thai and explains that Indians in Thailand, have faced fewer problems in Thailand as compared to other countries. It is well known that Thailand, also known as *Suvarnabhumi* has been at the centre of Southeast Asia. Its geographical proximity to India as well as the historical connection through the seas, made the country a centre for trade and commerce. The rivers on its east and west encouraged settlements of people and ethnic groups who moved around making contact with others. When Indian traders brought goods, they met the local rulers and pleased them with gifts and souvenirs. This resulted in the rulers becoming interested in Indian culture. Later, Brahmans were also invited from India. Their ideas, customs and rituals also influenced the local people. Indians in Thailand are now into the fourth generation and well-integrated in Thai society. The paper delineates the historical, cultural and religious ties of the Indian community with the Thai people and articulates possibilities for further deepening relations between our two countries.

The paper has also tried to explain the connections of India with Thailand through the occupation of Indians in Thailand including Sikh, Tamil and Hindu-Nepalese-Burmese people. The paper has also touched the preservance of Indian culture in Thailand with the explanation of constructed temples. The paper has well described the connections of the Indian diaspora in Thailand while stating, "Indians in Thailand are rich in religious, economic and social capital and this can serve as a role model and example of a successful diaspora in Thailand." It further suggests that the Indian communities in Thailand can be helpful in building connections with both countries.

The second chapter in this part entitled *India's Coverage on Connectivity Corridor with Southeast Asia* written by *Sunetra Ghatak* reviews the various transport corridors connecting India with South East Asian countries. The paper has tried to find out the impact of these corridors on the future growth of India with the help of a panel regression model. By taking the data of Trilateral Highway (TH), Kaladan Multi-modal Transit Transport Corridor (KMTTC), and Bangladesh–China–India–Myanmar Economic Corridor (BCIM-EC), and Mekong India Economic Corridor (MIEC) for the period of 2010-2017, the study finds that GDP and the freight of the regions having a corridor are positively related and the positive and significant relationship between road density and the freight. The study suggests that the countries connecting with the Trilateral Highway perform better than the countries not having that particular corridor. The results of Kaladan corridor and BCIM-

EC explains that the growth of freight is considerably higher across the countries compared to the corridor connecting countries, so may not perform as such. The third chapter entitled *Trans Asia Connectivity and Economic Corridors: Sustainable Financing for Economic Development* written by *Ayub Mehar* is based on the idea financing the corridors (and other infrastructure development) through long-term debt financing affects the economy negatively. It identifies the feasible modes of financing for the construction of economic corridors to connect the Asian economies by explaining the need for economic integration among Asian economies. In the light of explaining the connections through corridors, the study correlates the economic integration and macro financing activities with the economic welfare of the people in the participating countries. The study suggests that construction of economic corridors can establish the economic linkages if participating countries consider the formation of a fiscal union.

The second part entitled *Evaluating Role of China in India-East Asia Connections* is divided into four chapters. Fourth chapter entitled *India-China Maritime Cooperation: Avoiding Nuclear Rivalries* written by *Rajesh Kumar looks at India-China maritime cooperation in the 21st century. It analyses the challenges and prospects of their maritime cooperation/ competition assuming nuclear dimensions.* While explaining India's Maritime Diplomatic Activities in recent years, the article explains that the Indian Ocean remains as core of India's maritime diplomacy. It also provides insight on India- China- U.S.A. Stand-Off in the South China Sea (SCS) and East China Sea (ECS) Region and China's Belt Road Initiative (BRI)/One Belt One Road-OBOR. The article expresses that China does not want to engage in any nuclear dialogue with India as it might consider that India as a nuclear power. Thus it attempts to revisit the policy related to India- China maritime cooperation for making the India- East Asia Connections effectively.

The next chapter entitled *Sources of China's Export Growth: A Constant Market Share Analysis* is written by *Kulwinder Singh, Ajay Ranga & Rajiv Kumar* focuses on the sources of China's export growth for the period of 1984 to 2014 using the Constant Market Share (CMS) Model.

The study finds the two main factors i.e. competitiveness of Chinese exports growth and expansion of world demand are the main sources of China's export growth Model. Certain important facts of China's exports i.e. witnessing of the highest export growth rate during the period 2002-2007 due to the accession of WTO, shifting of commodity composition towards manufactured exports and increasing of exports in the relative contribution of developing countries have been explained by the chapter. It suggests that India should learn from the Chinese experiences and thus, makes an important contribution in Revisiting India- East Asia connections.

The next chapter entitled *An Analysis of India's Exports Instability to China* written by *Surinder Kumar Singla* explains the trade connections of India with the strongest economy of East Asia i.e. China well through the measurement of instability index of India's Exports with China. The growth and composition of Indian exports to China and the stabilisation effect of the Chinese market on India's export earnings has been analysed for the period of 1990-1991 to 2015-16. The study finds that Indian imports from China have grown faster than exports, resulted in a widening trade deficit of India. Using Coppock's instability indices, the study explains that Indian exports to China also remained more in stable than imports. The study explains the trade connections of India with the strongest economy of East Asia i.e. China well through the measurement of the instability index of India's Exports with China. The study suggests that there is a need to understand the demand and supply aspects of the commodities exported to China and try to explore the possibilities of shifting the exports from higher instable commodities and markets to lower ones.

The next chapter in this part entitled *An Analysis of Chinese Perspectives on Indian "Look East Policy"* written by *Shubham Karmakar*. speaks the current dynamics of Chinese perspectives on India's new "Look East Policy". The paper speaks that China faces a crucial period for the great rejuvenation of the Chinese nation. Properly handling the relationship between regional organisations and regional powers can contribute to the realisation of world regional cooperation and the writing of corresponding international rules. In the new stage, India's interest demands are no longer limited to economic and trade fields, and demand in the political and security fields is stronger than in the previous stage. India is eager to become a world power, which is the goal that it has always pursued. The areas of politics and security are related to the further cooperation between India and ASEAN countries. The paper concludes that as India and ASEAN have doubts about China's development, India's "Look East Policy", jointly with ASEAN, has the possibility of neutralise China's influence in the region. India's "Look East Policy" also brings many opportunities for China, so both countries China and India need a peaceful and stable external environment to achieve development.

The third part of the book entitled *Measuring Value Chain and Trade Relations in India- East Asia*, has further divided into five chapters. The chapter entitled *India's Participation in Global Value Chain with Selected East Asian Countries: Exploring the Facts* written by *Sandeep Kaur, Manpreet Kaur and Harpreet Singh* speaks about the growth and performance of India's Global Value Chain for the period of 1990 to 2018 with the help of Inter Country Input Output (ICIO) table for understanding the content of domestic and foreign value added overall and particularly Electrical and Machinery industry. It also makes the comparative picture of its exports with China, Indonesia and South Korea. The domestic value added share in gross exports of India with China has declined during 1995-2014. Alternatively, its foreign value added percentage share grew up for the same period. The similar trends have been observed for Indonesia and South Korea. India's Electrical and Machinery Industry Bilateral Sectoral Decomposition with China, Indonesia and South Korea has shown the growth of domestic value added (DVA) and foreign value added (FVA) in exports. But forward linkages (FL) of India with Korea has highly increased as compared to China and Indonesia. Vertical specialisation structure is very attractive in India's electrical and machinery industry. India has the potential to become an overall global value chain and also in the particular industry with these countries.

The next chapter in this part entitled *External Barriers to India's Agricultural Exports during WTO Regime* written by *Manpreet Singh & Dr. (Mrs.) Paramjit Nanda stresses that* India's share of agricultural exports in world exports and imports was 2.1 and 1.8 per cent respectively. India's agricultural exports also declined over the time period, which raises concern among policymakers. In this context, the paper tries to find out external barriers in the form of non-tariff barriers imposed on Indian agricultural exports by major countries namely USA, Russia, China, Japan, Australia, New Zealand, Iran, UAE, UK, EU, Bangladesh and Indonesia. The study reveals that the total share of all countries considered in India's total agricultural exports declined (i.e. share declined from 57.08 per cent in 1987-88 to 36.41 per cent in 2016-17). Of these 12 nations, six nations namely Russia, Japan, USA, UAE, UK and EU experienced a rapid decrease in India's exports of agricultural commodities. The study further finds out the non-tariff barriers imposed on Indian agricultural exports by these major countries. The residue of chemicals and pesticides in the Indian exports is the main problem raised by the chapter. The product standards are required to be built to make the connections not with India with East Asia but also with other important markets.

The next chapter in this part entitled *Measuring Concentration of India-East Asia Trade* was written by *Divya Vaid & Meenu* examines the growth and structural changes in India - East Asia trade by analysing export destinations and import sources during 1991-92 to 2014-15. The paper shows the need of revisiting India's Exports with East Asia as India faces a huge trade deficit with China, so there is a need to explore possibilities to boost the demand for top five exports to China and it is important to create possibilities to generate FTA specifically for the products in which India and China are trading. India should focus more on exports of Natural or cultured pearls and Electrical Machinery and Equipment to Hong Kong as these items have a prominent position in India's top five exports to Hong Kong and India should explore the Possibilities of Intra Industry Trade as these items are present in both India's exports to China and imports from China. There is a need to remove difficulties by reducing the time and cost of exports and imports in terms of documentary and border compliance.

The next chapter entitled *Export Diversification and Economic Growth: A Case Study of Some Selected Emerging Economies* written by *Vishal Sarin and Naveen Sood* is based on the hypothesis that more diversified countries tend to have faster and inclusive economic growth and this fact has been empirically proved and studies the causal relationship between export diversification and economic growth of selected emerging economies. For Argentina, India, Mexico, Korea and Turkey, economic growth and export diversification are independent. However, in the case of China, there exists bidirectional causality between GDP and export diversification.

The next chapter entitled *India and ASEAN Trade Relations: An Empirical Analysis* written by *Kuldeep Singh & Jaskiran Kaur* speaks about the trade patterns of India with ASEAN during 1995-96 to 2017-18. The Indian imports are more with ASEAN as compared to its exports showing an increase in overall trade balance and give suggestion to revisit the export with ASEAN.

The fourth part of the book lies under the sub- theme of *Building Economic Relations in India-East Asia* and comprises three chapters.

The chapter entitled *Knowledge economy, Institutions and Public Policy: The Case of East Asia and South Asian Economies written by Baldev Singh Shergill* speaks about the process of de-agrarian nation and deindustrialisation of some selected East Asian and South Asian Economies. The paper confirms the close relationship between innovation policies and knowledge economy perspective and a country's level of development in these economies and also, explains the reasons for performing East Asian Economies in better ways as compared to South Asian economies. The paper also highlights the weak knowledge economy indicators in the Asian countries, but they have developed local knowledge systems and skills which is helpful to turn the economy into a knowledge economy through the creation of technology. Thus this paper builds the economic connections of East Asia through the various approaches of Knowledge economy, which provide great lessons to South Asia including India.

The chapter entitled *Capital Goods Industry in East Asia: A Study of Indian Firms* is written by *Swaranjeet Kaur* and *Swati Mehta*. It speaks that Industrial sector affected due to global financial crisis in east Asia. In view of this, the study tries to find out the performance of the capital Goods Industry in India. The TFP growth of all sub-sectors of Capital goods sector remained negative except electronics industries during the pre-reform period. A slight increase of its growth in all sub-sectors except electronics during the post-reform period from 1991-92 to 2013-14. The greater values of growth rates for capital intensities and labour productivities in various sub sectors of the Capital Goods Sector are found. The study finds a decline in productivity in the Indian capital goods sector after the crisis of 2008. The machinery and electrical goods export of India was concentrated within East Asia, the study suggests for further investment in R&D and technology in this sector.

The last chapter entitled *Relationship between FDI Outflows and Economic Growth: Evidence from Developing Asia* written by *Vishal Sarin & Suresh Kumar* analyses the causal relationship between outward FDI and GDP by taking the data of developing economies of Asia for the period 1991-2017. The study finds the increasing share of Outward Foreign Direct Investment (OFDI) in the world OFDI. Only for the East Asian region, there is a short run causal relationship between these two variables running from OFDI to GDP. That means, in East Asia, higher OFDI leads to higher GDP. The east Asian region is the largest contributor in terms of OFDI from developing Asia. The study finds the important lesson from the analysis i.e. if the level of Outward FDI rises to a high level (as in the case of East Asia), only then it can positively affect GDP. The study suggests that the critical minimum level of Outward FDI can increase GDP.

As we are aware of the fact that India's recent economic acceleration and appropriate demographic dividend highlights that India also has a golden opportunity to "Look East Asia" and sustain high growth rates for years to come. India needs to reform its trade, infrastructure, education, and labor markets. What is needed now is the will to act rather than to look at East Asia and needs to hitch its wagon to East Asia's growth engine to admit herself to the Pacific Century. There are economic and geographic reasons for India to look and Act East Asia. Thus this volume raises these several issues of concern related to India- East Asia relations. Several practical suggestions relevant to both practionisers and policy makers have been made. China is clearly very much part of the border political and development discourse. So, the policy can be used as a balancing the power of China.

References

United Nations Conference on Trade and Development (2013). *World Investment Report 2013: Global value chains – Investment and Trade for Development. Sales No. E.13. II.D.5. Geneva.* Accessed from: *unctad.org/en/ Publications Library/wir2013_en.pdf* on August 2018.

IBEF. (2013). Growing Trade with Southeast Asia Evolving Business Relations Between India and Southeast Asia- A Study Report. India Brand Equity Foundations. Accessed from: https://www.google.com/url?sa=t&source=web&rct=j&url=https://www.ibef.org/download/growing-trade-with-southeast-asia.pdf&ved=2ahUKEwjO5LuH2ZLrAhU0yzgGHXB0BZ4QFjAAegQIAxAC&usg=AOvVaw2iEkG-WWATGY4dfbVRf3Rq on July 2018.

PART I

Building Diaspora, Infrastructure and Connections in India-East Asia Relations

1

Indian Diaspora in Thailand

Cementing Historical and Cultural Relations

Reena Marwah

Introduction

India has decisively shifted its policy stance for South East Asia from Looking East in the 1990s to Acting East, since 2014. This re-articulation, after a gap of more than two decades, brings an expectation from India for enhancing and deepening its engagement both with ASEAN and bilaterally with each of the member countries. The paper contextualises India's relations especially with Thailand, bringing to the fore our historical and cultural linkages not only through the Sanskrit language but through Brahmanism and Buddhism as well. Indian diasporic linkages are interwoven through Buddhism and Brahmanism, which are well documented. India and Thailand share unique civilisational links, especially through Buddhism. This is reflected in regular pilgrimages to places of Buddhist interest in India by a large number of Thai people. Hindu elements are reflected in Thai architecture, arts, sculpture, dance, drama and literature. The Thai language incorporates Pali and Sanskrit influences. A large Indian diaspora living and working in Thailand is another important bond. Indians were present in Thailand as far back as the 13th century, i.e. during the Sukhothai and Ayutthaya periods. Before India's partition, several Punjabi families migrated from Gujranwala now in Pakistan) to Thailand. Many Indian people go to South Asia; for work and South Asia is the hub of migrant workers. (Kaur, 2013). During the period 1942 to 1945, some Indians joined the Indian National Army in Malaya to fight for India's independence. Some among them gradually moved to Thailand and other South-East Asian countries. Thus, people from India have been settled there for more than 3-4 generations. The third and fourth generation families now see their children integrating with Thais, by marrying outside the Indian community. However, the majority of Indian families have not integrated and prefer to interact with members of their community. India Looks East Policy and Thailand Look West Policy complemented each other. The two countries completed 70 years of diplomatic relations in 2017. There have been several high-level visits of leaders of the two countries, with four Prime Ministerial visits from India to Thailand since 2001. In 2012, Prime Minister Yingluck Shinawatra was the chief guest on the occasion of India's Republic Day. H.R.H. Princess Sirindhorn herself is a frequent visitor to India. Moreover, both countries engage in various groupings like ASEAN, Mekong Ganga Cooperation (MGC), and Asia Cooperation Dialogue (ACD), among others. The partnership got a further boost with the 2010 India- ASEAN Trade in Goods Agreement. India in Thailand is viewed as a promising market with its large population and growing purchasing power. Thailand has also sought to diversify its export destinations and considers connectivity with India as a significant factor in boosting its economy. Similarly, Thailand's significance to India has begun to be appreciated as evident from the discussions relating to the Indo-Thai Free Trade Agreement (FTA) which moved faster than the wider Indo-ASEAN FTA. Thailand is also considered as India's partner for stimulating the economies of India's North-Eastern states. India also sends more than a million tourists every year, second only to China.

Review of Literature

To highlight the diasporic linkages, it is important to bring in a discussion of the relevant literature. Sastri's (1949) seminal work on South Indian influence in the far East underlines that higher-level cultural influences reached parts of Southeast Asia from China and India. He also discusses the role of the missionaries of Indian civilisation and the route they travelled. Sastri (1949) reveals that people from India could have come through Burma, or by sea (possibly after crossing the Isthmus of Kra). Wherever they went, their culture prevailed. The Khmers and Chams adopted Sanskrit as their official language. The missionaries also took with them the Vedic beliefs and Saivism. Hence, both Brahmanism and Buddhism reached Southeast Asian countries. Hence, the importance of Buddhism and Brahmanism has been explored in the present study.

V. Suryanarayan (2019) has written about the cultural indebtedness of all Southeast Asian countries to India. He also shared this personally with the author of this study.

Singh and Dhar (2014) provide a comprehensive account of Asian civilisational exchanges during the early modern periods through the dimensions of art, religion, commerce and politics. They add to the literature on culture studies and history even as they underline the multifaceted motivations for an understanding of connections between India and the rest of Asia. Their articulation underlines the importance of undergirding research on India Thailand cultural relations through the historical context in which they took place.

Manguin, Mani & Wade (2011), have also documented archaeological research carried out on both sides of the Bay of Bengal, in combination with renewed approaches to textual sources and art history. It details the exchanges between the two shores of the Bay of Bengal which led, among other processes, to the Indianisation of those parts of the region that straddled the main routes of exchange.

Pollock (1996), writes about the 'Sanskrit cosmopolis', which he dates approximately between the years 300 and 1300. He interrogates the reasons for the spread of Sanskrit from the Indian subcontinent to Southeast Asia and concludes that Sanskrit became the primary expression of the polities of Southeast Asia. The importance of Indianisation through language is underlined.

Wales (1931) has made a great contribution to the understanding of Hindu rituals and the presence of Brahmanas in the royal palaces. Wales himself had moved to Siam in 1924 and served as an adviser to the courts of King Rama VI and King Rama VII until 1928. His experiences provided the basis for his writings on the ceremonies and rituals followed by the monarchs, all of whom took the title of Rama.

Kusalasaya, K. (2013), writes of the Thailand India connection through Buddhism. As Buddhism impacts Thai society in diverse ways, the country is referred to as "The Land of Yellow Robes" by foreigners. Buddhist monks wear yellow robes. Given the increasing interest, the world is taking in Buddhism and because Buddhism thrives in Thailand; hence, it is important to understand how Buddhism reached here. The Thai people are forever grateful to India for enriching their culture.

Ghosh (2011) and Ghosh (2017) provide a detailed account of the aspects of India's cultural relations with Thailand. These include religion, art, artefacts, clothing, music—especially Indian classical music, cuisine, and the contemporary use of aspects of civilisation in the cultural diplomacy of both countries. However, historic underpinnings of the relations of the two countries and detailed aspects of Hinduism and Buddhism are not dealt with adequately. Moreover, the economic and strategic facets of the relationship are not within the scope of their study.

There are other important studies on soft power, religion and culture which merit attention. These include the following:

Chitrabongs, (2015), discusses the Omnipresence of the Ramayana in Thai Arts and Culture. It is well known that the imagery of Ramayana has influenced India's art and architecture. Even in modern art work, it has been depicted in many forms of art in Thailand. The study makes an important contribution to the importance of Hinduism in Thai rituals and ceremonies and these have been detailed in the present study.

However, Chitrabongs, (2015) does not discuss the entirety of India's relations with Thailand.

S. Srichampa (2015) has articulated the possibilities of cooperation through the harnessing of the soft power of India and Thailand. She describes the long-standing relationship between India and Thailand since ancient times. Indian influence has blended with the local beliefs and culture of the Thai people. Interestingly, no hard power tools were used to build the connection with countries of Southeast Asia, or Thailand. Rather, it was soft power that India used to forge ties with Thailand.

For an understanding of the Hindu diaspora in Thailand, Cohen's concept is instructive. There are mainly two key features of Cohen's concept of diaspora (2008), namely, first, the diaspora or their ancestors, have been dispersed from an original 'centre' to two or more foreign regions and second, their ancestral home is idealised and it is intended that, if the opportunity presents, either they or their descendants will return. Cohen also explains that the diasporic communities continue to relate to their home country and it is their consciousness of the community to which they belong that defines the existence of such a relationship.

Jangphanichkul (1993) delineates the sacredness and importance for Thai and Indian people. In the central area of Ratchaprasong in Bangkok, there is a highly revered and sacred Brahma shrine known as "Brahma Erawan Shrine". This shrine attracts many local and international believers in the hope of receiving blessings for success after making merit. The author describes how Hinduism influences Buddhism and is also influenced by it.

Poolthupya (2008) has written about rising India and Indian Communities in East Asia. She is a well-known scholar in India and has written about the multi-dimensional contribution of the Indian diaspora to Thailand.

Chhibber N.K. and Shishodia, S.K., (2013), provide merely a bird's eye view of the bilateral relations between India and Thailand; however, their work predates recent initiatives by India under India's Act East policy.

The Historical Connect

It is well known that "trade encouraged Indians to travel to Southeast Asia which has been a primary characteristic of Indians in Thailand since ancient times. Around 2,500 years ago, some Jambudvipa people (today called India) travelled via Bengal-Andaman sea-coast to Southeast Asia, then known as Suvarnabhumi (Thailand)".[1]

This has been until the commencement of general migration in the post-colonial period. But the Indian migrants arriving in Thailand differ from those choosing to go to neighbouring countries such as Malaysia as Thailand offers them greater freedom in their life. Trade has been the key factor in Indians success in Thailand. This chapter provides an overview of the migration of Indians to Thailand. It also discusses aspects of their adaptability in Thai society as well as their places of worship.

Hence, it is believed that Indian civilisation came to Thailand through trade. When traders brought goods, they met the local rulers and pleased them with gifts and souvenirs. This resulted in the rulers becoming interested in Indian culture. Later, Brahmans were also invited from India. This influenced the Rulers with respect to Devaraja concepts, literature and culture in the court. Their ideas, customs and rituals also influenced the local people.

Ancient Travel Routes

In the earlier times, there were two routes from India to Thailand: Sea Route and the Land Route. By the sea route, people came from India to Takuathung, then by land to Nakhon Si Thammarat; they also came from India by boat: i.e they came to the Malaya peninsula, after which they reached the Champa Kingdom, and then onwards to Thailand, via Khmer region.

By the land route: There were three ways through Burma to the western border of Thailand: The first was through the Mae Lamo border near Tak province, the second was at Phra Jedi Saam Ong border and

[1] www.tci.thaijo.org

to Kanchanaburi and the third was through Tavoy, Tenasserim and then onward to Singkhon border near Prajuab Khiri khan. This route was most popularly used by the migrants to reach Thailand.

It has been documented that Indian Brahmanas started to arrive in Thailand from the 3rd century A.D. (Srichampa, 2015: 126). This has been stated by Nan-chou I-wu Chih, a source from the 3rd century who tells us that southern Thailand practised Brahmanism as propagated by immigrant Brahmanas. India Thailand ties date back at least to the 3rd century AD. While traders came to Thailand, in the early times, Brahmanas also followed them. This is evident from the temples in Nakhon Si Thammarat, which is one of the southern provinces of Thailand. The three oldest groups of Vishnu statues in Thailand and other places in Southeast Asia, two of which were date back to the 3-4th centuries reflect the influence of Mathura and the final period of Amaravati Arts.

Indian art and culture from the 7th Century can be seen in the northern part of the Malay Peninsula, especially in Nakhon Si Thammarat. Here, the influence of Brahmanism can be traced by olden artefacts of Shaivism and Vaishnavism from Southern parts of India. The brief history of India-Thailand relations started from the very first kingdom of Siam known as Sukhothai, following the available evidence.

The importance of Brahmanas in the 7th century has been documented through the important ceremonial functions performed by the Brahmanas. Although the number of followers of Brahmanism was small, their services were offered to both the ruler and the ruled.

It was in the Ayutthaya period that witnessed the golden era of two-way trade relations with India. The products exported to India were mainly forest products including elephants and goods from India included mainly textiles and clothes. The influence of Indian textiles on the textile and prints of several Southeast Asian nations has been vividly described by Hema Devare, (Devare, 2016). During the period which followed, i.e. the Ratanakosin era, British colonisation from India spread to Southeast Asia.

Reign of Rama V (1853 – 1910): Open policy for foreigners

During the Ayutthaya period, Pali and Sanskrit were preferred in books and borrowed more Khmer words, especially using royal vocabularies for the king and royal members. It is important to point out that it was during the King Rama V's period of rule, (1853 – 1910) that it became popular to borrow Sanskrit names, hence making the names longer and adding to the prestige in naming. This process is referred to as "Thaksapakorn" which means 'Eight planets'.

Hence, the Government of Siam did business through the British raj established in this region. As the first monarch to travel outside his country, King Rama V visited Java and India to understand the British system of administration. After returning he introduced an open policy for welcoming foreigners to do business at an international level. In the early 20th century there were several push factors that resulted in Indians moving to other lands. The push factors among others included drought and rapid growth of population. Siam was a popular destination, as it had not been occupied by the British.

Indian Emigration to Siam

Indians were present in Thailand as far back as the 13th century, i.e. during the Sukhothai and Ayutthaya periods. Before India's partition, several Punjabi families migrated from Gujranwala now in Pakistan) to Thailand. During the period 1942 to 1945, many Indians joined the Indian National Army in Malaya to fight for India's independence. Some among them gradually moved to Thailand and other South-East Asian countries. Thus, people from India have been settled there for more than 3-4 generations. The third and fourth generation families now see their children integrating with Thais, by marrying outside the Indian community. However, the majority of Indian families have not integrated and prefer to interact with members of their community. This is in sharp contrast to the Chinese, who not only have integrated seamlessly into Thai society through wedlock but have also taken appended Thai names to their Chinese ones.

"Indian migrants like Hindus, Muslims, Sikhs came from many states such as Tamil Nadu, Sindhu, Punjab, Uttar Pradesh, Gujarat, Rajasthan, Pondicherry etc. of India".[2]

Once diplomatic relationships were established between India and Thailand in 1947, many Indians migrated to Thailand encouraged by their relatives, who were mainly settled in Bangkok. Nowadays, they have expanded their settlements to the suburbs of Bangkok (www.tci-thaijo.org). As stated earlier, Indians came through the ancient trade routes in the 2nd and 3rd centuries. "Indian merchants sold goods and offered them to local rulers who appreciated Indian culture. In the 3rd century, Brahmins came along with Indian traders on their travels, to perform religious rituals for them. Later, their faith spread to the local people of Siam, especially the rulers. Some people chose to follow Brahmanism. The Indian concept of revering the ruler as an incarnation of God was accepted by the local rulers. Thus, Indian language, culture and literature were engaged into Thai culture and society" (Srichampa, 2015).

The next generation of migrants came to Thailand in the aftermath of the India-Pakistan partition in 1947, due to the push factors of violence, poverty and political uncertainty. This migration to Thailand was by three routes:

1) By sea route from Madras and Calcutta, India to Malaysia and then to Thailand and on to Bangkok by train.
2) By land route to Chittagong in Bangladesh, through Burma by train, and by road to the north of Thailand.
3) By air from India to Thailand.

It has been noted that there are mainly five Hindu Indian groups who settled in Thailand. They are:

1) Uttar Pradesh group from the north of India, who first took up jobs as selling of groceries, delivering newspapers, and also employed as guards for foreign companies. These people worshipped the Hindu god, Vishnu and also established the first

[2] www.tci-thaijo.org

Hindu temple named "Vishnu Dhamma Sabha" which is now called "Wat Vishnu" of the temple of Lord Vishnu.

2) Sindh and Punjab group, also from the north of India, who started the textile industry in the Pahurat and Sampheng areas which are known as "Little Indias". The selling of textiles has been an important characteristic of the identity of the Indian diaspora in Thailand (Srichampa, 2015). Some of the succeeding generations are still running textile businesses today. Among this group of people, some are Sikhs. They built their gurudwara, Sri Guru Singh Sabha, at Phahurat in 1979. Another part of this group is Hindus. They constructed their mandir on Siriphong road called "Dev Mandir", in 1939.

Indians in Thailand: Occupational Pursuits

As stated earlier, it was following a royal visit to India, that King Rama V established a policy to wellcome people from abroad to do business at an international level. Due to push factors originating in India, especially drought and rapid growth of population, Indian emigration increased, with a policy to wellcome people from abroad. One reason for this was that Siam was an economic and commercial centre without British occupation. Indian migrants came from many states of India as follows: Hindus from Tamil Nadu, Sindh, Punjab, Uttar Pradesh, Lucknow, Ayodhya, Gujarat, Rajasthan and Bengal. Some had relatives or friends to help them settle, and others were total newcomers. People from the same town, with a common religion, would help each other (Srichampa, 2015). Learning the Thai language which includes some words of Hindi or Punjabi helped migrants to integrate more easily with the local people.

Most Hindus who initially migrated to Thailand sold cloth for a living. Some went about with their business on foot around Bangkok; some sold their goods throughout the country. Mostly, they were welcomed by local Thai customers and are well known for their entrepreneurial pursuits. Trading in textiles, real estate, gems and jewellery, they have made a significant contribution to the Thai economy.

Moreover, Thai people were not particularly interested in doing business so there was not much competition. The first and second generations who were hard working stayed in the business of textiles. Young people of succeeding generations were sent to be educated in India, to retain their language, religious-culture and social-links with the motherland. Moreover, India could offer their children better English skills than Thailand.

The identity of Indians as textile merchants in Thailand has long been recognised up to today. Moreover, many shops have Hindu-Nepalese-Burmese working as assistants. Some Hindu-Nepalese-Burmese manage to save money by working as assistants in Hindu or Sikh Indian tailor shops and, after some years, they set up their tailoring shops in tourist places. "Their target market, however, is different as Nepalese shops offer lower prices and quality than the Indian shops and so attract a different type of customer" (Srichampa, 2014).

Moreover, Hindu-Indian-Thais in the commercial areas of big cities can work together with the local people, including other ethnic groups such as Chinese-Thais, in commercial areas and undertake other social activities such as religious, charitable, national and academic events. Recently, however, "Chinese textiles have flooded the market with low prices posing a serious threat to the Indian Thai textile industry in Thailand".[3]

With the rise in the number of Indian tourists visiting Thailand, there is an increasing demand for Indian cuisine. These opportunities have been leveraged by migrants from India, Nepal and Bangladesh to sell Indian food. Hence, several Indian restaurants have been set up in places as Pattaya, Phuket and Chiangmai.

Given the fact that gems, jewellery and other precious metals are important during auspicious periods in an Indian's life, especially at a time of marriage, being in the business of jewellery has been an outstanding example of Indian expertise. Moreover, Thailand is a source of raw gems for production and export. Groups of Indians have been engaged in this

---

[3] www.forum-urban-futures.net

and invested in the jewellery business several decades ago. The areas of Bangkok where jewellery shops of Hindu-Indians can be found are Mahesak and Suriwong Roads.

Very often, Hindu Indians in Thailand mostly hire Hindu-Nepalese-Burmese, or Nepalese to work with them at home and their workplace/businesses. These workers with the same culture are better adapted. Hence, with Thai citizenship and the freedom to follow their customs and religion, migrants from India enjoy a comfortable living. A brief about the different communities which migrated from India to Thailand is given below.

Sikh Community in Thailand

It was in the latter half of the 19th century that Sikh families came as migrants to Thailand. Among the first Indians to arrive in Thailand was Kirparam Madan in 1884. He was from Bhadewal village in the district of Sialkot (which is now in Pakistan). He was joined by members of his family. Hence, they were among the first members of the "Indian diaspora in Thailand. The first Sikh person to travel to Chiang Mai was Ishar Singh, who travelled from India through Burma into Thailand in the year 1905 (or the year 2448 according to the Buddhist Calendar). Shortly after that, about four more families came to Thailand. They were Rattan Singh, Gian Singh, Wariaam Singh and Amanda Singh. It was by the year 1911, that many Sikh families had settled in Thailand".[4]

During the early 20th century, Bangkok was the centre of migrant Sikhs, but as there was no Gurdwara, their religious prayers were held in the homes of the Sikhs, usually on every Sunday and all their special religious days. In 1912, the Sikhs decided to establish a Gurdwara. The author of this study visited the Gurdwara Sri Guru Singh Sabha in Bangkok, which is located in the Phahurat area of Bangkok. This area is also known as Little India and is not far from the famous Chinatown. Over time the Sikh community built their temples or Gurudwaras in

[4] www.forum-urban-futures.net

various provinces of the country. In all, there are about 20 Gurudwaras in Thailand. Gurudwaras were also established in Chiang Mai, Nakhon Ratchasima, Pattaya, and Phuket, among others.

Sikhs are the largest community among Indians who made Thailand their home. The number of Sikhs is approx. 70,000/- according to recent sources. This was learnt through interviews held with members of the Indian community in Thailand in June 2018 and April 2019. The Sikhs have been involved in the business of textiles and garments. Sikhs are mostly settled in the area adjoining Pahurat Road. Most of them run real estate businesses, hotels or are engaged in readymade garments and textile business, including stitching/tailoring of made-to-order garments. The first Gurdwara in Phuket was constructed by the Sikhs who had come to Phuket to work in tin mining and railway engineering under the supervision of the British in 1939. Many of these groups of Sikhs were also involved during World War II in the Indian National Army. Later, many Sikh businessmen started migrating to Phuket to start businesses in such fields as tailoring and hotels. As Phuket became an attractive tourist hub, more Sikh families moved here. In 2001, a new Gurudwara was built in Phuket.

"Over the last three or four generations, the Indian expatriate population has risen to more than 150,000 residents, more than 70% of whom live in Bangkok. Some Sikhs have made their homes along Sukhumvit Road, but most run their businesses in the prominent community around Phahurat Road, near Chinatown. This is home to many descendants of Punjabi Sikhs from north-west India who settled in the early 20th century. The community's centrepiece is the enormous Sri Guru Singh Sabha temple, which was built in 1932 and is said to be the second-largest Sikh temple outside of India".[5]

"In terms of the Indian textile business, connections with related companies and factories, including shops in Thailand as well as with other foreign countries, have facilitated trade relations. In Thailand, Hindu-Indian businessmen and women are members of local associations such

[5] www.first worldnomnoms.com

as the Thai Textile Merchants Association; the Garments Industry Club; and the Synthetic Yarn and Fiber Association" (Srichampa, 2014).

There is an English magazine, called Masala Magazine. It is a bi-monthly publication that is free and is aimed at the Sikh population. "It serves the interests of Thai-Indians. It also covers stories on Indian expats working for multinational companies, such as the hotel chains, various international and UN organisations, banks, financial institutions and technology companies" (Srichampa, 2014).

Tamils in Thailand

The Tamil Nadu and north Sri Lankan group who came to Thailand became English teachers, foreign company staff or merchants. They worship the god Shiva and goddess Uma. Tamil migrants constructed the first southern Hindu temple called "Sri Mahamariamman" or "Wat Khaek" (literally "temple India") in the 1860s. Later, others from South India arrived in Thailand. "Sri Maha Mariamman temple was constructed in the 1860s by the southern Indian newcomers who settled along Silom Road, which is an area thronged by tourists. There are several stalls near the temple which sell decorative garlands, incense and Bollywood posters".[6]

"India is a vast country with a huge range of cultures, sub-cultures, communities and languages. This diversity is reflected in the Indian community here in Thailand where different identities subscribe to their respective associations" (www.firstworldnomnoms.com). Each Hindu community has a group leader who coordinates events and festivals.

Migrants from Gujarat, Rajasthan and Maharashtra

These people from the west of India, are keen on the jewellery trade. "They are mainly concentrated in the Silom and Sathorn areas of Bangkok. They both import and export gems and jewellery between Thailand, India and other parts of the world. There are some Hindus who frequent Wat Khaek and Silom road together with the South Indian group" (Srichampa, 2014).

[6] www.first worldnomnoms.com

The Hindu-Nepalese-Burmese people

These people are those who migrated to Burma in earlier times and later migrated to Thailand. It is interesting to understand their motivation for migration to Thailand. It was in 1814 the British made an unsuccessful attempt to take Nepal as a new colony, they tried to persuade the Gurkhas to join the East India Company on behalf of which they fought in several wars. Hence, Gurkhas came to be included in the British Indian Army and served in World Wars I and II. Post-independence of Burma in 1948, several Gurkhas joined the Burmese Army. Many among them were Hindu. They continued to serve the modern Myanmar Armed Forces. In addition to the Gurkhas who continued to live in Burma, workers from Nepal also migrated there in search of employment opportunities. They maintained their faiths, cultures and languages. A distinguishing feature of Gurkha Nepalese-Burmese identity is the celebration of festivals such as Diwali. They also built their temples. (However, when Burma came to be ruled by General Ne Win during the period 1962-1988, he instilled the nation with its own culture and nationalism. This led to foreigners seeking exile abroad, including the Nepalese. While some left the country to return to their homeland, others moved to Thailand. This policy also affected many Indians and led them to migrate to Thailand. It is interesting to note that some Nepalese women from Burma also moved with Indian families to Thailand and were employed as domestic servants or cooks. At some time, men also followed and worked in Indian-owned tailor or textile shops. Several families are of Hindu Nepalese-Burmese identity settled for several decades in the Thai-Myanmar area of Mae Sot district. There are approximately 40,000-50,000 Hindu-Nepalese people in Thailand.

There are other Hindu-Indians who came to Thailand. They started as employees of British people or other private companies, or in their businesses. Some were watchmen, milk-sellers, sellers and traders. Most were from eastern Uttar Pradesh. The next generation had opportunities to study at the University level and hence, could opt for diverse careers.

It is well known that over the past almost 70 years, many large corporations from India have set up businesses in Thailand. These include the "Aditya Birla Group, Indo Rama Group, Tata Group, Ranbaxy, Dabur, Lupin and NIIT. They are among other major Indian companies doing business in Thailand and contributing to a range of industries - chemicals, textiles, pharmaceuticals, steel, automotive, and IT. etc." (Srichampa, 2014). Most of the Indian workers are Hindus. Many of the companies have used Thailand as the springboard for entering new markets in the Southeast Asian region. Hence, these Thai-based Indian transnational companies have grown successfully. Indian Overseas Bank (IOB) is one of the oldest and major Public Sector banks in India with its Head Office located in Chennai. As on June 2014, the bank has 3315 branches (with overseas branches in Hongkong, Singapore, Seoul, Bangkok as well as Colombo with a Joint Venture Bank (India International Bank) in Malaysia).

The Bangkok branch of Indian Overseas Bank, one of the oldest foreign banks operating in Thailand, continues to be the only Indian Bank permitted to provide banking services in the Royal Kingdom of Thailand. It was opened on 23rd December 1947; hence the Bangkok branch of Indian Overseas Bank is almost as old as Independent India and has completed 7 decades of banking service.

The IOB has also partnered with the Indian business community in Thailand, thereby helping them meet their international trade and business-related banking requirements. The Bank has also been instrumental in providing easy and competitive remittance facilities to the large population of Indian expatriates working in Thailand. Another business which has established itself in recent years is the Information Technology sector. Some Indian IT specialists work with Thai or Indian companies and some have started their own IT businesses in Thailand. A few businesses have established their businesses in other countries of Southeast Asia. This has been due to the conducive business environment through the vibrant ASEAN Economic Community (AEC).

"Indian satellite broadcasts from India to Thailand attract an audience of Indian-Thais who also enjoy Indian DVD movies and other media from India available at Indian shops and through the internet" (Srichampa, 2014).

For a significant period, the Hindu-Indian associations headed by prominent Indians have been contributing to cultural and educational progress in Thailand. "Some of these Associations are Arya Samaj, Hindu Samaj, Geeta Ashram Thailand, Hindu Dharma Sabha, Maharashtra Mandal Bangkok, Radha Soami Satsang Beas foundation Bangkok, Shree Swaminarayan Satsang Mandal, Sri Maha Mariamman Temple, South Indian Association and Tamil Culture Association, etc. These associations perform socio-cultural activities and retain strong links with India. Besides, other business associations have also been set up, such as the India-Thai Chamber of Commerce and the Indian-Thai Business Association. They are also among the leading business groups of Thailand associated with the Indian Embassy and other related sectors. They play an important role in promoting business and attracting investment in India and Thailand using social media to publicise their initiatives and their contribution" (Srichampa, 2014).

There are several Universities that organise funfairs and other activities, including lectures, student exchanges and interactions. Prominent among them are Chulalongkorn University, Chiang Mai University, Silpakorn University and Mahidol University among others. Universities, by rotation, situated in Bangkok organise an annual Thai Indian funfair usually at a time when the tourists from India are in Thailand; i.e. especially during the summer months and winter months, i.e. during vacations. "The funfairs are jointly organised by the Indian Embassy in Thailand and the Indian Social Club of Thailand consisting of 65 Associations of Indian Diaspora in Thailand. More than 10,000 people, including students of the university, participate in the event. A variety of activities are planned such as Thai, Indian, & international cuisine; games, cultural program, lifestyle and northeast India cultural fashion show; Indian heritage corners, India-Thailand quiz contest; special folk dance troupe from Manipur Northeast India, India; exhibitions and other events are organised" (www.nationmultimedia.com). The 2019 Thai-Indian Fun Fair, held in February, was hosted by Srinakharinwirot University in Bangkok.

Language Preservation: Hindi and Sanskrit for Diasporic Communities

Children usually are seen accompanying their parents to the Dev Mandir. Discourses in Hindi and Sanskrit enable Hindu-Thais to preserve their language and encourage the new generation to learn and use it. Hindi or Punjabi languages and traditional customs including socialisation are taught in the family (Srichampa, 2014). While most of the young generation study at international schools and prefer to use English and Thai with their parents rather than their mother tongue, there is a strong sense among the elderly to ensure that the cultural identity of the coming generations is not affected (Srichampa, 2015). Hence, informal activities are organised in the temples or private homes to teach Hindi and Dharma to the children by the Brahmanas. "As for the Hindu-Nepalese, they prefer to set up home classes for Thai-born Nepalese children in the evenings to teach the Nepalese language and culture. Most Indian-Thais do not marry into Thai families due to their different social characteristics. Most marriages are arranged and brides are often from India, especially for those from conservative states and areas" (Srichampa, 2014). In most Indian families, at least one child is sent to India for education. It can hence be inferred that some Indian Thais are not able to speak the Thai language fluently, despite having Thai citizenship, because of staying away from Thailand for a long period.

Some Hindu families follow the customary family roles as in India, and after marriage, the wife stays with the husband's family. However, this trend is changing with young couples shifting out of their family homes. With Thailand's tourist-friendly policies and often waiving off the visa fee for tourists from India and some other countries, wedding ceremonies for Indians are being held in Thailand. These are being promoted by the Tourism Authority of Thailand in collaboration with hotels and Hindu-Indian-Thai event organisers who are understand the requirements and expectations of their Indian customers for destination weddings. While Thailand receives more than 1.5 million tourists from India every year, the Indian government is also wooing tourists from Thailand for the Buddhist circuit in India which is on the itinerary of increasing numbers of Thais.

Indians: Serving the Community

The majority of them do not involve themselves in politics. Therefore, they focus more on religion-socio-cultural activities. Although Hindu-Indian-Thais are Thai, their appearance, especially their faces identify them as Indians, but their socio-cultural and religious attitudes can be a mixture of Indian and Thai elements. Some characteristic features of Indian traditions are still followed within the family and community such as food, religious practices and festivals, women's dress and some customs. However, they do sometimes also participate in Buddhist ceremonies (Srichampa, 2014).

Although the present generations of Indians are well integrated into the Thai society, with some exceptions, the attitudes of the older age groups of Thais towards Indians has some prejudice. This was because, when Indians came to Thailand, many of them entered the business of money lending due to which they became very unpopular. Hence, in contrast with the Chinese, Indians have not easily mingled or been accepted among the Thai people. According to Srichampa, for the new generation, their sense of "Indian-ness" is weaker than it is for older generations. Moreover, with the ease of connectivity through the internet as well as the ease of travel, links between people around the world have been greatly enhanced. Indians like to maintain their identity, even as they participate in the festivals of the Thais. The intersection of Buddhism and Brahmanism has been well explained. Hence, many of the festivals of the Thai people have a lot of similarities with the Indian festivals. Indian gods as stated earlier, including Brahma, Vishnu, Shiva and Ganesha are very popular.

Several social organisations are undertaking charitable activities as well as activities of education. These include the Thai Bharat Cultural Lodge, TBCL, which has been supported by the Indian embassy for several years. The author also gave a lecture here on May 31st 2018 and interacted with members of the Thai and Indian community. Buddhist ceremonies and pujas are also held here. There is the Ramakrishna Vedant Association of Thailand, a women's friendship club, as well as schools that have been established by members of the Indian community. Sathya Sai School of Thailand helps in the teaching of English language to Thai students.

Conclusion

Evidently, given the historicity of India Thailand relations, the Indian diaspora in Thailand have assimilated within Thai society with greater ease than in other nations. It is believed, that this is due to the fact that the bilateral relations in terms of culture and language are very robust, translating further into religious bonding through Buddhism and Hinduism (Srichampa, 2014).

Hindu-Nepalese people also lives in Thailand peacefully because of their common religious roots. The Indian and Nepalese-Hindus have the same religious practices which can be performed at home, in the community, and at mandirs. At the same time, they integrate into Thai society by joining with Buddhists for religious activities and ceremonies. Other Thais also join them for religious ceremonies and other activities (Srichampa, 2015).

Thailand's experience leads us to the fact that Indians, as traders, merchants and investors, have exercised their expertise and skills as businesspersons throughout history. Hindu- Indian-Thais are mostly active in business in a few big cities in Thailand, and not widely throughout the country, unlike the Chinese-Thai. It is interesting to note also that new Indian transnational businessmen to Thailand are mostly Hindus (Srichampa, 2014). Moreover, through interviews of members of the Indian diaspora, it seems evident that Indian workers prefer to stay longer in Thailand, rather than going back to India. As Indian and Thai cultures share common religious-cultural elements, especially Hinduism and Buddhism, Thai people have no conflicts with any diaspora groups. Whereas some have more fully integrated into Thai society, Indians would prefer not to marry with Thais due to their distinct culture. This is one reason why Hindu Indians in Thailand have been able to preserve their identity. Most Hindus-Indians and Nepalese retain links with India and Nepal by visiting their relatives from time to time, and some even expect to return there for good in the future. Others, on the other hand, have become disconnected from the motherland and visit merely as tourists (Srichampa, 2015).

It is believed that the Hindu diaspora is an example of successful integration and settlement in another country. Indians in Thailand are rich in religious, economic and social capital and this can serve as a role model and example of a successful diaspora in Thailand (Srichampa, 2014).

The Indian communities in Thailand can help further India's interests in Thailand especially in terms of investment into their country, as well as investment from Thailand into India.

References

Chhibber, N.K. and Shishodia, S.K. (2013). India-Thailand Relations, in Kumar, Sanjay (ed), India-Thailand Bilateral Relations, New Delhi: Mohit publications, India.

Chitrabongs, M. R. C. (2015). The omnipresence of the Ramayana in Thai Arts and Culture. *India Studies Journal*, Special Issue, Thammasat University, Thailand.

Devare, Hema. (2016). *Ganga to the Mekong: A Cultural Voyage Through Textiles. Manohar Publishers, India.*

Ghosh, Lipi (Ed.). (2017). India-Thailand Cultural Interactions, Glimpses from the Past to Present., Springer, India.

Ghosh, Lipi (editor). (2011). Connectivity and Beyond-Indo Thai Relations through ages, The Asiatic Society, Kolkata.

Jangphanichkul, T. (1993). Brahma: God of Wealth and Prosperity. Bangkok, Thailand: Comma Publishing House.

Kusalasaya, K. (2013). Buddhism in Thailand: It's Past, and It's Present, *Access to Insight (BCBS Edition)*, 30 November 2013, Accessed from: http://www.accesstoinsight.org/lib/authors/kusalasaya/wheel085.html; accessed on November 20, 2018.

Kaur, S. (2013, January). 'Remittances, Trade and Growth in South Asia': A Panel Data Analysis. In *3rd Conference of IIFT and to be published in a commemorative volume on conference on empirical issues in international trade and finance* (pp. 10-11).

Manguin, P. Y., Mani, A., & Wade, G. (Eds.). (2011). Early interactions between South and Southeast Asia: reflections on cross-cultural exchange (Vol. 2). Institute of Southeast Asian Studies.

Pollock, S. (1996). The Sanskrit Cosmopolis, 300–1300: Transculturation, Vernacularization, and the Question of Ideology. Ideology and Status of Sanskrit: *Contributions to the History of the Sanskrit Language*, Leiden: Brill, pp. 197-247.

Kesavapany, K. & Mani, A. & Ramasamy, P. (2008). Rising India and Indian Communities in East Asia. ISEAS–Yusof Ishak Institute. Retrieved July 15, 2019, from Project MUSE database.

Sastri, K. A. N. (1949). *South Indian Influences in the Far East*. Hind kitabs.

Kulke, H., Bopearachchi, O., Sen, T., Singh, U., & Dhar, P. P. (2014). *Asian Encounters: Exploring Connected Histories*. Oxford University Press.

Smith, Adam, 1723-1790. (2000). *The wealth of nations/Adam Smith; introduction by Robert Reich; edited, with notes, marginal summary, and enlarged index by Edwin Cannan*. New York: Modern Library.

Srichampa, S. (2014). Hindus in the globalised Thai society. *Voice of Intellectual Man-An International Journal*, *4*(2), 31-52.

Srichampa, S. (2015). Hindu God Brahma in Thailand. Centre for Bharat Studies. Research Institute for Languages and Cultures of Asia, Mahidol University.

Srichampa, S. (2015). India and Thailand: Soft Power Ties. Humanities, Arts and Social Sciences Studies (Former name Slipakorn University Journal of Social Sciences, Humanities and Arts), 121-150.

Stark, M. T. & Allen, S. J. (1998). The Transition to History in Southeast Asia: An Introduction. *International Journal of Historical Archaeology*, *2*(3), 163–175.

Sugondhabhirom, A. (2018). The Kings and India: The Royal Thai Family and the Siam-Bharat relations. Retrieved from: http://newdelhi.thaiembassy.org/en/2018/07/kings-india-royal-thai-family-context-siam-bharat-relations

Wales, H. G. Quaritch (1931) *Siamese state ceremonies.* London, U.K.

www.forum-urban-futures.net

www.nationmultimedia.com

www.First worldnomnoms.com

www.forum-urban-futures.net

www.tci-thaijo.org

2

India's Coverage on Connectivity Corridor with Southeast Asia

Sunetra Ghatak

Introduction

Any discourse on regional economic integration is incomplete without the discussion of the importance of connectivity. It integrates the economies via trade promotion, brings people closer. Infrastructure improvement such as intra-regional corridor-based development bridge the geographical space and narrowed down the economic disparities within the region through reducing transportation costs and time (Ghosh and De, 2005; De and Iyengar, 2014; Sen, 2014; and De, *et al.* 2019). The potential gains from closer connectivity between India and Southeast Asia are no doubt large. "In the absence of adequate connectivity, enormous opportunities generated by the dynamic growth centres of Asia may stop at their international borders." (www.eria.org). Therefore a brief examination of India's initiation of connectivity corridors with Southeast Asian countries will help to understand India's approach towards regional connectivity frameworks in the light of 'Act East Policy' (AEP).

India's current relations with Southeast Asia began in the early 1990s when the country undertook the 'Look East Policy' (LEP) and later upgraded to 'Act East Policy' (AEP) in 2014 as an effort to strengthen economic and strategic relations. With a free trade agreement (FTA) in goods in 2010, India has created a versatile economic space and investment hub across the Southeast Asian region. In 2013, India became third dialogue partner in 2013 for initiating Connectivity Coordinating Committee- India Meeting of ASEAN. Now to utilise this space, regional connectivity, infrastructure development is a priority for India and central to its ties with Southeast Asia. Several studies showed that improved infrastructure (e.g. services links, logistics services) motivates micro-level production at the regional level, and enhances trade at the regional and global level to accelerate regional integration. (De and Iyengar, 2014; De *et al.*, 2018). States having better connectivity and access to the neighbouring markets through improved corridors may gain from Intra- and interstate economic activities as well as with neighbouring countries (De *et al.*, 2019). On the other, the states which have less proximity to the transport corridors might face more connectivity challenges and relatively little access to the international market (Pal, 2016).

India has also taken initiatives to upgrade and create new roads and highways, railways, airports, inland waterways, and ports, etc. under many infrastructure development projects which are believed to provide improved logistic services to promote trade and development and further minimise the cost of travel. "India also have a competitive advantage in computer and information related services". (Kaur et al. 2020). In the case of "India's connectivity issue with Southeast Asia, it has been looked through two ways: national connectivity, such as the Golden Quadrilateral (GQ) projects, the Delhi–Mumbai Industrial Corridor (DMIC), and the Dedicated Freight Corridor (DFC); and through regional connectivity, such as the Trilateral Highway (TH) and Mekong India Economic Corridor (MIEC)" (www.adb.org). India's connectivity with Southeast Asia, although at present at an initial stage of development, would ensure the time-bound creation of world-class infrastructure in the country. In the recent past, the government of India along with the Asian Development Bank, the World Bank, and the Japanese government have started many infrastructure projects in developing transport corridor to reach neighbouring countries, namely, Trilateral Highway (TH), Kaladan Multi-modal Transit Transport Project (KMTTP), and Bangladesh–China–India–Myanmar Economic Corridor (BCIM-EC), Mekong India Economic Corridor (MIEC), which are expected to bring potential benefits to the region. These corridors are significant for India and especially because of the ambitious AEP that aims to strengthen connectivity between India with Southeast Asia. In this context, this paper wants to review the overall presence of the transport corridor which connects India with Southeast Asian countries and to assess the impact of these corridors on the future growth of the connected areas.

The first objective is to analyse the impacts of specific infrastructure projects on the regional economy at the national level i.e. how these corridors are likely to impact on the economic development of the connected areas.

Second, it attempted to find out the potential of the existing freight over the economic corridor with the help of explanatory variables, like GDP and other infrastructure variables.

The rest of the paper is organised as follows. Section 2 presents the model adopted for the study. Section 3 discusses the results, and, the conclusions are briefed in Section 4.

The Model

Building up new corridors cause a progressive construction of space and minimise transportation cost which further increases the overall competitiveness of the system and allow the benefits of economies of scale by providing regional cooperation, clustering economic activities connecting nodal centres etc. (Ghosh and De, 2005; De, 2013; Sen, 2014; and De *et al.*, 2018; 2019). Literature-based on the economic impact of transport infrastructure talked about three approaches. The first approach believes in the social cost-benefit analysis with consumer surplus as the main object. This approach has been widely used in many countries with the objective of welfare economics. More recently a second approach has been evolved which is based on productivity rather than consumer surplus. The outcome of this approach is mainly based on travel time savings of the households which do not have direct implications for GDP. The third approach is far away from these above two views and mainly based on employment. In this approach investments in the transport infrastructure have spatially differentiated impacts on employment. Although these approaches are inter-linked and partially complemented but much not covered macro-economic benefits in terms of GDP. To fulfil this gap, this study tries to build a relationship between connectivity corridors with regional economic development (see Figure 2.1) and further will test that empirically. Improvement of transport corridors influences production and household consumption through lowering of transportation cost. This may generate a redistribution effect among economic groups and also among regions. The relationship between transport corridors and its impact on regional development is illustrated in Figure 2.1 while considering more than one sector. Improved and efficient transport infrastructure can minimise transportation cost and time employing a reduction of distances with higher average speed. This directly influences movements of freight and passengers by making the production process cheaper. This reduction helps a firm to increase productivity and accessibility. Therefore this increase in productivity and accessibility in a certain region (or country) may result in an expansion of economic activities. This further leads to influence the number of movements of freight and passengers as a result of the relocation of economic activities. The government invests in infrastructure to develop the associability for each region with a relatively positive economic development, for instance, to overcome congestion. Overall this improvement in transport infrastructure directly indirectly helps other sectors like technology, demography, economy and environmental and public policy to be mentioned.

To test this framework empirically, this study has taken India-Myanmar-Thailand Trilateral Highway (TH) which will connect Moreh, in the Manipur state of India to Mae Sot in the Tak Province of Thailand via Myanmar. India has deployed additional resources to complete this by 2020 to bridge the connectivity across India with Myanmar, and Thailand. Next is the Kaladan Multi-Modal Transit Transport (KMMTT) project, formulated to connect Kolkata port of India with Sittwe port of Myanmar, and is estimated to be operational by 2019-20. The third one is the Bangladesh-China-India-Myanmar Economic Corridor (BCIM-EC)

Figure 2.1: Model on the Relation between the Transport Corridor and its Economic Impact

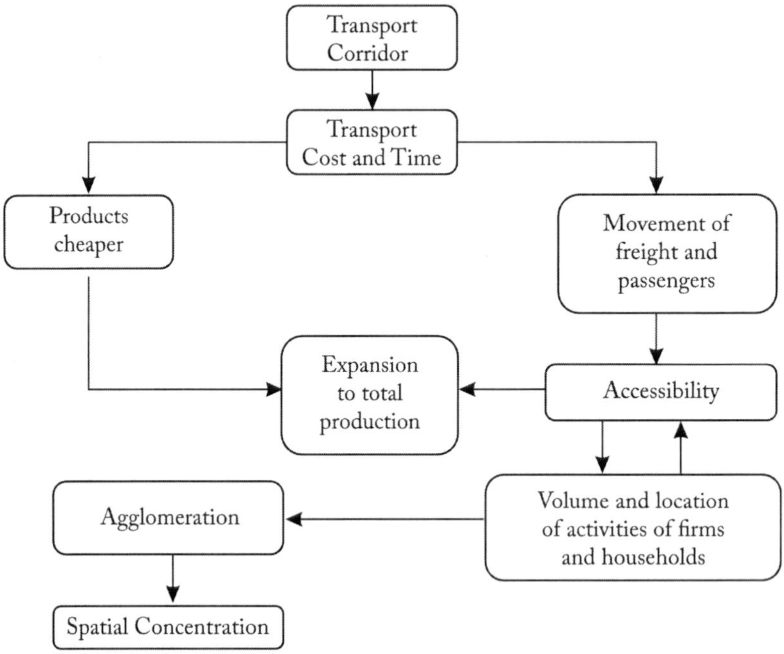

Source: Drawn by Author.

encompasses Kolkata in India to Kunming in China's Yunnan Province, passing through the Bangladesh and Myanmar. And last but not least is "the Mekong-India Economic Corridor (MIEC) involves integrating the four Greater Mekong Countries viz. Myanmar, Thailand, Cambodia and Vietnam with India through its east coast. It is proposed to connect the Ho Chi Minh City of Vietnam with Dawei in Myanmar through Bangkok in Thailand and Phnom Penh of Cambodia and further linking to Chennai in India. Integration with India is likely to add momentum to corridor development due to growing trade and investment linkages between India and Southeast Asian countries through the Myanmar border and the other coasts" (www.eria.org).

To assess the economic impact of transport corridors on economic activities we estimate the following baseline equation:

$$X_{it} = \alpha_0 + \alpha_i + \beta_1 Y_{it} - \beta_2 \tau_{ij} + \beta_3 I_{it} + \beta_4 C_{ki} + \beta_5 Z_i + \varepsilon_i \qquad (1)$$

where i represents a country, t time and ε_i is the error term. The dependent variable is total freight movement via land, air and sea routes. Y is the real expenditure where we have taken the Gross Domestic Product (GDP) and τ_{ij} is the trade cost. I is a vector of other independent variables such as road density, speed of vehicles which are taken to proxy the infrastructure, particularly these will give the essence of accessibility and quality of physical connectivity. Captures the effect of transport corridor on freight movement, where, corridor (k) is Trilateral Highway, Kaladan corridor, BCIM-EC, and MIEC respectively. We keep this corridor in our model as a categorical variable, where it takes '1' when the corridor (k) crosses the respective country or '0' otherwise. $Z$is the series of interaction variables to capture the effect of economic corridors on freight movement. All regressions include country-fixed effects α_i.

To carry out the future projections over a long time horizon, the growth rate of freight movement i has been obtained using equation (2) where an interaction term between GDP and freight have been taken.

$$\ln X_{it} = \sigma + \delta_{it1} \ln Y_{it} \tag{2}$$

Differentiation of the demand equation (1) for freight movement i with respect to time would yield the relation (where a hat (^) on the top of a variable denote its rate of growth):

$$\hat{X}_{it} = \delta \hat{Y}_{it} \tag{3}$$

This simpler equation can be used to project future freight demand $\hat{X}_{it}$, by using the income elasticity of the freight demand and the expected future growth rate, g, of GDP.

$$X_{it} = \alpha_0 + \alpha_i + \beta_1 Y_{it} - \beta_2 \tau_{ij} + \beta_3 I_{it} + \beta_4 (C_{ki} * \hat{Y}_{it}) + \beta_5 Z_i + \varepsilon_i \tag{4}$$

The study employ panel data model to analyse the relationship between the GDP and the freight in relation to corridors based on India, China, Thailand, Myanmar, Cambodia, Vietnam and Bangladesh for the period 2010 to 2017. The definitions of variables and their corresponding data source are given in Appendix 1.

Results and Discussions

Promotion of corridor is essential of a country's development as high transportation cost and low connectivity across regions are detrimental for trade and investments. Therefore, there is a bivariate association between income, infrastructure as any form of infrastructure development can boost the country's output by improving production and consumption.

To find the impacts of specific infrastructure projects on the regional economy at the national level i.e. how these transport corridors are likely to impact the economic development of the connected areas, this study has taken four corridors that are expected to connect India with the neighbour. The study estimated the generalised least squares (GLS) technique as the Hausman test (1978) reject random effect and select fixed effect. GLS also provides a higher R-square as compared to Ordinary Least Square (OLS). Therefore this technique is expected to fit better for our case to find out the potential of the existing freight over the economic corridor with the help of important explanatory variables. The estimated results are presented in Tables 2.1 and 2.2. Here we only report the significant results to discuss the estimated relations between the variables concerned.

Table 2.1 investigates the impact of different economic corridors on freight movement to capture the individual corridor effect in the regression models. Model 1 includes dummy for Trilateral Highway, Model 2 includes Kaladan corridor and Model 3 and Model 4 include BCIM–EC and Mekong India (MIEC) respectively. It is evident from Table 2.1 that the coefficients of the core variables are robust and consistent in all models. The good fit tells that GDP positively influences the freight of the regions having a corridor. Further results point out that GDP and road density (a proxy for infrastructure development) are the important determinants of freight flow. For every one per cent increase in GDP, total freight in the region is expected to increase by 0.8 per cent over time (see Model 1 in Table 2.1). The positive and significant relationship between road density and freight implies that the higher the road density, the higher would be the flow of freight between and within the countries. The trade cost has mixed results.

The existing Trilateral Highway shows a positive and significant coefficient, thereby suggesting that the countries connecting with the Trilateral Highway are expected to perform better than the countries not having that particular corridor. Dummy for the Kaladan corridor shows negative and insignificant estimates, whereas the dummy for BCIM-EC shows negative and significant results. This can happen when the growth of freight is considerably higher across the countries compared to the corridor connecting countries. The last corridor dummy of Mekong India shows a positive and significant sign believing that this will positively influence the country's freight.

Table 2.1: Estimated Results for Fixed Effect Model

Variable	Model 1	Model 2	Model 3	Model 4
Log of GDP	0.8** (-2.02)	0.5** (1.5)	0.3* (1.8)	0.4*** (2.8)
Trade Cost	-0.5 (1.2)	-0.1 (2.7)	0.4 (0.5)	-1.1* (1.3)
Log of Road Density	0.3*** (3.1)	0.4*** (2.8)	0.5** (3.6)	0.3*** (2.2)
Log of Speed	0.4 (0.4)	0.7* (0.5)	1.2* (1.1)	0.9** (2.3)
Trilateral Highway	1.2*** -	-	-	-
Kaladan Corridor	-	-1.9 (-3.7)	-	-
BCIM-EC	-	-	-1.6** (2.1)	-
Mekong India	-	-	-	1.1* (1.8)
Constant	-1.9 (-0.2)	-1.5 (0.6)	0.8 (-0.7)	0.2 (0.1)
N	35	35	35	35
R^2	0.718	0.802	0.813	0.689
Wald chi^2 (Prob> chi^2)	309.34 (0.00)	534.71 (0.00)	563.39 (0.01)	461.93 (0.00)
Country fixed effect	Yes	Yes	Yes	Yes
Time fixed effect	Yes	Yes	Yes	Yes

Notes: ***statistical significance at 1%, **statistical significance at 5%, *statistical significance at 10%; parentheses show standard error.

It is evident from Table 2.1 that GDP has a positive influence on freight. Therefore, we would like to investigate the contribution of GDP growth in corridors compared to non-corridor countries. Table 2.2 shows the interaction effect of GDP with a dummy for each corridor along with other core variables. The estimated coefficient of GDP shows the expected results, which has come out positive and significant in all the models. Trade cost again shows negative and significant in most of the models. The coefficient of road density has come out positive and significant in every model, thereby implying infrastructure is crucial to increase freight movement. The coefficient of speed shows mixed results.

Interestingly, in terms of GDP interaction, Models 1 to 4 in Table 2.2 clearly shows that the coefficients of corridor having countries and GDP interaction variable are positive and statistically significant. The size of the coefficient of interaction variable with GDP has come out greater than that of the coefficient of GDP in non-corridor countries, implying that the countries connecting with the corridors would gain relatively higher freight, compared to others. For instance, the coefficient of the interaction effect of GDP with a dummy for Trilateral Highway shows that a one per cent rise in GDP growth in corridor states would lead to 0.8 per cent rise in freight, compared to the non-corridor countries. Similarly, the interaction effect of GDP with the Kaladan corridor, BCIM-EC and Mekong India shows a significant higher impact on freight movement. Therefore this shows that in the future when these all corridors are in action then the countries will get higher freight movement with which the economic activities are expected to rise.

Conclusion

The benefits of better connectivity are enormous for both India and its neighbouring countries. In this study, we have analysed the importance of connectivity corridors. We empirically tried to see the impact of corridors, like Trilateral Highway (TH), Kaladan Multi-modal Transit Transport Corridor (KMTTC), and Bangladesh–China–India–Myanmar Economic Corridor (BCIM-EC), and Mekong India Economic Corridor (MIEC), on the economic development.

Table 2.2: Analysis Results of Corridors with GDP Interactions

Independent Variable	Model 1	Model 2	Model 3	Model 4
Log of GDP	0.4* (1.2)	0.3* (0.4)	0.3* (1.4)	0.2* (1.1)
Trade Cost	-1.3*** (4.3)	-0.9** (5.6)	-2.1*** (2.4)	0.8 (1.9)
Log of Road Density	0.4*** (2.9)	0.3*** (3.04)	0.5** (2.9)	0.5*** (2.9)
Log of Speed	1.6** (2.4)	2.3*** (4.4)	-0.2 (0.1)	0.6* (1.6)
Interaction of TH*GDP	0.8*** (2.9)	-	-	-
Interaction of Kaladan*GDP	-	1.4*** (3.4)	-	-
Interaction of BCIM-EC*GDP	-	-	1.3*** (6.1)	-
Interaction of Mekong India*GDP	-	-	-	0.9*** (3.8)
Constant	-38.4*** (0.8)	-21.6*** (6.8)	0.6*** (4.2)	0.4 (0.9)
N	35	35	35	35
R^2	0.818	0.792	0.690	0.634
Wald chi^2 (Prob> chi^2)	592.81 (0.00)	687.74 (0.00)	713.94 (0.00)	811.49 (0.00)
Country fixed effect	Yes	Yes	Yes	Yes
Time fixed effect	Yes	Yes	Yes	Yes

Notes: ***statistical significance at 1%, **statistical significance at 5%, *statistical significance at 10%; parentheses show standard error.

We found that GDP and road density is the positive and significant variables that have a significant impact on freight movement. Countries having corridors will get the benefit of freight with the higher flow of connectivity. For example, with better connectivity, countries can involve in the regional production network in an open economic framework. A stronger production network would enhance the trade and investment, and thereby deepen the Southeast Asian integration process. In the long-run, India connectivity would help to unlock the tremendous potential of Asia.

We found that when these international corridors will be functional then there will be a boost in the freight movements of the connected regions. "We have discussed that corridor based development projects are expected to generate further economic activities and regional development" (www.livemint.com). This further can influence the economic growth of the connected regions through the increase in the demand for production and consumption.

But this is not the only, air and maritime mode of transport are also crucial in deepening linkages between India and Southeast Asian countries. To add further, the need for not only physical connectivity but digital connectivity has also a role to play. India's regional connectivity with the Southeast requires the implementation of strong policy initiatives. Development and completion that all projects with Southeast Asia will bring significant opportunities for the creation of a functional single market in Asia.

References

De, P. (2013). Assessing barriers to trade in services in India: an empirical investigation. *Journal of Economic Integration,* 28 (1), 108-143.

De, P. and K. Iyengar, (2014). Developing Economic Corridors in South Asia. *Asian Development Bank,* New Delhi.

De, P., Ghatak, S., and Kumarasamy, D. (2018). Assessing the economic impacts of connectivity corridors: An empirical investigation. Research and Information System for Developing Countries.

De, P., S. Ghatak and K. Durairaj, (2019). Assessing Economic Impacts of Connectivity Corridors in Northeast India: An Empirical Investigation, *Economic and Political Weekly, Special Article Section, 54(11).*

Ghosh, B. and De, P. (2005). Investigating the linkage between infrastructure and regional development: Era of planning to globalisation, *Journal of Asian Economics,* 15(1), 1023-1050.

Kaur, S., Khorana, S., & Kaur, M. (2020). Is There Any Potential in Service Trade of South Asia?. *Foreign Trade Review,* 55(3), 402-417.

Pal, P. (2016). Intra-BBIN Trade: Opportunities and Challenges, *ORF Issue Brief*, 135.

Sen, K. (2014). Global Production Networks and Economic Corridors: Can They Be Drivers for South Asia's Growth and Regional Integration? *ADB South Asia*, Working Paper No. 33.

Appendix 2.1: Data Sources and Definition

Sl. No.	Variable Name	Description	Sources
1	F (Freight)	Total freight is calculated by aggregating the freight movement via land, air and sea routes in billion tonnes.	(i) Directorate General of Civil Aviation, Ministry of Civil Aviation (ii) Road Transport Year Book, Transport Research Wing, Ministry of Road Transport & Highways, Govt. of India (iii) World Development Indicators
2	Y (Gross Domestic Product)	Gross Domestic Product (GDP) at current prices are taken in US$ million.	(i) Reserve Bank of India (ii) World Development Indicators
3	Trade Cost	Trade cost measures based on the aerial distance between India's capital Delhi and respective country capital in km.	(i) Distance data has been collected with the help of the Google Map
4	Road Density	Ratio of total road in km to the total area in square km of that country. Road Density = $\frac{\text{Total available road in km in the respective country}}{\text{Total area in square km in the respective country}}$	(i) Ministry of Road Transport and Highways, Govt. of India (ii) Statistical Year Book India, 2016 (iii) Census of India, 2011
5	Speed	Average speed of the vehicle in km per hour	Based on literatures.

3

Trans Asia Connectivity and Economic Corridors

Sustainable Financing for Economic Development

Muhammad Ayub Mehar

Introduction

One of the desirable objectives of globalisation is reducing the global disparities in human welfare and development by the interaction of the peoples in a free world. This theory favours the participation and linkages among the nations. In this way, regionalisation is considered as the initiation of ultimate globalisation. The sociopolitical and economic histories of South Asia, Central Asia and Middle East are largely associated with the connectivity of their peoples, mutual trade, and transfer of natural and human resources. It describes the surprising consequences of economic linkages, and now it is a common opinion in the literature of Development Economics that Asia will re-gain its development rank in the New Economic Order. However, some analysts think that complicated barriers in economic integration will restrict Asian growth. These barriers limit the efficient utilisation of resources. In the presence of these barriers, the advantages of a big market from Almaty to Jakarta cannot be materialised. However, such barriers are quite removable by adopting liberal economic policies and regional economic integration. Notably, the history of the region denies the impossibilities of economic integration between the countries even in the presence of geopolitical tensions.

Here, it is notable that economic integration does not mean the economic linkages only. Economic linkage is a preliminary stage of economic integration. Economic integration is not similar to free trade. It is considered as the second-best option for mutual trade where barriers on free trade cannot be removed. Several politico-economic and social reasons may determine such irremovable barriers. Formation of preferential trading areas (PTAs), free trade areas (FTAs), customs unions (CUs), and economic and monetary unions (EMUs) are the earlier stages of economic integration. To implement an economic integration plan, mobility of the factors of production cannot be restricted. Business competitiveness is a requirement of free trade among the participating countries, while free mobility of the factors of production is a necessary condition to achieve a sustainable competitiveness in global environment. The sustainability of the free trade regime is always associated with the cross-border mobilisation of the factors of production including capital, labour, entrepreneurship and the utilisation of land. It implies also the mobility and migration of labour, cross borders listing of business enterprises, and the flow of investment.

Different levels of economic integration have been tested in various regions and groups of countries. Formation of preferential trading areas (PTAs), free trade areas (FTAs), customs unions (CUs), and economic and monetary unions (EMUs) are the interim stages to arrive at the complete economic integration. The North American Free Trade Area (NAFTA) which belongs to the second stage (free trade) has shown a successful model of resource allocations. The European Union (EU) has adopted an advanced version of integration after passing through earlier stages. The Euro-Zone has now embraced a single currency system, it is notable that economic integration does not mean the economic linkages only. Economic linkage is a preliminary stage of economic integration. Economic integration is something more than economic linkages. It is notable that free trade requires just frictionless cross the border movement of goods and services. However, economic integration builds a path for ultimate free trade. To develop cross the border infrastructure, transportation and custom facilities, easiness in documentation, introducing a visa free regime for business persons, and removing the non-tariff measures (NTMs) are included in this path.

"In the implementation of economic integration policies, mobility of the factors of production cannot be restricted. Free trade policy requires business competitiveness, while free mobility of the factors of production is a necessary condition to achieve sustainable competitiveness in the global environment" (www.tandfonline.com). The sustainability of the free trade regime is attached with the cross-border free mobilisation of the factors of production including capital, labour, entrepreneurship and the utilisation of land. The mobilisation of the factors of production is always associated with the mobility and migration of labour and the cross borders flow of investment.

There have been several integration attempts including ASEAN in Asia, Mercosur in Latin America, Ecowas/Comesa/SADC in Sub-Saharan Africa, and SAARC in South Asia. Some supranational institutions have played important roles in establishing economic integrations among the countries which have severe political disputes. For instance, the South Asian Association for Regional Cooperation (SAARC) played an important role in the implementation of the South Asian Free Trade Area (SAFTA).

Table 3.1: Stages of Economic Integration

No.	Degree of Integration	Scope of Integration
1	Preferential Trading Area (PTA)	A partial abolishment of custom tariffs on the inner borders of the member states
2	Free Trade Area (FTA)	A full abolishment of custom tariffs on the inner borders of the member states
Role of NTMs/NTBs and MFN Status		
3	Custom Union	A unified (common external) tariffs on the exterior borders of the union
4	Common Market	Inclusion of the movement of services, capital and labour into an FTA
5	Economic Union	A combination of the customs union with a common market
6	Fiscal Union	Introducing a shared fiscal and budgetary policy
7	Monetary Union	Introducing a shared currency
8	Complete Economic Integration	Unification of economic policies (tax, social welfare benefits, etc.), reductions in the rest of the trade barriers, the introduction of supranational bodies, and gradual moves towards the final stage, a "political union"

Source: Author Depiction.

Europe has already reached the highest level of economic integration by establishing a single currency and the European Central Bank, however, Asia has chosen loose economic cooperation based on free trade agreements, except for the Association of Southeast Asian Nations (ASEAN) which has created a common market. While it is obvious that the advantages of a big market from Almaty to Jakarta cannot be materialised in the presence of barriers in connectivity. So, there is a need to identify the complicated barriers in economic integration which restrict the economic growth and efficient utilisation of resources. The Three biggest barriers in the connectivity among Asian Countries are (1) Existence of the higher magnitude of NTMs/NTBs after removal of Tariff barriers, (2) Lack of Economic Corridors and (3) Lack of financing the infrastructure development and corridors.

Growing use of non-tariff measures (NTM) to restrict the imports from other countries has been observed after the formation of the World Trade Organisation (WTO). This practice has also been observed in South Asia with a higher magnitude. Such non-tariff measures (NTMs) are used to reinforce the market restrictions. They provide a substitute of tariffs to restrict imports. Theoretically, speaking, non-tariff measures (NTMs) cover a broad range of actions besides tariffs, which are used to protect a domestic economic activity. Such measures may be imposed or sponsored by the government. So, NTMs are more threatening than tariffs in restricting market access. Another important aspect from the basic understanding point of view is that if the basic objective of a measure is to protect the domestic economic activity, it will be known as an NTM. If this NTM is for a specific country and not applicable for all trading partners then it will be considered as a non-tariff barrier (NTB). Obviously, the tools and types of non-tariff barriers (NTBs) cannot be pre-determined or identified unless these are observed. The non-tariff barriers (NTBs) may be changed from time to time and varied from country to country. Such barriers may be hidden or invisible. It is too difficult to identify such invisible barriers. Regular monitoring and investigation is required to identify such barriers. The status of the 'Most Favored Nation (MFN)' can provide a simple and immediate solution of the 'NTBs' if these are identified (https://fp.brecorder.com). According to a survey (Mehar: 2013), more than 60 per cent NTBs in South Asia have been created through problems inland transportation, handling at ports and in banking transactions. The main area of concern of this study is to identify the sustainable sources for financing the corridors.

Economic Corridors for Regional Integration

One of the most important steps in the way of economic integration is the construction of economic corridors. Several projects are in progress to connect Europe with Asia through railways and highways. Trans Asia Railways (TAR) to link Malaysia to Turkey and then Western Europe and the 'One Belt, One Road' Project are included in these projects which are linking the Asian countries.

The 'Trans-Asian Railway (TAR)' project was initiated by the United Nations Economic and Social Commission for Asia and the Pacific (UNESCAP) to create an integrated freight railway network across Europe and Asia. This project was initiated in the 1960s, to provide a continuous 14,000-kilometer rail link between Singapore and Istanbul with possible further connections to Europe and Africa. This project was also seen as a way to the accessibility of landlocked countries like Laos, Afghanistan, Mongolia, and the Central Asian republics. The project promised to significantly reduce shipping times and costs between Europe and Asia. However, this Project cannot be considered a success story so far. Progress in developing the TAR was hindered by political and economic obstacles. By the 1990s, the end of the cold war and the normalisation of relations between some countries have improved the prospects of this project. By 2001, the four corridors had been studied as part of the plan: (1) The Northern Corridor: Germany, Poland, Belarus, Russia, Kazakhstan, Mongolia, China, and the Koreas, (2) The Southern Corridor: Turkey, Iran, Pakistan, India, Bangladesh, Myanmar, and Thailand, with links to China's Yunnan Province and, via Malaysia, to Singapore, (3) A Southeast Asian network, and (4) the North-South Corridor: Northern Europe to the Persian Gulf. Lastly, the 'Trans-Asian Railway Network Agreement' was signed in November 2006, by seventeen Asian nations as part of a United Nations Economic and Social Commission for Asia and the Pacific (UNESCAP) effort to build a transcontinental railway network between Europe and Pacific ports in China. The proposed 80,900-km railway network will originate from the Pacific seaboard of Asia and end on the doorsteps of Europe. Much of the railway network already exists, although some significant gaps remain. A big challenge is the differences in rail gauge across Eurasia. However, the fortune of this global mega plan must depend on the participation of Asian countries.

Another initiative of connectivity in Asia was introduced by China in 2013. This plan is called "One Belt, One Road (OBOR)". "It is an initiative which has been taken by the Chinese government to encourage connectivity and cooperation among the Asian countries. This plan (OBOR) consists of 6 trade corridors spread mainly over Eurasia but also touch the fringes of Pacific, North & East Africa" (https://fp.brecorder.com). The main corridors are:

One Belt, One Road (OBOR)

- China – Mongolia - Russia Corridor
- New Eurasian Land Bridge
- China – Central Asia – West Asia Corridor
- China – Indochina Peninsula Corridor
- China– Myanmar – Bangladesh – India Corridor
- China – Pakistan Economic Corridor (CPEC)

Corridor and Projects under ECO Initiatives

- Quadrilateral Agreement on Traffic in Transit (QATT), Islamabad
- Tehran-Istanbul (ITI) Train Network,
- Trilateral Transit Trade Agreement (TTTA),
- Pakistan - Uzbekistan Transit Trade Agreement,
- Pakistan – Iran – Turkmenistan Commerce Cooperation (PITCC),
- Afghanistan – Pakistan – India – Bangladesh - Myanmar (APIBM) Corridor,

- Pakistan – India - Nepal Integrated Network,
- Central Asia & South Asia (CASA) – 1000,
- Indus River Trade Corridor,
- North-South Transnational Corridor (Kazakhstan - Turkmenistan - Iran railway link),
- Iran - Pakistan – India Pipeline,
- Turkmenistan - Afghanistan – Pakistan and India (TAPI) Pipeline, and
- Trans-Iranian Canal

Demand-Derived Financing the Economic Corridors

The most important aspect of the construction of these economic corridors to materialise the strong economic integration among the participant countries belongs to the financing arrangements and their macroeconomic implications. The drastic side of infrastructure financing in Asian countries is the over-dependency on public sector fiscal resources. The participation of the private sector in infrastructure financing is not common in these countries. "The development and modernisation of physical infrastructure in developing countries during the bi-polar regime were largely based on the subsidised external debts and grants from industrialised countries" (www.abd.org). It was a global trend until 1990 that mega financing activities including infrastructure development have been considered as public sector responsibility. Even in a capitalist world, this was a common phenomenon. The developing world was habitual to get help from external sources for the development of infrastructure. "The statesmen and politicians in some countries still consider the foreign aid and external subsidised loans as an option for the infrastructure development, while the misuse of public funds, populism, corruption and inefficient planning have badly failed the economic governance in those countries" (www.abd.org). The inefficient utilisation of borrowed money adds a financial burden, while further borrowing at a higher cost to repay the external debts has become a common tradition in those economies. To improve the tax-to-GDP ratio through an increase in indirect taxes is a general consequent of this tradition.

In the current scenario, long-term debt has become the most popular source of financing for infrastructure projects. The share of debt financing in infrastructure projects with private participation in 2017 was 70 per cent, while 26 per cent came from equities and 4 per cent in the form of public subsidies. Out of 26 per cent equities, 23 per cent was from the private sector and 3 per cent from the public sector. While 70 per cent debt financing was divided between international and local (commercial) participants: 55 per cent financed by international and 15 per cent by local participants. Out of 55 per cent international debt financing, 30 per cent belong to DFIs (6 per cent multilateral and 24 per cent bilateral). In non-DFI debt financing, 18 per cent was contributed by the public sector and the remaining from the private (commercial) sector. This detail is enough to understand the patterns of infrastructure financing by the private sector. Long-term debt is the main source of infrastructure financing, while the share of short-term financing is declining globally. It is quite obvious that long-term debt by public sector entities creates fiscal problems in long-term because of the growing burden of payment. In this study, we tested the effects of an investment in infrastructure development and short-term financing. To estimate the impacts of infrastructure development and external financing on GDP growth we established the following model:

GROWTH=ß0 + ß1ENPM1217 +ß2TRPM1217 +ß3ELCLOS +ß4CRPTN + ß5STDBT16

Where, 'GROWTH' is GDP Growth in 2017, 'ENPM1217' is investment commitments in fuel and energy with private sector participation in million dollars during the last five years (2012-17), 'TRPM1217' is investment commitments in transport with private sector participation in million dollars during last five years (2012-17), 'ECLOS' is value lost due to electrical outage as a percentage of the sale, 'CRPTN' is bribery incidence as a percentage of firms, and 'STDBT16' is short-term debt as a percentage of total debt in 2016. The model has been tested in two different versions: with and without external debts. Investment with private participation in infrastructure for most of the countries belongs to FDI. The impact of five years investment has been tested and it is found that investment in fuel and energy has a significant positive impact on the growth of GDP. But the significant negative impact of investment in transportation is against the common logic. "In understanding the empirical analysis and statistical inferences, it is considered that investment in transport projects with private participation refers to the commitments to infrastructure projects in transport. Such projects should be reached at financial closure and directly or indirectly serve the public. Movable assets and small projects are excluded" (www.ceicdata.com). Data are in current U.S. dollars. The negative impact of investment in transportation may reflect the huge investment in popular public projects like the construction of motorways. Such projects are used by ruling political parties for fascination and enhancing public support and vote bank. But these can adversely affect economic growth. The value losses in business (ELCLOS) due to the electrical outage was introduced to capture the effect of deterioration in infrastructure. Its negative impact on GDP growth is significant. The negative impact of economic corruption (bribery) has also been proved statistically.

The data for these estimations have been extracted from the World Bank (2018), which covers 192 countries in 2017. The most important conclusion is the significant positive effect of the 'share of short-term financing in total external financing' on GDP growth. It concludes that long-term debts do not have a significant contribution to the growth of GDP. Based on global data it has been confirmed that a larger share of short-term financing in the total external debts has a significant role in the determination of GDP growth. This reflects an important phenomenon that more dependency on long-term debt for investment in developing projects by the public sector organisations encourages populism. The governments misuse these funds to gain public support by launching those developing projects which do not create the earning assets in the economy. These projects may be used for entertainment and fascination without creating the earning assets for sustainable development. These projects do not have commercial viability, so the governments have to arrange the redemption and interest payments through excessive taxations or further borrowing to repay the older debts. This practice affects the growth of GDP negatively. It is a common phenomenon that a large portion of the external outstanding debt of the developing countries belongs to their public sector. The effects of short-term debts seem positive for the growth of the economy, which indicates that such financings are used to manage the immediate requirements to maintain economic activities. Because these activities have to generate funds for repayment of short-term debt. In the majority of cases, long-term borrowing is spent through public entities. This conclusion is against not only common intuition.

Table 3.2: Dependent Variable= GDP Growth (GDPG17)

Variable	Model I		Model II	
	Coefficients	**T-Statistics**	**Coefficients**	**T-Statistics**
Intercept	3.513	2.073	-1.766	-2.104
ENPM1217	0.026	3.808	0.038	17.214
TRPM1217	-0.009	-2.887	-0.006	-7.562
ELCLOS	-0.352	-1.743	-1.201	-9.250
CRPTN	-0.369	-3.155	-0.380	-15.974
STDBT16	–	–	0.290	6.894
Adjusted R-Square	0.6804			0.9871
F-Statistics	4.184			90.730

Source: Authors Calculations.

Recommendations

Several studies have quantified the impacts of economic corridors and explained how these corridors affect the GDP growth, employment, pattern of investments, quality of life, globalisation, tax revenues and trade activities. This study has identified that financing the corridors (and other infrastructure development) through long-term debt financing may affect the economy negatively. The sovereign bonds to finance the corridors' infrastructure may be a considerable option but the success of these multilateral global projects requires the participation of all beneficiaries. The issuance of sovereign bonds to finance global or regional projects should not be based on the guarantees by a single country government.

If the objective of the construction of economic corridors is to establish the economic linkages then the participating countries should consider the formation of a fiscal union. The issuance of sovereign bonds jointly by the participants of a fiscal union will minimise the political risks and the cost of debt may be reduced. Otherwise, the sizeable subscription of sovereign bonds at appropriate cost cannot be successful in the countries where the private bonds market is inactive and its size is negligible. Another possibility of the financing of regional infrastructure projects is the formation of autonomous entities to govern, operate and finance the projects. International investors can participate in those corporate entities through equities.

The study shows the favourable role of 'Short-term Financing' in creating economic efficiencies. The higher share of long-term debts in total debt financing affects GDP growth negatively. It aggravates poverty and the burden of indirect taxes. The study recommends equity (participation) financing for cross the border economic corridors and other infrastructure projects.

The study is based on a development financing model (Mehar: 2018) which recommends that the cost of external debt (investment) must be less than incremental growth in GDP. The external capital becomes a problem only if the government has to generate funds from the public to pay the cost of external capital. So, external financing is still a viable option for developing countries.

These recommendations minimise the role of government and public finances in the construction of economic corridors, while these corridors will be considered as 'international properties'. This approach minimises the political risk. In this way the government responsibilities concerned with these corridors will be limited to the following points:

1. To manage the law and order situation and the provision of justice without any political, sectarian or ethnic bias;
2. To ensure transparency and sustainability in the economic policies and international economic agreements; and
3. To provide complete freedom to economic activities without any unnecessary bureaucracy.

References

Asian Development Bank (2017); 'Country Partnership Strategy: Pakistan: 2015–2019', Manila: Public Private Partnership in Pakistan: 2017.

Bhattacharyay, B. N. (2012); 'Estimating Demand for Infrastructure 2010–2020', In 'Infrastructure for Asian Connectivity', edited by B. N. Bhattacharyay, M. Kawai, and R. Nag. 19–79. Cheltenham: Asian Development Bank Institute (ADBI)/ADB and Edward Elgar.

Håvard Halland, John J. Beardsworth, Bryan C. Land and James A. Schmidt (2014); 'Resource Financed Infrastructure: A Discussion on a New Form of Infrastructure Financing' in 'Public-Private Infrastructure Facility (PPIAF)', Washington: 2014.

Inderst (2013); 'Private Infrastructure Finance and Investment in Europe', EIB Working Paper 2; Luxembourg: 2013.

Inderst, Georg (2018); 'Infrastructure Investment, Private Finance, and Institutional Investors: Asia from a Global Perspective', Luxembourg: 2018.

Asian Development Bank Institute (2018); 'Financing Infrastructure in Asia and the Pacific Capturing Impacts and New Sources'; Tokyo: 2018.

Mehar, Ayub (2005); 'Is debt a substitute of equity? Relevancy of Financial Policy in New Economic Scenarios'; Applied Financial Economics, 15 (1); 337-366.

Mehar, Ayub (2015); Infrastructure Development by Liberalizing Economic Policies: The Straight Path of Economic Prosperity; Islamabad, Economic Freedom Network: 2015.

Mehar, Ayub (2017); Infrastructure Development, CPEC and FDI in Pakistan: Is There any Connection? Transnational Corporation Review; 2017 (6); 2-10.

Mehar, Ayub (2018); Global Financial Architecture and Growing Poverty: Is There a Connection? (unpublished paper)' MPRA: 2018.

Michael, Regan (2018); 'Infrastructure Financing Modalities in Asia and the Pacific Region: Strengths and Limitations' in 'Financing Infrastructure in Asia and the Pacific Capturing Impacts and New Sources'; Tokyo, Asian Development Bank Institute: 2018.

Naoyuki Yoshino, Peter J. Morgan, and Pradumna B. Rana (2018); 'Global Shocks and the New Global and Regional Financial Architecture: Asian Perspectives'; Tokyo, Asian Development Bank Institute: 2018.

Organization for Economic Co-operation and Development (2012); 'Strategic Transport Infrastructure Needs to 2030'; Paris, OECD Publishing: 2012.

Singh, A. and Hamid, J; (1992), Corporate Financial Structures in Developing Economies; IFC Technical Paper No. 1, IFC; Washington: 1992.

The Economists (2012); 'Real Wealth of Nations'; 30th June 2012.

UNU-IHDP and UNEP (2012); 'Inclusive Wealth Report 2012: Measuring progress toward sustainability'; Cambridge: Cambridge University Press: 2012.

US Department of Transportation, Federal Highway Administration- FHWA (2010); 'Project Finance Primer - Update to the Innovative Finance Brochure' Washington: 2010.

World Bank (2007); 'Government Guarantees: Allocating and Valuing Risk in Privately Financed Infrastructure Projects', Timothy C Irwin; Washington: 2007.

World Bank (2017); 'Private Participation in Infrastructure (PPI)- Annual Report 2017'; Washington: 2017.

https://fp.brecorder.com

www.abd.org

www.Leicdata.com

PART II

Evaluating Role of China in India-East Asia Connections

4

India-China Maritime Cooperation

Avoiding Nuclear Rivalries

Rajesh Kumar

Introduction

India's Maritime Diplomacy in the 21st Century

India is not known for following British geographer Mackinder's heartland thesis. But it's fully aware of the importance of safeguarding its large maritime area. It also realises that maritime areas have the potential of emerging as fresh points of conflict on part of nations. It is in light of new realities of the 21st century, the paragraphs mentioned in the Government of India (GOI) Annual Report of Ministry of Defence 2014-15 are very significant and they indicate about India's maritime posturing in years to come. The report says, "India is a maritime Nation and the country sits astride a very large number of busy International Shipping Lanes, that criss-cross the Indian Ocean. More than 90% of our trade by volume and 70% by value are transported over the seas" (Lalremsiami and Patnaik, 2020). For a rapidly growing economy seeking new markets worldwide, these trade figures will only spiral upwards in the future. Another Indian Navy policy document of October 2015 defines maritime diplomacy in terms of engagement with different countries to mitigate traditional and non-traditional threats. (Indian Navy 2015: 84). India's maritime diplomacy has been well explained by Pradeep Chauhan, a retired Vice Admiral. According to him "India's 'Maritime Diplomacy' is a function of the desire of the nation to preserve, protect and promote her maritime interests". (Chauhan, 2015) He adds that maritime diplomacy is not merely about naval power but has a wide spectrum that involves political, economic and military power exerted through the use of the sea. (Chauhan, 2015) Accordingly, the conduct of maritime diplomacy is undertaken by the Ministry of Foreign Affairs and the Indian Navy and maritime security engagement have become the cornerstone of India's regional foreign policy initiatives.

Today India is over whelmingly busy in getting its maritime presence enhanced in the Indian Ocean Region as well as the Asia Pacific region. India is also impacted by developments beyond its immediate neighbourhood and the Indian Ocean region. Developments in West Asia, Central Asia, South East Asia and the Asia Pacific have a direct bearing on India's interests. At the international level, a great geopolitical game across the globe is being played out. Russia is attempting to bring all adjoining maritime areas under its influence like; Black Sea, Caspian Sea, Baltic Sea and the Mediterranean. China is redefining its maritime strategies in areas like South China Sea (SCS), East China Sea (ECS), Yellow Sea, Indian Ocean (IOC), Bay of Bengal (BOB), Persian Gulf and it has also succeeded in getting its presence established as far as the Gulf of Aden.

In light of the global trend, India is also known for interacting more actively with littoral states of the Indian Ocean Region and employing maritime security engagements as a cornerstone of her regional foreign policy initiatives. India's maritime economic activities have continued to expand across a large range, including energy security, seaborne trade, shipping and fishing, with substantial Indian investments and citizens overseas. For external trade and energy needs, India has continously dependent on the seas. (Sheliya and Joshi, 2019). These include crude and liquefied hydrocarbon imports, the export of refined products, offshore development and economic partnerships across the world. India's trade and energy security, development of its deep-sea mining areas, and supporting its scientific research stations in Antarctica, are all dependent on its Sea Lines of Communication (SLOCs). This has lent a pivotal role to the security of India's SLOCs and increased the importance of the sea routes, international shipping and *freedom of navigation* to India's national interests. "On the whole, the safety and security of seaborne trade and energy routes, especially in the IOR, considering their effect on global economies and India's national interests; The importance of maintaining freedom of navigation and strengthening the international legal regime at sea, particularly the United Nations Convention on the Law of the Sea (UNCLOS) are on to high agenda of Indian Navy" (Limaye, 2017).

India's Maritime Diplomatic Activities in Recent Years

Today emergence of new maritime flash points is being witnessed in the South China Sea, the Malacca Straits, Black Sea, the Arabian Sea and Piracy in the Gulf of Aden. All such issues form the basis of our maritime diplomacy with countries like Singapore, Japan, Australia, Vietnam, U.S.A. and Sri Lanka. Under the complex maritime security environment, India's maritime role has increased. India's maritime strategy is experiencing pressure from China, Pakistan and other maritime powers besides the United States and Russia. The new issues like piracy and terrorism have made its maritime diplomacy ever challenging and multifaceted. Conduct of naval exercises with countries like Vietnam, Philippines, Japan, China, U.S.A., Malaysia and Brunei has become an important way of maritime engagements with littoral nations regularly.

"India has major strategic interests as well as economic and commercial stakes in continued peace and stability in the Asia Pacific region. India's view is that all countries must exercise restraint and resolve bilateral issues diplomatically and without recourse to the use or threat of use of force. India supports freedom of navigation in international waters and the right of passage, following international law. India believes that the current regional security landscape calls for a cooperative and inclusive approach. On its part, under the 'Act East' policy which places renewed emphasis on engagement with the Asia Pacific, India has been an active participant in various bilateral as well as multilateral fora with a focus on security matters such as the East Asia Summit, ADMM – Plus and ASEAN Regional Forum (ARF)". (Annual report of MOD, 2014-15)

There is also a need to further improve regional responses to challenges such as transnational crime, terrorism, natural disasters, pandemics, cybersecurity as well as food and energy security. The report focuses on the linkages between local groups and terrorist organisations outside the region are a matter of concern. India has historic ties with several African nations and has sought to deepen its bilateral ties with African countries through the strategic initiative of the India-Africa Forum Summit (IAFS) mechanism that seeks to promote regional and continent-level political and economic cooperation with African countries (Annual Report of MOD, 2014-15).

The Indian Ocean Remains as Core of India's Maritime Diplomacy

"A new struggle for dominance over the Indian Ocean has started with the rise of major economic powers in the Asia-Pacific that relies on energy imports to sustain their growth. Not only does most oil and gas shipping transit through the Indian Ocean, but these energy resources are also produced in the littoral states. The seabed of the Indian Ocean is rich in mineral resources. It is in the interests of the world economy that a free and uninterrupted flow of oil and goods through the ocean's Sea Lines of Communication (SLOCs) is maintained. The world today relies on the US to maintain peace and stability in the region". (Kumar, 2012)

The aim to maintain stability in the Indian Ocean goes to the heart of India's economic interests. More than 95 per cent of its exports are shipped through the surrounding waters. Up to 81 per cent of the oil volume that India consumes is provided via the Arabian Sea. India drills up to 70 per cent of its hydrocarbons in offshore blocks. Since the late 1990s, state-owned energy companies have discovered more promising offshore deposits of gas and oil. Apart from energy, the Indian Ocean is precious for several other assets, such as mineral ores and fishing grounds. "Besides hydrocarbons, the Indian Ocean contains several other valuable minerals. Titanium, Zirconium and Thorium are found in the Indian Mannar Gulf and the Bengal Gulf. In several million of square kilometres, the Ocean floor is also covered with so-called poly-metallic nodules; these are volcanic composites that hold manganese, iron, and nickel. Several of these areas are commercially exploitable" (Jonathan, 2009).

India Holds Annual Joint Naval/Tri services Exercise with the IOC Littoral States as Part of Sagar Outreach Programme and Maritime Diplomacy

India continued to remain engaged with IOC littoral states in 2017-18. The MOD Annual Report 2017-18 pointed out that "Indian Navy synergising their Humanitarian and Disaster Relief efforts with that of our neighbours, the Indian Navy invited 'Observers' from Sri Lanka, Maldives, Bangladesh and Myanmar to participate in the 'Annual Tri-Service HADR Exercise' conducted by the Indian Navy from May 18–20, 2017 on the Western Coast". Further, to expose mid-level leaders of IOR littoral nations to Blue Water operations, the Indian Navy conducted 'Exercise SAMBANDH', from October 24–27, 2017, wherein the Indian Navy's capabilities were showcased to 'Observers' from 18 Friendly Foreign Countries, which included, Sri Lanka, Bangladesh, Vietnam, Mauritius, Maldives, Seychelles, Mozambique, Oman, Myanmar, Thailand, Indonesia, Iran, Kenya, UAE, Malaysia, Qatar, Tanzania and Madagascar (Annual Report MOD, 2017-18). India continued to maintain closer cooperation with Indian Ocean Littoral Navies like Thailand and the Indonesian Navy under the *CORPAT* programme. India carried out the 21st edition of 'Malabar-17' naval exercise with U.S. and Japan Self Defence Maritime Forces in July 2017. It also held a joint naval exercise under SIMBEX-17 with Singapore in May 2017. This year only, India also became a full member of SCO which is to provide closer cooperation with all five Central Asian republics besides Russia and China. India held INDRA series of tri-services exercise with Russia also in October 2017Annual Report

MOD, 2017-18). The Indian navy thus remains engaged in multiple, increasingly institutionalised, naval exercises with a plethora of both regional and extra-regional navies, ranging from France to Singapore.

Chinese interests and strategies in the Indian Ocean under 'string of pearls' and India-China Maritime Security Competition

India-China relations continue to remain stable in recent years, barring the 2017 Dokalam episode. Except for the last 3 years, China remained India's largest trading partners until the U.S.A. replaced it. Post Indian 1998 May nuclear explosion, China's foray into Indian Ocean waters have increased and at ties, China has openly stated that the Indian Ocean does not belong to India without providing any reasonable answer to its similar assertion in SCS, ECS and Yellow sea region. Undoubtedly, the last two decades of the 21st century has witnessed more competition between two Asian neighbours in each other's maritime territory. Both the countries are under pressure to ingrain new factors into their maritime policies: like energy security goals; climate change targets; keeping sea lanes open on 365 days basis; exploitation of sea minerals/resources; dealing with piracy; threats attributed to non-state actors etc.

Scholar's view that China's foremost interest in the Indian Ocean is to protect its increasingly important supplies of energy that need to transit that region. In recent times non-conventional security threats such as piracy have also emerged. They have plagued the Strait of Malacca and more recently the region off the coast of Somalia. Besides, "the Chinese have gone into Africa in a big way. China also sees itself as a possible long-term competitor of India and the US. Such Chinese strategic planning is reflected in 'string of pearls' which includes the Gwadar port in Pakistan, naval bases in Burma, electronic intelligence-gathering facilities on islands in the Bay of Bengal, funding the construction of a canal across the Kra Isthmus in Thailand, a military agreement with Cambodia and the building up of forces in the South China Sea" (Pant, 2016). Thus there is no denying the fact that the Chinese thrust into the Indian Ocean is gradually becoming more pronounced. "The term 'string of pearls' was coined in 2003 by a team of Booz Allen consultants, in a report for the Pentagon, to describe China's attempts to gain a strategic foothold in the Indian Ocean. Soon 'string of pearls' came to mean the encirclement of India by China" (Kumar, 2012).

Despite political controversies in each of these countries, China has built container ports in Bangladesh at Chittagong and in Sri Lanka at Hambantota (Pant, 2016). It is suspected that at Hambantota the Chinese have also constructed a naval facility, or at least are going to use the deep seaport for this purpose in case of need. One could witness the pace at which Chinese companies have also acquired a terminal for 30 years in Colombo port just opposite to posh area of Colombo having topmost sky rise hotels and other financial companies towers. The deep sea ports at Gwadar and Hambantota will allow the Chinese to monitor Indian and US naval activity in the region. All these new Chinese maritime threats find mention in the 2003 Govt. of India, Annual Defence Report stressed that "the seas surrounding India have been a theatre of superpower rivalry in the past, and continue to be a region of heightened activity from and by extra-regional navies on account of global security concerns (Annual Report of MOD, 2003-04). India's readiness to meet these new threats is mentioned in the 2006 Annual Defence Report which said that India will continue to monitor "China's military modernisation, including in the maritime sector" (Annual Report of MOD, 2004-05).

"China is reluctant to depend on US naval power to keep sea lanes open in the Indian Ocean, through which 80 per cent of its oil passes through. It has decided to boost its naval power at 'choke points' along the sea routes from the Persian Gulf to the South China Sea" (Pant, 2016). China has deployed its Jin-class submarines at a submarine base near Sanya on the southern tip of Hainan Island in the South China Sea. As a result of changing Chinese naval doctrine, the Sino-Indian relationship is becoming competitive. China is becoming more assertive in playing a greater role in the Indian Ocean region, protecting and advancing its interests, especially Chinese commerce, as well as countering India (Pant, 2016). The Chinese presence in the Indian

Ocean has significantly expanded China's strategic depth in India's backyard and is likely to reduce the manoeuvrability of the Indian navy ((Pant, 2016), and Kumar, 2012).

In the light of ever-increasing threats, since 2000, the Indian Navy has been conducting more and more exercises in the eastern part of the Indian Ocean, even in the South China Sea. Officials from the Ministry of Defence also acknowledge that the Far Eastern Command will expand its capacity beyond maritime policing and that India "should maintain control over the Andaman Sea as China's principal maritime gateway" (Navy, 2015). Thus, Asia's industrialising and urbanising giants, India and China, represent the greatest growth trajectory for the demand for energy and minerals in the world, both today and into the foreseeable future.

South Asia remains caught into geo-strategy and geopolitics of powers like India, Pakistan, China and the USA. Overall, China has been working constantly to keep Indian influence at bay through coercive policies like openly opposing India and favouring other South Asian countries, especially, Pakistan. China's ambitions in the Indian Ocean region and the Arabian Sea further complicate the situation. For China, the deepening of Indo-US strategic cooperation in recent years is seen as strengthening of the balance of power against it and containing its influence in Central, South, South-East Asia and South Pacific region. At the same time, Sino-Pak strategic cooperation puts strain and pressure on India's security policy. China's 21st century flagship projects like One Belt and One Road (BRI) and CPEC have the potentials to aggravate the Indian security complexities further.

India-China Maritime Cooperation: The Nuclear Dimension

It is only in the South Asia region in the world where three countries India, China and Pakistan all sharing borders with each other are also nuclear powers. A large portion of their annual defence budget gets spent on account of developing new strategic weapons. All these countries also remain the largest importers of arms at the world level. Since the Indo-U.S. nuclear agreement of 2008 that allowed the Nuclear Suppliers Group (NSG) to permit trade in civilian nuclear materials with India, nuclear cooperation dynamics among India, U.S.A., China and Pakistan have become highly competitive. The pending border disputes between India-China and India-Pakistan continues to impinge upon their nuclear policies which have taken military orientations in the present era. The World over nuclear policies of countries remains influenced by such theories. China has entered into a nuclear agreement with Pakistan for compensating for the advantage India gained in the aftermath of the Indo-U.S. nuclear agreement. India-Pakistan continues to pursue its declared nuclear doctrines. India continues to pursue No First Use (NFU), whereas, Pakistan's doctrine says that it may use nuclear weapons against India without caring for India's NFU in case of protecting its supreme national interest. At the same time, India continues to remain sceptical about China's nuclear and missiles cooperation with Pakistan. For China, Pakistan is a key ally for neutralising India's ever-increasing nuclear weapons capabilities. China wants Pakistan to offer credible deterrence to India thereby restricting India from ever posing a serious threat to China.

Moderation of China's Conventional and Nuclear Forces and Growing Indian Concerns

China has been trying to enhance its global reach. PLA global operations in recent years included counter-piracy patrols, humanitarian assistance and disaster relief, exercises and sea lane security. Highlights include "the deployments of the 17th and 18th Naval Escort Task Forces to the Gulf of Aden, PLA Navy frigates escorting cargo ships carrying chemical weapons materials out of Syria, search and rescue support for Malaysia Airlines MH370, participation in UN peacekeeping missions, circumnavigation of the African continent, and the first-ever deployment of a SHANG-class nuclear-powered submarine (SSN) and SONG-class diesel-electric submarine (SS) to the Indian Ocean" (Annual Report, 2015). "The Second Artillery Force possesses at least 1,200 short-range ballistic missiles (SRBMs) in its inventory. China is increasing the lethality of its conventional missile force by fielding a new ballistic missile, the CSS-11 (DF-16), which possesses a range of 800-1,000 km. The CSS-11, coupled with the already deployed conventional variant of the CSS-5 (DF-21) medium-range ballistic missile (MRBM), will improve China's ability to strike not only Taiwan but other regional targets" (Navy, 2015). All such developments are sufficient to worry not only the U.S. but also Indian policymakers. Chinese media raised a lot of hue and cry during the recently defused Dokalam crisis. It boasted a lot of China's newly attained nuclear missiles capabilities and issued several warnings to the Government of India for withdrawal of its armed forces from Dokalam. China's considered Dokalam to be Bhutan's territory and claimed that it had the right to settle a border dispute with Bhutan where India had strong reservations and it sent its armed forces into Bhutan's territory as it has been India's duty to take appropriate measures in case of Bhutan's security and foreign affairs related matters. However, the entire crisis got defused by the withdrawing of their forces from the area in the last week of August 2017 bilaterally.

China's Changed Nature of Nuclear Doctrine in the 21st Century

China's nuclear weapons policy prioritises maintaining a nuclear force able to survive an attack and respond with sufficient strength to inflict unacceptable damage on an enemy. A new generation of mobile missiles, with warheads consisting of MIRVs and penetration aids, are intended to ensure the viability of China's strategic deterrent in the face of continued advances in the U.S. and, to a lesser extent, Russian strategic ISR, precision strike, and missile defence capabilities. Similarly, India's nuclear force is an additional driver behind China's nuclear force modernisation.

Indeed, "India's no-first-use stance is not open-ended as it leaves open the possibility of retaliation in the event of an attack on it or its forces by nuclear, biological or chemical weapons. Nevertheless, there can be no mistaking the purely defensive role accorded by India to nuclear weapons" (IDSA Task Report, 2010) *The nuclear weapons policies of the United States are the most prominent external factors influencing Chinese advocates for raising the alert level of China's nuclear forces.* "China maintains a small nuclear arsenal-well under 300 warheads-that is kept off alert: the warheads are separated from the missiles" (Kristensen and Norris 2015). It has a clear message for the U.S. and India both in the 21st century. Overall, China has a nascent nuclear triad, but one that remains limited primarily by range, arsenal sise, and operational experience. India in recent years also has been trying to develop its nuclear triad capability at the earliest to counter threats from China and Pakistan both.

All such developments have serious bearings on India's overall security and strategic environment. All such capabilities have emboldened China towards Asia-Pacific, South Asia, South-East Asia and Central Asian countries. Its assertiveness is being experienced in the Indian Ocean region, the South China Sea, East China Sea and the Yellow Sea region. No such mechanism of Arms Control measure exists among China and South Asian Nuclear Powers like India and Pakistan.

India's Preparedness to Counter China-Pakistan Dual Threat

After testing Agni III intermediate-range ballistic missile (IRBM) in April 2007, which is India's first missile that could reach China's entire territory, and in its 3,500 to the 4,000-kilometre range, India is also continuing to work on Multiple Independently-targetable Re-entry Vehicle (MIRV) technology to enable the Agni III to circumvent Chinese missile defence countermeasures (Bedi, 2006). India has also expedited the development of longer-range missiles like the Agni-V and the Agni-VI and the quest for the sea leg of the nuclear "triad" has been propelled by China's concern only. Thus, China, India and Pakistan are deeply caught in a strategic triangular relationship that share a history of conflicts and border disputes. Most recently in February 2019, India also tested anti-satellite weapons the first time. It is all set to carry out a simulated space war exercise in late 2019.

Indian Recent Arms Procurement for Reducing Strategic Gap with China

The U.S.A. sold India ten C-17 heavy-lift aircraft worth US$4.1 billion. In March 2009 the US government authorised the US$2.1 billion sales of eight Boeing P-8I long-range maritime patrol aircraft to the Indian Navy. Before that, in January 2008, Washington approved the US$1 billion sales of six Lockheed Martin C-130J Super Hercules military transport planes. Similarly, in 2007 the Indian Navy purchased the USS for US$48 million. The Trenton is a landing-dock vessel and was also the Indian Navy's first-ever US-built naval vessel. In 2005, India and the US signed a historic defence framework that, for the first time, included joint production of arms. Previously, in 2002, the US sold to India 12 Raytheon-manufactured weapon-locating radars in a deal worth $200 million. (Desilva-Ranasinghe) Based on projections over the next five years, India is expected to spend upwards of US$30 billion on advanced weapons systems. Although Russia and Israel remain India's two leading defence suppliers, arms sales from the US are set to expand over the coming years. India is also likely to start receiving the supply of 36 French-made Rafale fighter aircraft on an outright purchase basis.

In the light of China's sustained military build-up, India has also been speeding up its defence procurement. "The Indian Army is raising two new specialised infantry mountain divisions (35,000 soldiers) and an artillery brigade for Arunachal Pradesh, designed to redress the imbalance on the Sino-Indian border" (Pant, 2016). It is also revising its conventional war-fighting doctrine that is aimed at deterring as opposed to dissuading-China, though its meaning in operational terms remains far from clear. The Indian military is currently refining a "two-front war" doctrine to fend off Pakistan and China simultaneously (Pant, 2016). The 2017 Dokalam crisis expedited the process of infrastructure projects getting completed soon. It is in this context Army Chief General Rawat said that India is fully capable of fighting two and a half battles as of today. India most recently carried out airstrikes inside Pakistan's Balakot area in May 2019 in aftermath of the Pulwama terrorists attack against its par-military forces in which 40 soldiers were killed. It showed India's determination for taking risks of higher nature including a war with Pakistan or China or both.

India has also taken many steps for reducing China's threat to the Indian Ocean region. "The development of the first-ever Indian maritime doctrine contemplating a 'blue-water' role for the fleet and nuclear-armed submarines for strategic deterrence for which India has already Asia's most powerful fleet, is planning to add about 100 warships to its navy within 2020" (Lamont J. & Sood V., 2009) and to enlarge its naval footprint.

The Indian Navy is aiming for a total fleet of 140-145 vessels over the next decade, built around two carrier battle groups: *Admiral Gorshkov* which is now inducted in the navy since 2013 and the indigenous carrier, the 37,500-tonne STOBAR Air Defense Ship got inducted by 2015 (Pant, 2016). India's naval power stands multiplied with two aircraft carriers over the next decade, as well as the commission of its first indigenous nuclear submarine ARIHANT Class in 2016, has been very crucial for power projection and to achieve a semblance of strategic autonomy. India's emerging capability to put a carrier task force as far as the South China Sea and the Persian Gulf has given a boost to the Indian Navy's blue-water aspirations and India hopes to induct a third aircraft carrier by 2017, ensuring that the Indian Navy has two operational carriers at any given point. "The deployment of the Jin-class submarine at Hainan by China will also force India to speed up its indigenous nuclear submarine project that has been in the making for more than a decade now with the Indian Navy, rather ambitiously, aiming at the induction of five indigenous Advanced Technology Vehicle (ATV) nuclear submarines" ((Till and Bratton, 2012) and Pant, 2016). "A submarine-based nuclear arsenal is considered critical by Indian strategists to retain a second-strike capability" (Pant, 2011).

"The United States has also recognised the importance of India's role in the region, viewing it as crucial in maintaining peace and stability in the Indian Ocean and its vast periphery. The U.S. and Indian navies have stepped up their joint exercises and the United States has sold India the USS *Trenton* (renamed INS *Jalashwa*), the first of its class to be inducted into the Indian Navy" ((Till and Bratton, 2012) and Pant, 2016). India is seen as a balancer in the Asia-Pacific where the U.S. influence has waned relatively even as China's has risen. India's ties with Japan have also assumed a new dynamic with some even mooting a "concert of democracies" proposal involving the democratic states of the Asia-Pacific working towards their common goals of a stable Asia-Pacific region. While such a proposal has little chance of evolving into anything concrete in the near term, especially given China's sensitivities, "India's decision to develop natural gas with Japan in the Andaman Sea and recent military exercises involving the United States, Japan, India and Australia under proposed QUAD does give a sense of India's emerging priorities" (Navy, 2015).

India- China- U.S.A. Stand-Off in the South China Sea (SCS) and the East China Sea (ECS) Region

Another area of a flashpoint between India-China and U.S.A. in recent years has erupted in the South China Sea and the East China Sea region. China's actions for asserting and defending its maritime territorial and Exclusive Economic Zone (EEZ) claims in the ECS and SCS, particularly, since late 2013, have heightened concerns among observers that China may be seeking to dominate or gain control of its near-seas region, meaning the ECS, the SCS, and the Yellow Sea. Chinese domination over or control of this region could substantially affect U.S. strategic, political, and economic interests in the Asia-Pacific region and elsewhere. China has recently completely rejected the verdict pronounced by the Permanent Court of Arbitration, Hague in favour of the Philippines, thereby raising serious concerns within the minds of many countries of the region.

The United States supports the principle of freedom of the seas, meaning the rights, freedoms, and uses of the sea and airspace guaranteed to all nations in international law. The United States opposes claims that impinge on the rights, freedoms, and lawful uses of the sea that belong to all nations. The U.S. is of view that Territorial disputes should be resolved peacefully, without coercion, intimidation, threats, or the use of force, and in a manner consistent with international law (Annual Report

MEA, 2015-16). China in recent years has also succeeded in developing artificial islands and defence bases in the SCS region. All kinds of reports and pictures have been appearing in media that the artificial island has been converted into PLA Naval Base.

India faces a Herculean challenge in protecting its interests in the South China Sea. As discussed in the preceding paragraphs, China has been laying claim on almost the entire South China Sea without recognising similar rights of countries like Vietnam, Philippines, Malaysia, Taiwan and Brunei. Vietnam has already allocated oil blocks to India from where India's ONGC Videsh Limited supplies oil to Vietnam. China has expressed its reservations over the presence of Indian company ONGC Videsh in SCS for oil exploration. India's view is that all countries must exercise restraint and resolve bilateral issues diplomatically, according to principles of International law and without recourse to the use or threat of use of force. India is of the view that in the current regional security landscape, there is a need to promote a cooperative approach. Hence, we remain actively engaged with the Asia Pacific community through a web of bilateral as well as multilateral fora like the East Asia Summit, ADMM – Plus and ASEAN Regional Forum (ARF), to contribute to peace and stability in the region (Annual Report MOD, 2014-15). India has entered into several agreements with the U.S.A. to cope up with the emerging maritime threats from China. The U.S. also sees that India can play an important role in its 'Asia Pivot' policy.

The South China Sea is strategically important for India as 5 Trillion Dollar of global trade passes through the South China Sea annually and over 50 per cent of India's trade with the South East Asian and the East Asian Nation passes through it. India fears that the complete dominance of the South China Sea region by China in future will control India's trade route. Therefore India has joined the United States and Japan in voicing concern on China's unilateral moves and at the same time, India also supports freedom of navigation in the region. Since mid-July 2016, countries have been witnessing assertive postures of China by totally rejecting the verdict given by the Permanent Court of Arbitration, Hague in favour of the Philippines thereby rejecting China's claim over disputed island belonging to the Philippines. Thus, the situation in the entire region remains grim.

China's Belt Road Initiative (BRI)/One Belt One Road-OBOR

During various state visits in 2013, Chinese president Xi Jinping announced the Silk Route Economic Belt (SREB) and the 21st-century Maritime Silk Route (MSR). These two major initiatives were initially packaged and labelled under the overarching term 'One Belt, One Road' (OBOR), in short: 'Belt & Road'. These two different routes ultimately connect China with Europe, Africa and Southeast Asia. This impression is further enhanced by a map published by the news agency, depicting both a land route running from inner China to Southern Europe (via the Netherlands) and a sea route connecting the port of Shanghai ultimately with the endpoint of the land-based route in Venice, via India and Africa (Derleer, 2016) Ongoing and planned projects will focus on the development of a wide array of assets, including ports, roads, railways, airports, power plants, oil and gas pipelines and refineries, and Free Trade Zones, etc., as well as a supporting IT, telecom and financial infrastructure. To date, PwC has tracked the equivalent of c. US$250 billion in projects that have either been built already, recently started construction or have been agreed on and signed in relation to B&R (Navy, 2015) India's answer to China's OBOR is the International North-South Transport Corridor (INSTC) which has made significant progress during the year. Following up on the dry run study conducted by the Federation of Freight Forwarders' Association in India (FFFAI) on the INSTC Route, India hosted an interactive session on INSTC at Mumbai in June 2015, followed by Expert Level and INSTC Council Meetings in Delhi in August 2015 and a conference to popularise the INSTC route in Mumbai in December 2015. Customs officials of India, Russia and Azerbaijan also met in Astrakhan, Russia in November 2015. (Annual Report MEA, 2015-16)

Conclusion

India-China relations are passing through a very historical phase as India under PM Modi is all set for assuming the role at the global level. India is on the way to emerge as a global leader. India is ready to take risks in its foreign and security affairs. The actions of the Indian government in the aftermath of the Pulwama attack in May 2017 showed its determination to cross the borders of Pakistan and carried out the airstrike at Balakot in Pakistan. India also did not move back on the issue of the Doklam crisis in June 2017. Defusing of 2017 Dokalam crisis is an example where India did not care for the Chinese threat for several weeks together. India became Part of QUAD at the same time China facilitated India's membership to SCO. However, China is still opposed to India's entry into NSG. India's multi-prong approach for dealing with the China-Pakistan joint threat has started paying dividends in recent years. Post-Doklam and Post Pulwama, India needs to work with China and Pakistan both for reducing the dangers of nuclear war completely. Already the tensions are building up in the Persian Gulf and Arabian Sea region between the USA and Iran. The threats of war are looming large between USA and Iran over the nuclear issue only. The role of Russia and China on the issue of Iran's nuclear programme has been ambivalent. India needs to convince China which refuses to discuss nuclear issues with India so far. Till date, China has refused to engage in any nuclear dialogue with India that might give the impression it recognises India as a nuclear power. For the same reason, China refuses to discuss nuclear confidence-building and risk reduction measures with India. It is high time that India-China-Pakistan agrees to a mechanism for slowing down of regional missiles and other strategic arms race into the sub-continent ((Till and Bratton, 2012) and Pant, 2016).

As both, countries are the two largest populated countries of the world they need to maintain restraints over nuclear and maritime security issues. Closer Developmental Partnership which is at the core of India-China bilateral relations has received a further boost in June 2019, when PM Modi after winning the General Elections second time visited Bishkek, Kazakhstan during the SCO Annual summit where he also had one to one meeting with Chinese President Xi-Xin-Ping. Before this, both leaders had signed several agreements/MOUs in areas including railways, trade and commerce, science and technology, space and people to people exchanges along with 26 commercial/business agreements amounting to US$ 22 billion. Significantly, while New Delhi is increasingly apt to engage in naval cooperation, India is an active member of several regional forums and institutions, such as the Indian Ocean Rim Association for Regional Cooperation, which focuses on trade issues and was launched in 1997, or Both have been cooperating on global forums like BRICS, G-20, and BASIC. Both countries need to remain ever ready for engaging each other in serious discussions to avoid any flashpoint in sea waters. Both need to chalk out maritime CBMs matching with the kind of CBMs both have for maintaining peace and tranquillity on the Line of Actual Control. Both also need to remain ready for accommodating each other's legitimate aspirations to avoid confrontations over complex issues like SCS, ECS, CPEC and OBOR initiatives. There is enough space for both of them to grow and prevent direct conflict with each other by accommodating each other's aspirations and both have a great chance to reaffirm their full faith in the policy of 'Panchsheel' and 'Peaceful Co-existence'.

References

Indian Navy. (2015). Ensuring Secure Seas: Indian Maritime Security Strategy. Naval strategic publications. Retrieved from: http://indiannavy.nic.

Chauhan, P., Khurana, G.S. (2015). "Maritime Diplomacy", South Asia Defence & Strategic Review, 12 September 2015, Website accessed 11 February 2016, URL: http://www.defstrat.com/exec/frmArticleDetails.aspx?DID=602

Integrated Headquarters, Ministry of Defence (Navy). (2015). "Ensuring Secure Seas: Indian Maritime Security Strategy" accessed from www.mod.nic.in

Govt. of India, Annual Report MOD 2014-15.

Kumar, A. (2012). Chinese engagement with the Maldives: Impact on security environment in the Indian Ocean region. *Strategic Analysis*, *36*(2), 276-289.

Holsag, J. (2009). China, India and the Military Security Dilemma, BICCS Asia Paper 3 (5), 18.

Govt. of India, Annual Report, MOD 2017-18, pp. 34-35.

Govt. of India, Annual Report, MOD 2017-18, pp. 30-31.

Govt. of India, Annual Report, MOD 2003-04.

Govt. of India, Annual Report, MOD 2005-06.

Kumar, A. (2012). Chinese Engagement with the Maldives: Impact on Security Environment in the Indian Ocean Region, Strategic Analysis, 36(2), 276-289. accessed from http://www.tandfonline.com/page/terms-andconditions.

Integrated Headquarters, Ministry of Defence (Navy). (2015). "Ensuring Secure Seas: Indian Maritime Security Strategy" accessed from www.mod.nic.in

Office Of The Secretary Of Defence Annual Report to Congress: Military and Security Developments Involving the People's Republic of China 2015.

Nuclear Disarmament A Way Forward, IDSA Task Report, 2010. p. 20.

Bedi, R. (2006). 'India Holds Back from Test Firing Agni III', Jane's Defence Weekly, 24 May 2006; in Holslag, Jonathan (2009) Ranasinghe, S.D. (2012). Fact Sheet: The Indian Ocean Region and Australia's National Interests. South And West Asia Research Programme.

Pant, H. V. (2011). China and India: A Rivalry Takes Shape. *Foreign Policy Research Institute*. Accessed from www.fpri.org on June 25, 2018.

Pant, H.V. (2011). China And India: A Rivalry Takes Shape. *Foreign Policy Research Institute*. Accessed from www.fpri.org on June 29, 2018.

Ronald O'Rourke. (2015). Maritime Territorial and Exclusive Economic Zone (EEZ) Disputes Involving China, Congressional Research Service 7-5700 accessed from www.crs.gov R42784, 18-20 on May 25, 2018.

Govt. of India, Annual Report MOD 2014-15, p. 3.

Yeroen van der Leer. (2016). China's new silk route The long and winding road. Accessed from www.pwc.com/gmc on July 10, 2018.

Govt. of India, Annual Report MEA 2015-16.

Lalremsiami, C., & Patnaik, J. K. (2020). India in the South China Sea: Role and Implications.

Sheliya, M., & Joshi, H. (2019). India's Maritime Wall in the Indo-Pacific Region. Sigma Iota Rho Journal of International Relations.

Limaye, S. (2017). Weighted West, Focused on the Indian Ocean and Cooperating across the Indo Pacific: The Indian Navy's New Maritime Strategy, Capabilities, and Diplomacy. Center for Naval Analyses Arlington United States.

Till, G., & Bratton, P. (Eds.). (2012). Sea Power and the Asia-Pacific: The Triumph of Neptune? (Vol. 47). Routledge.

Vaughn, B. (2018). China-India Great Power Competition in the Indian Ocean Region: Issues for Congress.

5

Sources of China's Export Growth

A Constant Market Share Analysis

Kulwinder Singh, Ajay Ranga & Rajiv Kumar

Introduction

China has astonished the world by becoming the largest exporter in the global export market surpassing Germany and the US in a very short period. Also, it is known as the world's manufacturing factory. A shift in the commodity composition of China from primary to manufacturing products has resulted in a substantial rise in its exports. Share of China's total merchandise exports of manufacturing products in its total export earnings has risen to 80 per cent in 1990s from 40 per cent in late 1970s and to 92 per cent in 2005-06 (Athukorala, 2009).

The rising share of high-tech and medium-tech exports in China indicates its increasing specialisation in producing such products (Jenkins and Edwards, 2015). Various factors may be responsible for such outstanding changes not only the export sector but also in the whole external sector and the overall economy. Because of its outstanding export performance, the present paper aims at examining China's export performance and explores various sources of exports.

After the implementation of economic reforms and participation in globalisation, China has emerged as a shining star in the sky of economic growth and development. China's entry into the global market has had an important effect on the rules of the world trading system (Bown and Crowley, 2010). China started witnessing export-led growth in the mid-1980s, much inspired by the success stories of its East Asian neighbours.

In the mid-1980s, China began witnessing export-oriented growth, inspired much by its East Asian neighbours' success stories. In the 1980s, the use of the export-led growth model was facilitated by two theories, namely, Gradient Theory and Great International Circulation theory. The gradient theory splits China into three regions, east, central and western, and gives priority over the development process to different levels (www.paftab.org). According to this theory, the development process will be initiated by the eastern region and then central and western regions will play their roles subsequently. China utilised this understanding in her seventh five-year plan (1986-90) (Yao, 2010). After three decades of inward-oriented trade and foreign investment policies, in 1979 China witnessed a paradigm shift in its development strategy by shifting from 'close door' to "open-door" market-oriented policy regime. Accordingly, China has introduced a series of policy changes related to the external sector (trade and foreign investment reforms) and internal reforms which have resulted in persistent, albeit gradual, liberalisation in its trade and foreign investment regime. This has resulted in spectacular growth in GDP and foreign trade (Panagariya, 1993). On account of these developments, China has not only recorded high export and GDP growth but also became the first choice of international firms as FDI inflows increased from the US$ 3.49 billion in 1980 to US$ US$ 40.71 billion in 2000 to US S133.70 billion in 2016. The unprecedented expansion of the external sector contributed to the growth of China. China became a star performer with averaging 8.5 per cent GDP growth during the 2000s. Most SAARC nations have higher imports of transport services (Kaur, 2020).

Amongst others, the export sector is a major part of the external sectors of China, has assumed a place of paramount importance and started playing a significant role in the economic development process. China had integrated into the world economic system after its accession to WTO rules and commitments and thereby materialised the gains of its comparative advantage especially cheap availability of labour. Structural change and demographic transition, collectively termed as China's double transition, has helped China to achieve rapid export-led growth. China has achieved spectacular growth in export volume in the past three decades. Equally impressive is China's rapid up-gradation of its export structure (Xu, 2010). China had a share of 2 per cent in world exports in 1990 and it had jumped to 13.8 per cent in 2014. Thus, the main change in the global arena is the emergence of China as an economic powerhouse (IEA, 2016). Recently China is known as World's Manufacturing Factory and emerged as one of the major exporter and importer in the global market after the USA and UK and become the second-largest economy of the world after the USA. Structural change has a dampening effect on the Balassa-Samuelson effect to sustain China's competitiveness in the world market (Yao, 2010). Over time Chinese trade is expanding with a double-digit growth rate of more than 10 per cent. Chinese imports are also rising simultaneously but the growth of exports has been much higher than that of its imports which gets reflected in its trade surplus.

Generally, the export performance of a nation is determined by (i) demand of its exports in the world market (ii) specialisation of the country in those commodities that are in high demand (iii) rising demand for countries exports in its export destination countries and last but least (iv) competitiveness of export (Nayyar, 1976). There are no such systematic studies which would have decomposed sources of Chinese export growth in the context of aforesaid determinants. However, there are some studies decomposing the quality and quantity effects of Chinese exports. In the existing literature, there is no study decomposing Chinese export performance using constant market share analysis. Against this understanding, the present study is an attempt to decompose Chinese export performance using the Constant Market Share (CMS) model. This study covers the period from 1984 to 2014 that is characterised by the implementation of trade liberalisation in the Chinese economy that was initiated in 1978. Further, this period is also important due to increasing multilateralism in the world economy having a great impact on trader economies particularly giant exporters. Beginning in 1984, the Uruguay round of trade negotiation was concluded during this period, leading the establishment of WTO in July 1994. Particularly for China, this period was very crucially significant due to accession to WTO rules and commitments those made her active trade partner in new economic order created through WTO and other international economic institutions. It is in this context, it is of utmost important to sketch-out China's exports performance as well as the sources of its export growth. The present paper contributes to the existing knowledge by analyzing the above issues using constant market share analysis for the period 1984-2014.

The export performance of China by the CMS model has not been analysed earlier using constant market share analysis. However, some studies have attempted to decompose Chinese exports using various other methods. Chen, Mai, and Yu (2006) have studied the behaviour, by using the Cournot quantity competition model, of the Chinese exporters between the mid-80s and 2001, to investigate the effect on the export performance of export refund policy using the Spearman rank correlation coefficient. Results have shown a significant positive correlation between China's export-tax rebate policy and its exports, final domestic consumption and foreign reserve. Cerra and Chaman (2003) estimated export supply price elasticities of different industry groups of China on basis of panel data set of aggregate export unit price and volume indices. Overall, the data show that export supply has been more sensitive to market price signals in recent years after reforms. Yao (2010) studied the influence of structural change on China's export competitiveness and found that it dampens the Balassa-Samuelson effect, allowing China to remain competitive in the global market. However, a variety of literature on various aspects of China's export performance is available, but it lacks in terms of decomposition of sources of its export performance. It provides a good case to study sources of China's export performance using the Constant Market Share (CMS) Model.

This paper has been organised into four sections. Beginning with section I, introductory remarks about the Chinese exports are presented and the objective of the study has been discussed. Section II explains issues pertaining to data and methodology used in the analysis of Chinese export performance during the concerned period. Sections III presents results and discussion pertaining to China's export performance and its sources. Lastly concluding remarks are presented and some important lessons for Indian exports are discussed.

Major Changes in China's EXIM Policy

It is critical because China's integration with the world economy was very gradual manner. In the initial years of liberalisation, the Chinese government allowed FDI in some coastal cities and also established Special Economic Zones in those provinces (Fung, Lizaka and Tong, 2004). In the second half of the 1980s, the government of China encouraged FDI and special treatment was given to export-oriented foreign investors as well as investors using advanced technology. For instance, the government provided preferential treatment to such kinds of foreign investment. Similarly, in the 1990s, China allowed FDI in several sectors including agriculture, hydropower, energy, communications and raw material sector. To attract high FDI, China adopted a favourable tax policy and also extended financial support to selective units (Fung, Lizaka and Tong, 2004). Finally, in December 2001, China became a member of WTO and accordingly eliminated many restrictions which were not in line with WTO commitments. In this context, it is interesting to analyse its trade performance in different phases of liberalisation as the focus of the government was and remains to increase export by regulating the operations of foreign and local firms.

Methodology and Data

The Constant Market Share Model is widely used methodology to analyse the export performance of a country (Tyszynsky, 1951, Baldwin, 1958; Spiegeeglas, 1959; and Naya, 1967). The model has been improved by Leamer and Stern (1970 and 2006). Following Leamer and Stern (2006), India's export performance was examined by Virmani (2007) and Singh (2014). In the present study, the methodology used by Singh (2014) has been followed for decomposing sources of Chinese export performance. The equation of CMS method decomposes country's export performance into four parts: (i) World Demand Effect (WDE), (ii) Commodity Composition Effect (CCE), (iii) Market Distribution Effect (MDE) and (iv) Residual Competitiveness Effect (RCE). The following is the main equation of the CMS model in terms of actual export growth.

$$\Delta X = \underbrace{\sum_{i=1}^{n} rX_i}_{(i)} + \underbrace{\sum_{i=1}^{n} r_i X_i - \sum_{i=1}^{n} rX_i}_{(ii)} + \underbrace{\sum_{i=1}^{n} \sum_{j=1}^{n} r_{ij} X_{ij} - \sum_{i=1}^{n} r_i X_i}_{(iii)} + \underbrace{\Delta X - \sum_{i=1}^{n} \sum_{j=1}^{n} r_{ij} X_{ij}}_{(iv)}$$

Where,

ΔX = actual change in country's exports

r = percentage increase in total world (excluding China) exports from period 1 to period 2

r_i = percentage increase in the world (excluding China) exports of commodity i from period 1 to period 2

r_{ij} = percentage increase in the world (excluding China) exports of commodity i to region j from period 1 to period 2

X_i = China's exports of commodity i to the rest of the world in period 1

X_{ij} = China's exports of commodity i to region j in period 1.

The expression (i) refers to the overall growth in the world exports and thus termed as the "World Demand Effect (WDE)."

The "Commodity Composition Effect (CCE)" is captured by expression (ii). The "Market Distribution Effect (MDE)" is reflected in expression (iii). The difference between the actual export growth of the focus country (X) and the growth that would have occurred if the country maintained its export share of each commodity to each market (Σi ΣjrijXij) is reflected in expression (iv). As a result, it's known as the "Residual Competitiveness Effect (RCE)." (See Singh, 2014, for further information.)

This study covers the period from 1984 to 2014 that is characterised by the implementation of trade liberalisation in the Chinese economy that was initiated in 1978. Further, this period is also important due to increasing multilateralism in the world economy having a great impact on trader economies particularly giant exporters. Beginning in 1984, the Uruguay round of trade negotiation was concluded during this period, leading to the establishment of WTO in July 1994. Particularly for China, this period was very crucially significant due to accession to WTO rules and commitments those made her active trade partner in new economic order created through WTO and other international economic institutions. It is in this context, it is of utmost important to sketch-out China's exports performance as well as the sources of its export growth. The present paper contributes to the existing knowledge by analyzing the above issues using constant market share analysis for the period 1984-2014.

For explaining Chinese export performance, the whole period under consideration is divided into four sub-periods. The first sub-period ranges from 1984 to1994; it shows China's export performance before the establishment of WTO; the second sub-period covers the following seven years (1995-2001). It explains Chinese export performance during the new economic order created with the establishment of WTO; however, China was not its member until 2001. The third sub-period ranges from 2002 to 2007; it reveals China's export performance after it acceded to WTO rules and commitments and before the global financial crisis began in late 2007. Fourth sub-period ranges from 2008-2014. It is justified against the fact that the subprime crisis has adversely affected the economic growth of the world economy, as well as world trade, which has witnessed a slowdown. These developments would have negatively contributed to the export performance of China as many developing and developed nations have temporarily heightened the restrictions on imports of goods to revive their industrial sector.

This study is based on secondary data which is mainly obtained from World Development Indicators (WDI) published by World Bank

(WB); International Financial Statistics (IFS)and Direction of Trade Statistics (DOTS) brought out by International Monetary Fund (IMF); and UN-Comtrade Database printed by United Nations Organisations (UNO). The analysis is undertaken at the aggregate level (i.e. at digit I) of SITC Revision-1. Leading export destinations (both developed and developing) covering more than 75 per cent share of China's exports have been selected for highlighting changing directions of China's exports and estimating market composition effects. Countries selected for comparison of export growth with China are the major growth players in the global export market covering more than 80 per cent of world exports during the reference period.

A Glimpse of China's Export Performance

The emergence of China in the world economy is the key event in the recent phase of economic liberalisation and globalisation. It is evident as China's GDP remained fairly above the GDP growth of the world economy during the reference period. The highest growth was registered during the period 2002-07 i.e. after WTO accession and before the incidence of global slowdown; however, there was a the mild decline in growth after 2007 which may be due to global financial crisis. China's trade was recorded as highest of US$ 23714 during 2008-2014. The highest growth of merchandise trade was noticed during 2002-07. In the period (2002-07), China's trade of merchandise grew at 28.05 per cent per annum whereas world trade of merchandise grew at 16.64 per cent in the same period. Interestingly, China's exports have experienced phenomenal growth during the period under study. It was recorded at the highest of 30.16 per cent during 2002-2007 and 17.33 per cent during 1984-2014.

The rate of export growth was recorded much higher than that of its import growth during the whole study period and even during selected sub-periods. Comparing the growth of China's GDP, exports, imports and trade growth performance with that of the world, it comes out that China has outperformed the world economy in all these growth aspects. Moreover, the export growth rate of China was recorded quite higher

Table 5.1: Growth of National Income and Merchandise Trade in China from 1984 to 2014

Period/Sub-periods	GDP (US $ Billions)		Exports (US $ Billions)		Imports (US $ Billions)		Total trade (US $ Billions)		China's BOT (+/-) (US $ Billions)
	World	China	World	China	World	China	World	China	
1984-94	324286 [3.01]	5864 [9.58]	37113 [9.14]	656.437 [16.97]	38713 [8.78]	688.31546 [13.27]	75825 [8.96]	1345 [14.98]	-32
1995-2001	225129 [3.24]	7067 [8.42]	38625 [3.55]	1378 [10.56]	39625 [3.97]	1188 [11.12]	78249 [3.76]	2566 [10.82]	190
2002-2007	320335 [3.76]	14857 [11.57]	58285 [16.72]	4307 [30.16]	60243 [16.76]	3677 [25.64]	118528 [16.74]	7985 [28.05]	630
2008-2014	379574 [2.28]	29543 [8.73]	115194 [5.37]	12713 [11.17]	118062 [5.12]	11001 [12.28]	233255 [5.24]	23714 [11.67]	1712
1984-2014	1319393 [2.87]	58082 [9.92]	249216 [8.34]	19120 [17.33]	256642 [8.25]	16617 [15.97]	505858 [8.30]	35736 [16.64]	2503

Source: Authors' calculations based on WDI, WB; IFS-IMF and DOTS-IMF databases.
Note: Figures in parentheses are Average Annual Growth Rates (AAGR) during the respective period.

than that of import growth resulting in an ever-increasing trade balance during the study period (Table 5.1).

Figure 5.1 exhibits China's share in world GDP, exports, imports and total trade during the reference period. China's share in world GDP has reached above10 per cent in 2014 from about 1 per cent in 1984. Similarly, their share in world trade, exports and imports have recorded a phenomenal increase over the period under consideration. It is evident as Chinese accounted for less than 2 per cent of world exports in 1984 which increased to 12 per cent in 2014. Besides, China's also witnessed a remarkable increase in other indicators (Figure, 5.1). The fabulous export performance of China could be an outcome of twin changes: (i) China's double transition and (ii) its full integration into the world system world economy. Export-led growth will continue for another 10 to 15 years before China finishes the double transition in demography and industrialisation (Yao, 2010).

Figure 5.1: China's Share in World Exports, Imports, Total Trade and GDP during 1984-2014

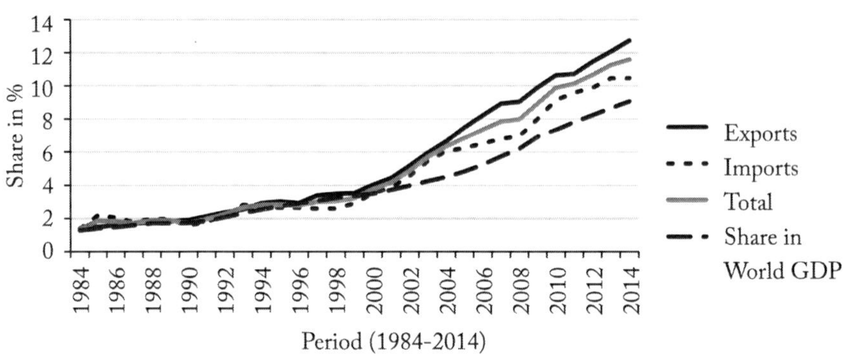

Source: Authors' calculations based UN-Comtrade data.

Depicting export growth of China vis-à-vis selected developed and developing countries during 1984-2014, Table 5.2 and Table 5.3 reveal China's exceptional growth performance of exports. Export growth of China has been found to be highest as compared to all the selected

Figure 5.2: China's Export Growth vis-à-vis Selected Developed Countries during 1984-2014

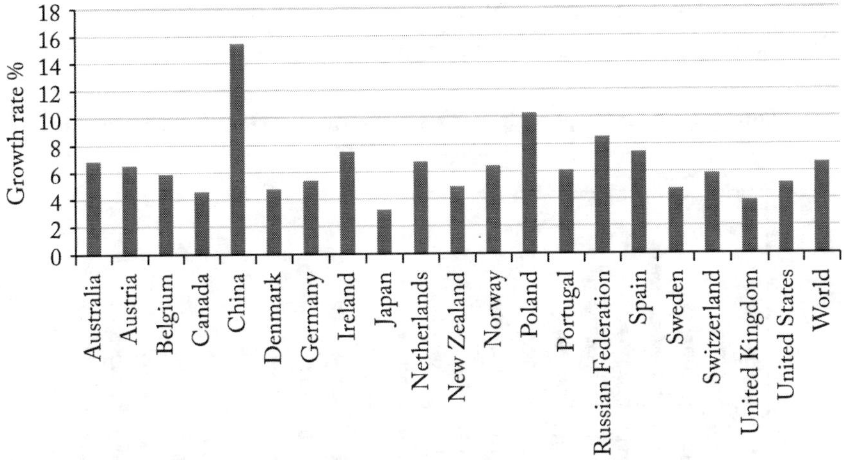

Source: Based on Authors' Calculations using UN-Comtrade data.

developed countries (see Figure 5.2) as well as developing countries (See Figure 5.3). It was also fairly more than the growth of world exports during the same period. Analysis of export growth affirms that China has outperformed the majority of its developing and developed counterparts in the period under consideration. An interesting point is that the export growth of China remained highest in the sub-period (2002-2007). It was the period of China became a member of WTO. It could be because China's entry in WTO provided a large diverse market for Chinese products. Given its comparative advantage (or competitive edge), China has efficiently catered for the expanding world market, especially in emerging countries. Further, it was a phase when a large number of leading international firms has shifted their production base in China on account of high and rising manufacturing in advanced countries. Accordingly, the share of international firms in China's manufacturing exports reached above 55 per cent in recent years.

The aftermath of the global crisis has resulted in a deceleration of Chinese export growth as it was recorded in a single digit (9.79 per cent) as compared to the double-digit growth in previous sub-periods. Moreover, trends in changing share of selected developing and developed countries in world exports highlighted the far better performance of China's exports in the global export market.

Figure 5.3: China's Export Growth vis-à-vis Selected Developing Countries during 1984-2014

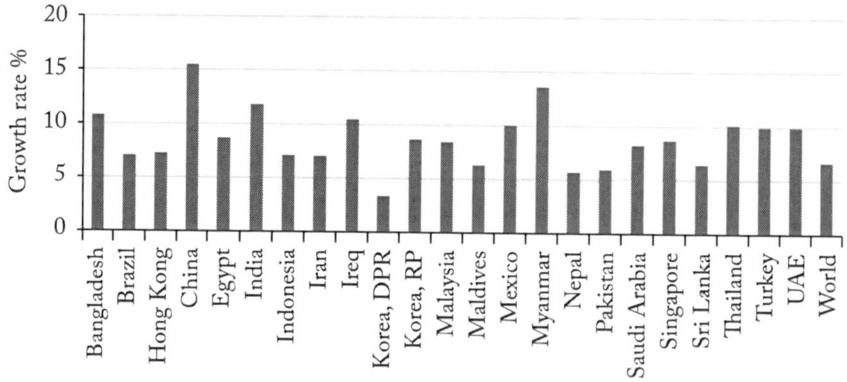

Source: Based on Authors' Calculations using UN-Comtrade data.

Decomposing Sources of China's Export Performance

Table 5.2 brings out the decomposition of China's export growth during various periods since 1984. Data show that China's export performance was mainly attributed to its competitive strength during the period 1984-2014 as RCE turned out to be 92.16 per cent followed by MDE of 11.98 per cent and WDE of 7.65 per cent during 1984-2014. However, CCE contributed negatively to the export performance and, thus, exhibits the wrong specialisation pattern of exports in China. But, this is justified in today's context as a new theory of international trade explains economies of scale and monopolistic competition as the basis of incidence from trade from any country rather than its resources endowment. During the pre-WTO accession period (1984-2001), Chinese export performance was attributed to their competitive strength backed by world demand and marginally positive market distribution effect.

Table 5.2: Decomposition of China's Export Growth during Various Periods during 1984-2014. (Values in US $ Billions)

Period/s	Actual Change in Exports		World Demand Effect (WDE)		Commodity Composition Effect (CCE)		Market Distribution Effect (MDE)		Residual Competitiveness Effect (RCE)	
1984-2014	2317.47	[100]	177.35	[7.65]	-7.7	[-0.33]	11.98	[0.52]	21035.85	[92.16]
1984-2001	241.23	[100]	62.71	[26.00]	-6.9	[-2.86]	5.67	[2.35]	179.74	[74.51]
2001-14	27.67	[100]	16.75	[60.54]	-2.89	[-10.45]	2.87	[10.36]	10.94	[39.56]
1984-94	145.09	[100]	58.44	[40.28]	-11.36	[-7.83]	-11.01	[-7.58]	109.01	[75.13]
1994-2001	2076.24	[100]	348.3	[16.78]	-43.1	[-2.08]	-23.29	[-1.12]	1794.34	[86.42]
1994-97	953.96	[100]	299.31	[31.38]	-41.75	[-4.38]	-33.71	[-3.53]	730.11	[76.53]
1997-2001	83.31	[100]	23.35	[28.02]	-6.94	[-8.33]	-7.71	[-9.25]	74.61	[89.56]
2001-14	1311.66	[100]	331.24	[25.25]	-59.28	[-4.52]	-12.32	[-0.94]	1052.02	[80.21]
2001-07	357.7	[100]	68.9	[19.26]	-62.88	[-17.58]	51.65	[14.44]	300.03	[83.88]
2007-10	1122.28	[100]	105.7	[9.42]	-15.8	[-1.41]	29.5	[2.63]	1002.87	[89.36]
2007-14	96.13	[100]	34.19	[35.56]	-5.79	[-6.02]	12.12	[12.61]	55.62	[57.85]
2010-14	764.58	[100]	45.05	[5.89]	65.36	[8.55]	-33	[-4.32]	687.17	[89.87]

Source: Authors' calculations based UN-Comtrade data.
Note: Values in parentheses are the percentages from the total.

On the other hand, CCE was found to be negative stating the wrong specialisation pattern. The analysis also reveals world demand as the primary sources of export performance followed by residual competitiveness effect during post-WTO accession period (2001-2014). Integration of the Chinese economy with the world economic order has enabled it for capturing gains of comparative advantage and gaining export competitiveness (Yao, 2010). The magnitude of CCE and MDE was similar to that of during the pre-WTO accession period. During the post-global crisis period (2007-2014), there was a little bit of decline in the competitiveness of China's exports but they grew to have a world demand effect of 35.56 per cent during this period. Moreover, RCE was regained at the level of 89.87 per cent during 2010-14. Thus, it can be concluded that Chinese export was achieved outstanding performance based on their competitive strengths and utilizing the world demand effect provided by processes of globalisation and liberalisation in the world economy. However, market diversification has also contributed to its marginally positive impact.

Table 5.3 shows the commodity wise decomposition of China's exports growth during the whole study period (i.e. 1984-2014). Chinese exports are mainly dominated by manufacturing commodities which are represented b commodity groups SITC 6, 7 & 8. Among these, SITC 7 showed the highest increase followed by SITC 8 & 6. No wonder, the growth of these commodity groups is mainly attributed to China's competitive strength as the residual competitive effect was found to be 98.56 per cent, 93.14 per cent and 93.04 per cent for commodity groups namely SITC 7, 8 & 6 respectively. Besides, commodity groups SITC 1 & 0 also grew due to the competitive strength of China. The remaining groups grew due to the world demand effect. Whereas the market distribution effect remained negative for most of the commodity groups and for remaining commodities it was negligible.

Tables 5.4 and 5.5 show the commodity wise decomposition of Chinese exports during two sub-periods i.e. 1984-2001 and 2002-14. The results are more or less the same as during the total period of the study. During both the sub-periods, three major commodity groups were

Table 5.3: Commodity-wise Decomposition of China's Export Growth during 1984-2014 (Values in US $ Billions)

Commodity Codes*	Actual Change in Exports		World Demand Effect (WDE)		Market Distribution Effect (MDE)		Residual Competitiveness Effect (RCE)	
0	55.76	[100]	17.51	[31.41]	9.68	[17.36]	28.56	[51.23]
1	2.78	[100]	0.74	[26.71]	-0.07	[-2.5]	2.11	[75.78]
2	12.91	[100]	12.37	[95.81]	-2.15	[-16.65]	2.69	[20.84]
3	28.44	[100]	35.09	[123.36]	-6.29	[-22.12]	-0.35	[-1.24]
4	0.54	[100]	0.56	[103.03]	-0.09	[-16.89]	0.07	[13.86]
5	133.19	[100]	13.9	[10.44]	-1.35	[-1.02]	120.65	[90.58]
6	397.17	[100]	25.7	[6.47]	1.93	[0.49]	369.54	[93.04]
7	1053.21	[100]	11.12	[1.06]	4	[0.38]	1038.09	[98.56]
8	632.66	[100]	34.02	[5.38]	9.39	[1.48]	589.25	[93.14]
9	0.81	[100]	18.64	[2298.21]	-3.06	[-377.87]	-14.76	[-1820.34]

Source: Authors' calculations based UN-Comtrade data.

Note: Values in parentheses are the percentages from the total.

Table 5.4: Commodity-wise Decomposition of China's Export Growth during 1984-2001(Values in US $ Billions)

Commodity Codes*	Actual Change in Exports		World Demand Effect (WDE)		Market Distribution Effect (MDE)		Residual Competitiveness Effect (RCE)	
0	9.68	[100]	3.78	[39.1]	2.23	[23.05]	3.66	[37.85]
1	0.77	[100]	0.25	[32.35]	-0.1	[-12.6]	0.62	[80.25]
2	1.78	[100]	1.83	[102.83]	0.4	[22.53]	-0.45	[-25.36]
3	2.68	[100]	8.07	[301.62]	-1.2	[-44.77]	-4.2	[-156.85]
4	-0.03	[100]	0.05	[-204.41]	0.08	[-326.42]	-0.16	[630.84]
5	12.07	[100]	3.91	[32.43]	0.33	[2.73]	7.82	[64.84]
6	39.41	[100]	9.54	[24.22]	1.58	[4.01]	28.28	[71.77]
7	85.54	[100]	4.88	[5.7]	1.62	[1.9]	79.04	[92.4]
8	90.26	[100]	15.35	[17.01]	1.92	[2.13]	72.99	[80.87]
9	-0.93	[100]	3.85	[-414.2]	-1.2	[129.25]	-7.86	[845.66]

Source: Authors' calculations based UN-Comtrade data.
Note: Values in parentheses are the percentages from the total.

Table 5.5: Commodity-wise Decomposition of China's Export Growth during 2001-2014 (Values in US $ Billions)

Commodity Codes*	Actual Change in Exports		World Demand Effect (WDE)		Market Distribution Effect (MDE)		Residual Competitiveness Effect (RCE)	
0	46.08	[100]	25.51	[55.36]	-4.41	[-9.58]	24.98	[54.22]
1	2.01	[100]	1.22	[60.69]	0.64	[31.62]	0.15	[7.69]
2	11.13	[100]	10.41	[93.53]	-1.57	[-14.13]	2.29	[20.6]
3	25.77	[100]	16.45	[63.84]	2.84	[11.01]	6.48	[25.16]
4	0.57	[100]	0.3	[52.08]	-0.17	[-30.24]	0.44	[78.15]
5	121.13	[100]	25.6	[21.14]	-1.51	[-1.24]	97.03	[80.11]
6	357.76	[100]	49.77	[13.91]	-4.81	[-1.35]	312.8	[87.43]
7	967.67	[100]	86.06	[8.89]	-7.08	[-0.73]	888.69	[91.84]
8	542.4	[100]	89.23	[16.45]	-7.26	[-1.34]	460.43	[84.89]
9	1.74	[100]	0.65	[37.31]	0.06	[3.36]	1.03	[59.33]

Source: Authors' calculations based UN-Comtrade data.

Note: Values in parentheses are the percentages from the total.

SITC 6, 7 & 8. The value of these commodity groups grew mainly due to the competitive effect. During both the sub-periods, the competitive the effect remained positive for most of the commodity groups. Similarly, the world demand effect also remained positive for most of the commodity groups. However, during both the sub-periods, market distribution effect remained either negative or minuscule.

Table 5.6 shows the market-wise decomposition of China's exports during the whole study period. As is clear from the data, China's major exports destinations were the USA, Hong Kong, Japan and the Republic of Korea. It is surprising to note that in the case of most of the countries China's competitiveness effect for all the countries remained above 90 per cent. Whereas the world demand effect and commodity composition effect remained well below the competitiveness effect for all the countries. Though for Germany, Singapore and Japan world demand effect remained somewhat significant but for the remaining countries, it remained very low. Similarly, the commodity composition effect remained negative or miniscule for all the countries. Hence, the growth of China's exports to various countries is attributed to its competitive strength which other countries like India must also learn.

Tables 5.7 and 5.8 explain the market-wise decomposition of China's exports growth during two sub-periods i.e. 1984-2001 and 2002-14. During both the sub-periods, the competitiveness effect of China for most of the countries remained stronger as compared to world demand effect and commodity composition effect. There was not much change in the direction of China's exports during both the sub-periods. For major trade partners, China's competitiveness effect remained even stronger. However, in the first sub-period, the world demand effect remained quite significant in the case of Brazil, Singapore and Germany. Hence, it can be said that China's exports to these countries increased mainly due to increased demand for these countries. During both the sub-periods, the commodity composition effect remained either negative or very low. Thus, like the whole study period, during both the sub-periods, China's competitive strength played a crucial role in increasing its exports to the selected countries.

Table 5.6: Market-wise Decomposition of China's Export Growth during 1984-2014 (Values in US $ Billions)

Export Destinations	Actual Change in Exports		World Demand Effect (WDE)		Commodity Composition Effect (CCE)		Residual Competitiveness Effect (RCE)	
Brazil	34.49	[100]	6.07	[17.6]	-1.44	[-4.18]	29.86	[86.58]
Germany	71.93	[100]	5.41	[21.15]	-0.48	[-1.3]	67.01	[80.15]
Hong Kong	356.5	[100]	75.39	[7.51]	-4.62	[-0.67]	285.74	[93.16]
India	54.18	[100]	0.55	[1.01]	0.05	[0.09]	53.59	[98.9]
Italy	28.45	[100]	1.51	[5.32]	0.14	[0.49]	26.8	[94.2]
Japan	144.29	[100]	18	[12.48]	-3.64	[-2.53]	129.93	[90.05]
Jordan	3.36	[100]	0	[0]	0	[0]	3.36	[100]
Netherlands	64.61	[100]	1.88	[2.92]	-0.34	[-0.53]	63.07	[97.61]
Others	842.22	[100]	59.07	[7.01]	1.2	[0.14]	781.95	[92.84]
Republic of Korea	100.33	[100]	0	[0]	0	[0]	100.33	[100]
Russia	53.08	[100]	2.67	[5.03]	-0.85	[-1.6]	51.27	[96.57]
Singapore	47.67	[100]	9.21	[19.33]	0.98	[2.06]	37.47	[78.61]
Syria	0.98	[100]	0	[0]	0	[0]	0.98	[100]
UK	56.81	[100]	1.71	[3.01]	-0.26	[-0.45]	55.36	[97.44]
USA	394.8	[100]	10.41	[2.64]	-1	[-0.25]	385.39	[97.62]
Vietnam	63.73	[100]	0	[0]	0	[0]	63.73	[100]

Source: Authors' calculations based UN-Comtrade data.

Note: Values in parentheses are the percentages from the total.

Table 5.7: Market-wise Decomposition of China's Export Growth during 1984-2001 (Values in US $ Billions)

Export Destinations	Actual Change in Exports		World Demand Effect (WDE)		Commodity Composition Effect (CCE)		Residual Competitiveness Effect (RCE)	
Brazil	0.97	[100]	1.77	[183.17]	-1.1	[-113.79]	0.3	[30.61]
Germany	8.98	[100]	1.93	[72.42]	-0.34	[-14.14]	7.39	[41.72]
Hong Kong	39.95	[100]	28.93	[21.49]	-5.65	[-3.79]	16.67	[82.3]
India	1.86	[100]	0.08	[4.3]	0.01	[0.47]	1.77	[95.23]
Italy	3.69	[100]	0.67	[18.12]	0	[-0.07]	3.02	[81.95]
Japan	39.82	[100]	10.41	[26.14]	-2.84	[-7.14]	32.26	[80.99]
Jordan	0.23	[100]	0	[0]	0	[0]	0.23	[100]
Netherlands	6.96	[100]	0.66	[9.51]	-0.21	[-3.05]	6.51	[93.54]
Others	59.06	[100]	18.31	[31]	1.34	[2.27]	39.41	[66.73]
Republic Of Korea	12.52	[100]	0	[0]	0	[0]	12.52	[100]
Russia	2.12	[100]	0.14	[6.56]	-0.15	[-6.98]	2.13	[100.42]
Singapore	4.55	[100]	3.99	[87.77]	-2.17	[-47.71]	2.73	[59.94]
Syria	0.22	[100]	0	[0]	0	[0]	0.22	[100]
UK	6.45	[100]	0.81	[12.58]	-0.2	[-3.13]	5.84	[90.55]
USA	52.05	[100]	5.73	[11.01]	-0.63	[-1.21]	46.95	[90.21]
Vietnam	1.8	[100]	0	[0]	0	[0]	1.8	[100]

Source: Authors' calculations based UN-Comtrade data.

Note: Values in parentheses are the percentages from the total.

Table 5.8: Market-wise Decomposition of China's Export Growth during 2001-14 (Values in US $ Billions)

Export Destinations	Actual Change in Exports		World Demand Effect (WDE)		Commodity Composition Effect (CCE)		Residual Competitiveness Effect (RCE)	
Brazil	33.53	[100]	2.7	[8.04]	-0.15	[-0.45]	30.98	[92.42]
Germany	62.95	[100]	12.56	[19.23]	-1.46	[1.78]	51.85	[82.12]
Hong Kong	316.55	[100]	60.87	[19.95]	5.64	[-2.32]	259.96	[82.37]
India	52.32	[100]	7.55	[14.43]	0.19	[0.36]	44.58	[85.21]
Italy	24.77	[100]	3.47	[14.02]	-0.18	[-0.74]	21.48	[86.72]
Japan	104.47	[100]	21.98	[21.04]	-8.53	[-8.16]	91.02	[87.12]
Jordan	3.14	[100]	0.57	[18.18]	-0.16	[-5.17]	2.73	[86.99]
Netherlands	57.65	[100]	9.07	[15.74]	-2.79	[-4.85]	51.37	[89.11]
Others	783.16	[100]	106.69	[13.62]	-8.98	[-1.15]	685.45	[87.52]
Republic of Korea	87.82	[100]	23.71	[27]	-0.76	[-0.86]	64.86	[73.86]
Russia	50.96	[100]	9.4	[18.45]	-1.09	[-2.14]	42.65	[83.69]
Singapore	43.12	[100]	5.78	[13.4]	0.58	[1.34]	36.77	[85.27]
Syria	0.76	[100]	0	[-0.33]	-0.06	[-7.66]	0.82	[107.99]
UK	50.36	[100]	5.34	[10.6]	-1.44	[-2.85]	46.46	[92.25]
USA	342.75	[100]	31.68	[9.24]	-10.1	[-2.95]	321.18	[93.71]
Vietnam	61.93	[100]	10.89	[17.58]	-1.04	[-1.68]	52.09	[84.1]

Source: Authors' calculations based UN-Comtrade data.

Note: Values in parentheses are the percentages from the total.

Conclusion

The present study examines China's export performance and highlights the decomposition of its sources during the period 1984-2014. The findings of the study reveal that China has registered outstanding export performance. Export growth of China was found to be fairly higher than that of world exports as well as its developing and developed countries counterparts. Its share in world exports has risen to more than 12.72 per cent in 2014 from 1.38 per cent in 1984. The growth of exports was higher compared with the growth of GDP, imports and total trade during the study period. China has cultivated the benefits of accession to WTO which is very evident from its highest export growth rate during the period 2002-2007. Commodity composition showed a shift towards manufactured exports, however, seven out of ten broad product groups registered outstanding exports performance in the world export market registering a rapid increase in world exports. China has registered an increase in the relative contribution of developing countries in its total export earnings indicating increasing competitiveness in respective markets. Results of the decomposition of exports growth provide useful insights in terms of sources of export growth. Competitiveness of Chinese exports comes out as the primary source of their rapid growth in the global export market. Besides world demand for Chinese exports has also contributed significantly. Commodity composition has turned out to be a negative source of Chinese export performance. However, it can be justified in the context of new theory international trade stating economies of scale in imperfect competition as an important source for the participation of the nations into international trade. Marginally positive market distribution is indicative of increasing market diversification of China's exports during the concerned period. As globalisation has opened a large and diverse export market for all the participating countries, analysis of China's export performance proclaims more emphasis on export competitiveness to achieve outstanding export performance. The analysis also demands further examination of China's export sector for identification of sources of its competitive strength.

The outstanding export performance of China proposes useful directions to countries like India for making their export competitive to expand their share in the global export market. Otherwise, there is no other alternative available to sustain a high rate of exports and GDP in the globalised era. So more emphasis might be given to be competitive at the global level for which efforts at the end of the states and exports are required. Globalisation has provided huge capital inflow and free imports of modern technologies at the doorsteps of developing countries like India. Using these sources, the miraculous export performances based on competitive advantage can be materialised. China has written its success story through the rapid transition from its primary exports to manufactured ones using SEZ strategy of promoting exports effectively. India might also have a critical analysis of the performance and strategy of SEZs so to transform its commodity composition. Also, attention might be given to the identification of rapidly growing markets that was not taken care of during the post-reform period (Singh, 2014). Having a proactive attitude towards the globalizing competitive environment and making relevant arrangements for export promotion by the state and exporters, India too can raise its place in the world export scenario.

References

Athukorala, P. C. (2009). The rise of China and East Asian export performance: Is the crowding-out fear warranted? *World Economy, 32*(2), 234-266.

Baldwin, R. E. (1958). The commodity composition of trade: selected industrial countries, 1900-1954. *The Review of Economics and Statistics*, 50-68.

Bown, C. P., & Crowley, M. A. (2010). *China's export growth and the China safeguard: threats to the world trading system?* The World Bank.

Cerra, V., & Saxena, S. C. (2003). How responsive is Chinese export supply to market signals?. *China Economic Review, 14*(3), 350-370.

Chen, C. H., Mai, C. C., & Yu, H. C. (2006). The effect of export tax rebates on export performance: Theory and evidence from China. *China Economic Review, 17*(2), 226-235.

Fung, K. C., Iizaka, H., & Tong, S. Y. (2004). Foreign direct investment in China: Policy, recent trend and impact. *Global Economic Review, 33*(2), 99-130.

Jenkins, R., & Edwards, L. (2015). Is China 'Crowding Out' South African Exports of Manufactures?. *The European Journal of Development Research*, *27*(5), 903-920.

Kaur, S., Khorana, S., & Kaur, M. (2020). Is There Any Potential in Service Trade of South Asia?. *Foreign Trade Review*, *55*(3), 402-417.

Leamer, E. E., & Stern, R. M. (1970). Constant-market-share analysis of export growth. *Quantitative international economics. Boston: Allyn and Bacon*, 171-183.

Leamer, E. E. and Stern, R.M. (2006). Quantitative International Economics, Aldine Transaction Ltd, New Brunswick and London.

Naya, S. (1967). The commodity pattern and export performance of developing Asian countries to the developed areas. *Economic development and cultural change*, *15*(4), 420-437.

Nayyar, D. (1976). India's Export and Export Policies in the 1960s, Cambridge University Press, Cambridge.

Panagariya, Arvind. (1993). China's Export Strategy: What Can We Learn From It? Retrieved from: http://www.econpapers.repec.org/RePEc:wpa:wuwpit:0309014.htm.on March 20, 2018.

Singh. (2014). A constant market share analysis of India's export performance. *Foreign Trade Review*, 49 (2), 141-161.

Spiegelglas, S. (1959). World exports of manufactures, 1956 vs 1937. *Manchester School of Economic and Social Studies*, *27*(2), 111-139.

Tyszynsky, H. (1951). World Trade in Manufactured Commodities 1899-1950, *The Manchester School of Economic and Social Studies* 19(3), 272-304.

Veeramani, C. (2007). Sources of India's export growth in pre- and post-reform periods. *Economic and Political Weekly*, 2419-2427.

Xu, B. (2010). The sophistication of exports: Is China special ? *China Economic Review*, 21(3), 482–493. Retrieved from: http://doi.org/10.1016/j.chieco.2010.04.005 on March 30, 2018.

Yao, Y. (2013). Double transition and China's export-led growth. In *China's New Role in the World Economy* (pp. 65-88). Routledge. Retrieved from: http://www.paftad.org/files/34/01_YANG YAO_Growth.pdf. on April 20, 2018.

6

An Analysis of India's Exports Instability to China

Surinder Kumar Singla

Introduction

Liberalisation policies, in India, brought major changes in the growth, and pattern of its exports. Though, over the last two and half decades, the value of India's merchandise exports has increased significantly yet its share in world exports is low. Therefore, the importance of increasing exports is always recognised by the planning authority of India. A very important feature of India's trade is its growing ties with China. In fact, India-China relations, today, are evident with the rapid growth of trade, which has already crossed US$ 70 billion in 2015-16. China has already overtaken the UAE to become India's largest trading partner. Thus, the importance of India and China in international trade is becoming clearer with each passing day. In fact, "India-China trade is a fascinating subject for a very simple reason that the two countries are close neighbours, have large populations and enjoy endless cultural ties. Any effort to strengthen economic ties between the two countries will be most fruitful for their rapid development. Moreover, since 1991, China has emerged as a major destination for Indian exports" (Singla, 2015). Although, in recent years, India's exports to China have suffered a setback, China's share in India's global exports has increased substantially. There have been significant changes in the Indian export basket to China. Although it is still dominated by few items, many new items have also been added. In fact, it has been a legacy that a lot of items disappear from the export list after a short look. The volume of major commodities also fluctuated rapidly (Singla, 2015). Due to all this, India experienced volatile export earnings from China and it is a proven fact that fluctuations in export earnings can be dangerous for the growth of any economy. Hence, it becomes an important topic to investigate the stabilisation effect of China on India's export earnings. The present study examines the performance of India's exports to China by exploring their growth and stabilisation effect.

Objectives and Methodology

The present study is based on the following three objectives: (i) to examine the growth and composition of Indian exports to China; and (ii) to analyse the stabilisation effect of the Chinese market on India's export earnings. The analysis has been made for the period from 1990-1991 to 2015-16. However, due to some methodological limitations and unavailability of data, the instability index has been computed for the period from 1996-97 to 2015-16.

Instability Index is the measure of assessing the degree and extent of stability of export as well as examining the risk associated with profitability and export earnings of a particular commodity. It refers to the degree of short-run, year-to-year fluctuations in the export earnings. In this study, the extent of export instability has been calculated by using Coppock's Instability Index (Devkota, 2004). The algebraic form of it is:

$$V_{log} = \frac{\Sigma\,[(\log X_{t+1} - \log X_t) - m]^2}{N-1}$$

The Instability Index (I-I) = [Anti-Log ($\sqrt{V_{log}}$) – 1] × 100

Where X_t is the value of a country's exports in year t; N is the number of years; m is the arithmetic mean of the difference between the logs of X_t and X_{t+1}, X_{t+1} and X_{t+2}, etc.; and V_{log} is the logarithmic variance of the series. The analysis of export instability has been made for two different periods i.e. from 1996-97 to 2005-06 and from 2006-07 to 2015-16. As the regular presence of the commodity is mandatory for the calculation of the index, the analysis is confined to India's top fifteen exports to China during both the sub-periods. The instability of the selected Indian exports to China has been calculated in terms of value, volume and unit value. Along with this, the indices of instability have also been constructed with reference to India's exports to the whole world and the Rest of the World (RoW) for the various commodities involved. Here, RoW stands for India's exports to all countries minus China. The criterion applied is that if the overall instability index for the world is lower than that of RoW, then the movement of exports to China has been compensatory.

Growth of India's Exports to China

"India and China are two of the world's oldest civilisations. Economic relations between the two countries, in the realm of trade, date back to a very long time when merchant adventurers crossed the barriers of mountains, seas and deserts in search of markets in any country" (Ganguli, 1956 and Singla 2015). The most important aspect of the old contacts was the establishment of Buddhism in China. "Indian monks acted like bees carrying cultural pollen to China. In addition to the development of religion and philosophy, they also promoted the development of economics, astronomy, medicine, chemistry and physical exercise in China" (Acharya, 2000 and Singla, 2015). Thus, historically, economic dialogue between India and China has been far less important than their cultural interactions. Trade and cultural ties between the two countries increased through the Silk Road. This road played an important role in rebuilding the history of cultural and economic ties between the two countries. Chinese traders used the Silk Road to sell silk, tea, porcelain and other goods to India and take pepper, perfume, jewelry, horses, etc. from India (Singh, 2005 and Singla, 2015). The first decade, after independence, witnessed peaceful and harmonious relations between the People's Republic of China and the newly independent Government of India. In 1954, the two countries signed a Sino-Indian Agreement on Trade. However, the trade agreement between the two countries ended in 1962 due to the

Sino-Indian war. Since the resumption of diplomatic relations in 1976, bilateral relations have improved gradually (Singla, 2015). With the resumption of diplomatic relations, India-China economic relations strengthened significantly. In the late 1980s, China moved forward on the economic reform front and made major changes in its foreign trade regime. The reforms greatly boosted the growth of China's foreign trade, which in turn contributed to the country's rapid economic growth (Yin, 2004). India-China relations deepened in August 1984 with the expansion of the Most Favored Nations (MFN) doctrine. However, "one of India's biggest problems was the growing trend in Indian trade deficit with China in the 1980s, a phenomenon that seems to have started since the beginning of China's reform process" (Debroy, 1989 and Singla, 2015). Since the 1990s, trade between the two countries has grown exponentially. During this period, India also began the process of liberalisation and opened up its economy to the world. China also seized the opportunity and deepened its trade ties with India. The spectacular growth in their bilateral trade is evident from Table 6.1. In 1990-91, India's exports to China were merely Rs. 33 crore which increased to Rs. 87471 crore in 2011-12. However, after that Indian exports to China declined continuously except in 2013-14 when it was on its top i.e. Rs. 90561 crore. In 2015-16, it reached the previous six-year lowest i.e. Rs. 58933 crore. Similarly, during the study period, India's imports from China also rose quite tremendously, without any substantial decline (Singla, 2015). Indian imports from China increased fabulously from Rs. 64 crore in 1990-91 to Rs. 404043 crore in 2015-16. It declined only once i.e. during 2009-10 when it fell by Rs. 1557 crore over the previous year. Though India's exports to and imports from China have experienced few ups and downs during the study period its total trade increased continuously (except during 1998-99 when it fell by 5.74 per cent). India's exports to China remained more unstable than imports. Recently, the substantial fall in Indian exports is not experienced with China alone but with the rest of the world as well. The Indian government blamed the RBI for refusing to devalue the rupee to compete with other emerging economies. As the outcry grew louder, the government quickly targeted the low hanging fruit – the rupee – as a quick fix solution. However, the data makes it clear that between January 2013 and March 2016 Indian rupee was down by 17 per cent as compared to only 3.4 per cent down of the Chinese Yuan. Similarly, the currencies of some other countries like Singapore, Philippines and Thai have also lost less than Indian currency. Thus, India is suffering from export deceleration and currency devaluation simultaneously. It is, therefore, doubtful that another bout of the rupee weakness is to compensate for the revival of exports. Former RBI Governor Raghuram Rajan said that the real reason for the depressing state of Indian exports is the decline in global trade and the shifting patterns of imports in global economies (Hindu, 2016). So far as the fall in Indian exports to China is concerned, the biggest reason is the sharp decline in one important commodity group i.e. ores, slag and ash. There was a time when this commodity alone comprises about half of India's total exports to China. But, due to a substantial fall in Chinese steel production, its global demand for the commodity reduced significantly. Iron and Steel Association of China has predicted that it will probably contract further in the years to come. Moreover, like other industrialised nations, China is becoming more competitive and advancing the value chain. China is becoming a source of raw material used for the production of many end products which reduces external dependence. This may be another reason for the decline in Chinese demand for Indian goods. Another major problem from India's point of view was its growing trade deficit with China. At large, the balance of trade has been in China's favour, with the exception of 1991-92 and 1992-93, when India adjusted the balance of trade with China to Rs. 67 crore and Rs. 44 crore respectively. But apart from these two years, India has faced an unfavourable balance of trade with China. Moreover, during 1990-91, India's trade deficit with China accounted for only 0.29 per cent of its total trade deficit, which reached its maximum during 2015-16, at 44.59 per cent. So it is very surprising that China alone contributes more than 2/5th of India's trade deficit which is a serious cause for concern.

Table 6.1: Value of India's Merchandise Trade with China (Crore Rs.)

Years	Exports	Imports	Balance of Trade	Total Trade	Annual Percentage Change
1990-91	33	64	-31 (0.29)	96	-
1995-96	1113	2716	-1603 (9.88)	3829	20.14
2000-01	3798	6863	-3065 (11.23)	10660	35.03
2005-06	29925	48117	-18192 (8.92)	78042	36.61
2006-07	37530	79009	-41479 (15.44)	116538	49.33
2007-08	43597	109116	-65519 (18.38)	152713	31.04
2008-09	42661	147606	-104944 (19.66)	190267	24.59
2009-10	54714	146049	-91335 (17.63)	200763	5.52
2010-11	64315	198079	-133764 (20.48)	262394	30.70
2011-12	87471	265466	-177995 (20.24)	352936	34.51
2012-13	73530	284385	-210855 (20.38)	357914	1.41
2013-14	90561	309235	-218674 (26.98)	399796	11.70
2014-15	73030	369565	-296535 (35.27)	442596	10.71
2015-16	58933	404043	-345110 (44.59)	462976	4.60

Note: Figures in parentheses show the percentage share in India's overall negative balance of trade.

Source: Calculated from Monthly Statistics of Foreign Trade of India, DGCI & S; Kolkata, (Various Issues).

The end of the Cold War and the emergence of a vibrant Asian economy have altered the global balance of power during the 1990s. Both India and China have emerged as the two fastest-growing economies in the world and have become major trade partners (ITPO, 2003 Singla, 2015). It is also observed that China has become one of the major destinations for Indian exports. Table 6.2 shows the growth of India's exports to China and the world. During the study period, India's exports to China increased at a much higher rate than India's overall exports (31.90 per cent and 17.83 per cent, respectively). A similar trend could also be seen during the sub-periods, except the last one, i.e. from 2010-11 to 2015-16, when the growth rate of Indian exports to China remained less than that of her global exports. During the last sub-period, the growth rate of India's global exports remained positive i.e. 8.90 per cent but the growth of her exports to China remained negative i.e. -2.18 per cent. Thus, it shows that Chinese demand for Indian exports dampened more seriously as compared to global demand.

Table 6.2: Growth Rate of India's Exports: China and Overall

Period	China	Overall
1990-91 to 1999-2000	52.77	18.95
2000-01 to 2009-10	35.81	19.56
2010-11 to 2015-16	-2.18	8.90
1990-91 to 2015-16	31.90	17.83

Note: Figures represent the average annual percentage growth of India's exports to China and to world.
Source: Calculated from Monthly Statistics of Foreign Trade of India, DGCI & S, Kolkata, (Various Issues).

The usefulness of foreign trade depends upon the composition of trade which is determined by the nature of commodities exported and imported by a country (Singla, 2015). The *composition* of Indian exports to China has undergone substantial changes, particularly after the liberalisation process. Table 6.3 shows that the total share of selected commodities, in India's total exports to China hovered between 93.58 per cent (during 1992-93) and 46.49 per cent (during 1997-98). Hence, India experienced sharp fluctuations in the share of selected commodities. As is clear from the table, during the first decade of the new century, Indian exports to China were mainly driven by one major commodity group i.e. ores, slag and ash. During 2007-08, about 3/5th of India's total exports to China were comprised by this commodity group. The reason for this sharp rise was the heavy dependence of China's front-running steel industry on Indian iron ores so that it could meet the growing demand for steel of its construction and defence industries. However, during the recent period, Chinese steel production has reduced significantly which has dampened Indian exports of ores, slag and ash. Presently, the share of this commodity group has been reduced to only 5.82 per cent. Hence, ores, slag and ash have lost their comparative

Table 6.3: Percentage Share of Selected Commodities in India's Exports to China

Commodities	1990-91	1995-96	2000-01	2005-06	2006-07	2007-08	2008-09	2009-10	2010-11	2011-12	2012-13	2013-14	2014-15	2015-16
1. Ores, slag & ash	18.77	33.78	18.68	51.26	45.89	56.88	51.35	47.80	33.67	25.39	13.98	10.51	4.27	5.82
2. Iron & steel	0.61	11.43	3.29	6.28	5.76	2.06	4.02	2.65	5.30	3.15	2.23	2.18	0.99	1.62
3. Cotton	0.68	6.65	8.47	7.62	9.04	9.98	4.07	10.76	13.30	22.98	25.11	25.95	19.11	18.69
4. Organic chemicals	0.77	7.43	13.00	6.81	6.25	5.78	4.27	4.40	4.95	4.92	7.56	6.17	8.77	9.37
5. Inorganic chemicals	28.94	2.94	0.46	4.86	4.24	1.45	2.22	0.95	1.21	0.60	0.31	0.77	2.08	1.98
6. Plastic	0.00	3.57	9.74	4.05	5.18	2.13	1.53	2.70	2.83	3.38	4.66	3.75	2.98	3.41
7. Copper	29.59	0.01	1.87	1.74	6.43	3.71	1.28	4.69	9.61	11.16	14.87	12.59	15.83	12.71
8. Salt, sulphur, earths & stone	0.83	1.67	5.77	2.24	2.49	1.85	2.93	2.40	2.63	2.63	4.51	4.51	5.20	6.00
9. Nuclear reactors & boilers	0.15	0.78	2.11	1.88	1.88	2.16	2.52	2.67	2.25	2.09	3.22	3.24	4.18	5.11
10. Animal or vegetable fats & oils	0.00	5.96	1.67	0.48	0.68	0.64	1.08	1.51	1.66	1.86	2.79	1.95	2.28	3.28
Total	**80.34**	**74.22**	**65.06**	**87.22**	**87.83**	**86.64**	**75.27**	**80.52**	**77.41**	**78.16**	**79.25**	**71.62**	**65.70**	**67.98**

Source: Calculated from Monthly Statistics of Foreign Trade of India, DGCI & S; Kolkata, (Various Issues)

relevance in Indian exports basket to China. It is interesting to note that during recent times three commodity groups have made their presence realised. These are cotton; copper; and organic chemicals. During 2015-16, these three commodity groups comprised 40.77 per cent of India's total exports to China. The share of other commodity groups remained low and fluctuating.

Stabilisation Effect of Chinese Market on Indian Exports

It is a fairly widespread view that underdeveloped countries typically suffer from wider fluctuations in their export earnings which produce short-term instability of domestic income and prices and also inhibit long-term growth (Macbean, 1966). Heavy and sudden fluctuations in exports may create serious problems in the balance of payments (BoP), national income, investment and then may also create a severe adverse impact on the overall growth of a country. Not only may this, but the export instability of a country also create income instability in other countries because this world has been synchronising by the process of globalisation (Sinha, 1999). Further, there has been a strong debate about the exact causes and consequences of exports instability. Most of the existing literature has generally agreed that excessive fluctuations in foreign trade originate from variations in supply or demand or other economic and non-economic factors. It is also a fact that the developing countries have a substantially higher degree of export earnings instability than that of developed countries (Macbean, 1966; Savvidos, 1984; and Lanceiri, 1987). Though few researchers have examined the instability of Indian export earnings (Gill,1983; Singhal and Kaur, 1986; Das and Pant, 1989; Kaur, 1993; and Brar, 1996) none of them have touched the relevance of the Chinese market for Indian export earnings. As China has emerged as one of the major destinations for Indian exports, it becomes an important exercise to examine the stabilisation effect of the Chinese market on Indian export earnings. Like most of the studies, the present study is based upon the Coppock's instability indices which have been calculated for two different sub-periods for the selected fifteen export items.

First Sub-Period (1996-97 to 2005-06)

(a) Value Instability

Instability indices pertaining to the value of India's major commodity groups exported to China, to the world, and RoW have been worked out and presented in Table 6.4. As is clear from the table, all the export items do not exhibit a uniform pattern of instability. The extent of instability varied from commodity to commodity. With China, the magnitude of the instability was highest in the case of the commodity called oil-cake & other solid residues, obtained from soya-bean oil (206.51) and lowest in the case of shrimps & prawns frozen (21.66). China had a destabilising effect upon the value of five commodities, i.e. oil-cake & other solid residues, obtained from soya-bean oil; chromium ores & concentrates; iron ores & concentrates (non-agglomerated); granite crude or roughly trimmed; and organic compounds, because for these five commodities, the world instability indices (i.e. 29.08, 62.58, 35.94, 28.03 and 13.94 respectively) were higher than those for RoW (i.e. 25.78, 32.13, 25.93, 25.52 and 13.74 respectively). But, in the case of the rest of the ten commodities, China had a stabilising effect.

(b) Volume Instability

Table 6.5 shows instability indices pertaining to the volume of India's exports to China, to the world, and RoW. The instability indices of the volume of exports to China for fifteen commodities varied between 26.36 and 658.66. The lowest degree of instability was marked in the case of shrimps & prawns frozen and the highest was in the case of iron ores & concentrates (agglomerated). Further, out of the fifteen commodities studied, in the case of seven commodities, i.e. oil-cake & other solid residues, obtained from soya-bean oil; chromium ores & concentrates; granite crude or roughly trimmed; aluminium oxide; simply cut or sawn granite with a flat or even surface; organic compounds; and mucilages thickeners, whether or not modified the world instability indices (i.e. 30.50, 274.60, 26.33, 51.48, 15.58, 8.17 and 9.10 respectively) were

Table 6.4: Instability Indices Pertaining to the Value of India's Major Exports to China, World and RoW (1996-97 to 2005-06)

Commodities	China	World	ROW	Effect of Chinese Market
1. Oil-cake & other solid residues, obtained from soya-bean oil	206.51	29.08	25.78	Instable
2. Chromium ores & concentrates	91.81	62.58	32.13	Instable
3. Frozen fish excluding livers & roes	23.23	22.96	25.49	Stable
4. Iron ores & concentrates (non-agglomerated)	38.88	35.94	25.93	Instable
5. Iron ores & concentrates (agglomerated)	43.12	57.00	215.38	Stable
6. Granite crude or roughly trimmed	34.92	28.03	25.52	Instable
7. Aluminium oxide	95.39	50.06	50.14	Stable
8. Shrimps & prawns frozen	21.66	4.01	4.12	Stable
9. Simply cut or sawn granite with a flat or even surface	35.59	13.96	14.11	Stable
10. Phthalic anhydride	41.51	39.25	40.62	Stable
11. Organic compounds	55.61	13.94	13.74	Instable
12. Mucilages thickeners, whether or not modified	29.78	13.66	14.73	Stable
13. Cotton yarn containing 85% or more by weight	83.58	98.73	100.35	Stable
14. Granite merely cut, into blocks or slabs of a rectangular shape	42.32	22.29	28.20	Stable
15. Appliances of taps, cocks, valves etc.	78.14	11.70	13.83	Stable

Source: Calculated from Statistics of Foreign Trade of India by Countries and Monthly Statistics of Foreign Trade of India, DGCI & S, Kolkata, (Various March Issues).

higher than those for RoW (i.e. 24.76, 139.82, 23.89, 36.98, 15.36, 7.95 and 8.03 respectively). It indicates that, in volume terms, India's trade with China had a destabilising effect on her overall trade of these seven commodities. While for the rest of the eight commodities, China had a stabilising effect.

Table 6.5: Instability Indices Pertaining to the Quantity of India's Major Exports to China, World and RoW (1996-97 to 2005-06)

Commodities	China	World	RoW	Effect of Chinese Market
1. Oil-cake & other solid residues, obtained from soya-bean oil	191.36	30.50	24.76	Instable
2. Chromium ores & concentrates	303.42	274.60	139.82	Instable
3. Frozen fish excluding livers & roes	30.44	26.87	31.39	Stable
4. Iron ores & concentrates (non-agglomerated)	606.79	699.70	835.70	Stable
5. Iron ores & concentrates (agglomerated)	658.66	810.87	2689.48	Stable
6. Granite crude or roughly trimmed	41.09	26.33	23.89	Instable
7. Aluminium oxide	196.02	51.48	36.98	Instable
8. Shrimps & prawns frozen	26.36	5.11	5.31	Stable
9. Simply cut or sawn granite with a flat or even surface	27.73	15.58	15.36	Instable
10. Phthalic anhydride	39.89	25.94	26.81	Stable
11. Organic compounds	29.23	8.17	7.95	Instable
12. Mucilages thickeners, whether or not modified	39.08	9.10	8.03	Instable
13. Cotton yarn containing 85% or more by weight	75.61	99.98	101.40	Stable
14. Granite merely cut, into blocks or slabs of a rectangular shape	40.15	34.69	35.39	Stable
15. Appliances of taps, cocks, valves etc.	146.38	11.15	14.17	Stable

Source: Calculated from Statistics of Foreign Trade of India by Countries and Monthly Statistics of Foreign Trade of India, DGCI & S, Kolkata, (Various March Issues).

(c) Unit Value Instability

Instability indices pertaining to the unit value of India's exports to China, to the world, and RoW have been presented in Table 6.6. In terms of unit value, the extent of instability, with China, varied between 9.53 and 731.54. The lowest degree of instability was marked in the case of the commodity namely granite crude or roughly trimmed and the highest was in the case of iron ores & concentrates (non-agglomerated). China had a destabilising effect upon the unit value of eight commodities, i.e.

oil-cake & other solid residues, obtained from soya-bean oil; chromium ores & concentrates; frozen fish excluding livers & roes; aluminium oxide; phthalic anhydride; organic compounds; mucilages thickeners, whether or not modified; and granite merely cut, into blocks or slabs of a rectangular shape, because for these eight commodities, the world instability indices (i.e. 14.55, 154.03, 4.85, 13.24, 13.73, 13.93, 14.83 and 7.41 respectively) were higher than those for RoW (i.e. 14.54, 147.14, 4.56, 12.19, 12.97, 13.22, 14.53 and 7.01 respectively). But for the rest of the seven commodities, China had a stabilising effect.

Table 6.6: Instability Indices Pertaining to the Unit Value of India's Major Exports to China, World and RoW (1996-97 to 2005-06)

Commodities	China	World	RoW	Effect of Chinese Market
1. Oil-cake & other solid residues, obtained from soya-bean oil	17.66	14.55	14.54	Instable
2. Chromium ores & concentrates	130.07	154.03	147.14	Instable
3. Frozen fish excluding livers & roes	7.29	4.85	4.56	Instable
4. Iron ores & concentrates (non-agglomerated)	731.54	790.75	949.20	Stable
5. Iron ores & concentrates (agglomerated)	693.38	733.53	949.58	Stable
6. Granite crude or roughly trimmed	9.53	2.87	3.05	Stable
7. Aluminium oxide	87.20	13.24	12.19	Instable
8. Shrimps & prawns frozen	12.58	5.73	6.83	Stable
9. Simply cut or sawn granite with a flat or even surface	28.22	1.53	2.03	Stable
10. Phthalic anhydride	21.33	13.73	12.97	Instable
11. Organic compounds	46.20	13.93	13.22	Instable
12. Mucilages thickeners, whether or not modified	16.25	14.83	14.53	Instable
13. Cotton yarn containing 85% or more by weight	15.88	3.85	3.88	Stable
14. Granite merely cut, into blocks or slabs of a rectangular shape	17.85	7.41	7.01	Instable
15. Appliances of taps, cocks, valves etc.	30.14	8.42	8.63	Stable

Source: Calculated from Statistics of Foreign Trade of India by Countries and Monthly Statistics of Foreign Trade of India, DGCI & S, Kolkata, (Various March Issues).

Thus, it can be said that out of fifteen commodities, China had stabilised the value of ten commodities, the volume of eight commodities and the unit value of seven commodities. In terms of value, the ten commodities for which China had a stabilising effect constituted only 16.84 per cent share and the rest of the five commodities for which China had a destabilising effect constituted 34.70 per cent share of India's total exports to China. Thus, China had more of a destabilising effect on India's exports than the stabilising effect. Further, from the above tables, it can also be observed that the index of instability pertaining to volume was higher than that of unit value for 11 major export commodities considered during the period from 1996-97 to 2005-06. This implies that the instability in the value of exports was more due to the instability in the volume of the commodities exported rather than due to the fluctuations in the unit value obtained because the value of a commodity would be its volume multiplied by its unit value.

Second Sub-Period (2006-07 to 2015-16)

(a) Value Instability

Table 6.7 shows instability indices pertaining to the value of India's exports to China, to the world, and RoW. With China, the magnitude of the instability was highest in the case of the commodity called other petroleum oils and oils obtained from bituminous minerals etc (181.32) and lowest in the case of menthol (16.18). China had a destabilising effect upon the value of six commodities, i.e. cotton, not carded or combed; granite crude or roughly trimmed; other petroleum oils and oils obtained from bituminous minerals etc; polypropylene; castor oil and its fractions; and single yarn of uncombed fabrics measuring <714.29 but >= 232.56 dctx, because for these six commodities, the world instability indices (i.e. 50.73, 9.38, 18.76, 35.77, 20.15 and 40.03 respectively) were higher than those for RoW (i.e. 34.74, 5.13, 18.39, 23.49, 13.63 and 33.38 respectively). But, in the case of the rest of the nine commodities, China had a stabilising effect.

Table 6.7: Instability Indices Pertaining to the Value of India's Major Exports to China, World and RoW (2006-07 to 2015-16)

Commodities	China	World	RoW	Effect of Chinese Market
1. Iron ores & concentrates (non-agglomerated)	69.99	51.72	350.14	Stable
2. Cotton, not carded or combed	59.62	50.73	34.74	Instable
3. Cathodes and sections of cathodes	87.75	17.94	93.48	Stable
4. Granite crude or roughly trimmed	11.31	9.38	5.13	Instable
5. Other petroleum oils and oils obtained from bituminous minerals etc	181.32	18.76	18.39	Instable
6. Polypropylene	73.97	35.77	23.49	Instable
7. Ferro-chromium carbon contng>4% by wt	37.67	35.75	60.18	Stable
8. Castor oil and its fractions	22.04	20.15	13.63	Instable
9. Single yarn of combed fabrics measuring<192.31 but >=125 dctx	42.81	23.69	25.94	Stable
10. Single yarn of uncombed fabrics measuring<714.29 but >= 232.56 dctx	96.53	40.03	33.38	Instable
11. O-xylene	21.16	24.08	31.66	Stable
12. Aluminium oxide other than artificial corundum	144.17	49.06	73.52	Stable
13. Diamonds other than industrial, not mounted	148.35	13.73	14.08	Stable
14. Human hair and animal hair/other textile materials, for making wigs/the like	17.67	12.80	12.95	Stable
15. Menthol	16.18	16.87	20.87	Stable

Source: Calculated from Statistics of Foreign Trade of India by Countries and Monthly Statistics of Foreign Trade of India, DGCI & S, Kolkata, (Various March Issues).

(b) Volume Instability

Table 6.8 shows instability indices pertaining to the volume of India's exports to China, to the world, and RoW. The instability indices of the volume of exports to China for fifteen commodities varied between 11.65 and 232.34. The lowest degree of instability was marked in case of human hair and animal hair/other textile materials, for making wigs/ the like and the highest was in case of diamonds other than industrial, not mounted. Further, out of the fifteen commodities studied, in the case of five commodities, i.e. iron ores & concentrates (non-agglomerated); cathodes and sections of cathodes; other petroleum oils and oils obtained from bituminous minerals etc; ferro-chromium carbon contng >4% by wt; and aluminium oxide other than artificial corundum, the world instability indices (i.e. 38.45, 14.36, 71.46, 22.04 and 52.45 respectively) were lower than those for RoW (i.e. 217.52, 72.40, 71.70, 33.66 and 74.39 respectively). It indicates that, in volume terms, India's trade with China had a stabilising effect on her overall trade for only these five commodities. While for the rest of the ten commodities, China had a destabilising effect.

Table 6.8: Instability Indices Pertaining to the Quantity of India's Major Exports to China, World and RoW (2006-07 to 2015-16)

Commodities	China	World	ROW	Effect of Chinese Market
1. Iron ores & concentrates (non-agglomerated)	46.01	38.45	217.52	Stable
2. Cotton, not carded or combed	59.15	53.89	43.37	Instable
3. Cathodes and sections of cathodes	70.82	14.36	72.40	Stable
4. Granite crude or roughly trimmed	14.74	12.21	7.15	Instable
5. Other petroleum oils and oils obtained from bituminous minerals etc	171.23	71.46	71.70	Stable
6. Polypropylene	90.71	51.02	34.09	Instable
7. Ferro-chromium carbon contng>4% by wt	33.56	22.04	33.66	Stable
8. Castor oil and its fractions	17.78	7.28	7.23	Instable
9. Single yarn of combed fabrics measuring<192.31 but >=125 dctx	46.56	19.15	15.57	Instable
10. Single yarn of uncombed fabrics measuring<714.29 but >= 232.56 dctx	82.98	35.76	32.10	Instable
11. O-xylene	25.51	28.72	18.43	Instable
12. Aluminium oxide other than artificial corundum	182.73	52.45	74.39	Stable
13. Diamonds other than industrial, not mounted	232.34	11.06	9.51	Instable
14. Human hair and animal hair/other textile materials, for making wigs/the like	11.65	9.70	2.44	Instable
15. Menthol	26.19	14.14	14.05	Instable

Source: Calculated from Statistics of Foreign Trade of India by Countries and Monthly Statistics of Foreign Trade of India, DGCI & S, Kolkata, (Various March Issues).

(c) Unit Value Instability

Instability indices pertaining to the unit value of India's exports to China, to the world, and RoW have been presented in Table 6.9. In terms of unit value, the extent of instability, with China, varied between 5.49 and 131.24. The lowest degree of instability was marked in case of the commodity namely cotton, not carded or combed and the highest was in the case of diamonds other than industrial, not mounted. China had a destabilising effect upon the unit value of five commodities, i.e.

Table 6.9: Instability Indices Pertaining to the Unit Value of India's Major Exports to China, World and RoW (2006-07 to 2015-16)

Commodities	China	World	ROW	Effect of Chinese Market
1. Iron ores & concentrates (non-agglomerated)	27.39	27.38	38.17	Stable
2. Cotton, not carded or combed	5.49	12.07	19.18	Stable
3. Cathodes and sections of cathodes	12.67	18.54	25.70	Stable
4. Granite crude or roughly trimmed	16.00	11.10	7.05	Instable
5. Other petroleum oils and oils obtained from bituminous minerals etc	30.34	65.25	66.39	Stable
6. Polypropylene	7.94	7.66	8.00	Stable
7. Ferro-chromium carbon contng>4% by wt	9.61	15.88	23.10	Stable
8. Castor oil and its fractions	9.49	9.01	9.46	Stable
9. Single yarn of combed fabrics measuring<192.31 but >=125 dctx	11.14	11.72	12.52	Stable
10. Single yarn of uncombed fabrics measuring<714.29 but >= 232.56 dctx	11.17	9.32	8.83	Instable
11. O-xylene	10.75	10.57	12.33	Stable
12. Aluminium oxide other than artificial corundum	8.53	8.24	16.06	Stable
13. Diamonds other than industrial, not mounted	131.24	9.90	9.88	Instable
14. Human hair and animal hair/other textile materials, for making wigs/the like	17.43	16.33	15.60	Instable
15. Menthol	36.54	26.71	15.04	Instable

Source: Calculated from Statistics of Foreign Trade of India by Countries and Monthly Statistics of Foreign Trade of India, DGCI & S, Kolkata, (Various March Issues).

granite crude or roughly trimmed; single yarn of uncombed fabrics measuring <714.29 but >= 232.56 dctx; diamonds other than industrial, not mounted; human hair and animal hair/other textile materials, for making wigs/the like; and menthol, because for these five commodities, the world instability indices (i.e. 11.10, 9.32, 9.90, 16.33 and 26.71 respectively) were higher than those for RoW (i.e. 7.05, 8.83, 9.88, 15.60 and 15.04 respectively). But for the rest of the ten commodities, China had a stabilising effect.

Thus, during the second 2006-07 to 2015-16, out of selected fifteen commodities, China had stabilised the value of nine commodities, the volume of five commodities and the unit value of ten commodities. In terms of value, the nine commodities for which China had a stabilising effect constituted 43.24 per cent share and the rest of the six commodities for which China had a destabilising effect constituted 18.96 per cent share of India's total exports to China. Thus, in the second sub-period, China had a more stabilising effect on India's exports than destabilising effect. Further, as in the first sub-period, the index of instability pertaining to volume was higher than that of unit value for 12 major export commodities considered during the second sub-period i.e. from 2006-07 to 2015-16. Hence, it again implies that the instability in the value of exports was more due to the instability in the volume of the commodities exported rather than due to the fluctuations in the unit value obtained.

Conclusion

The trade relations between India and China are developing at their own momentum and dynamism. Since the 1990s, India's merchandise trade with China increased at a tremendous pace. Over the last 25 years period, there has been seen thousands fold increase in India's total trade with China (Singla, 2015). However, the mutual trade between the two neighbouring countries seems to be getting one-sided as the Indian imports from China have emerged much faster than exports. In the year 2015-16, India's exports were a mere 14.59 per cent of her imports with China. This has widened the already existing trade deficit for India. Presently, China is contributing a little less than half of India's overall trade deficit. This is not a new experience for India. India's trade balance with China remained negative during the whole study period except for two years.

Indian exports to China also remained more unstable than imports. In the recent past, there has been seen a substantial fall in India's exports to China. However, this reduction is not experienced with China alone but with the world as well. The Indian government has blamed the RBI who refused to devalue the rupee to make it competitive against its other emerging market peers. As the cries are getting louder, the Government has been targeting the low hanging fruit – the rupee – as a quick fix solution. However, the explanation of former RBI Governor, Raghuram Rajan, seems to be more appropriate who stated that the actual reasons for the sad state of affairs of Indian exports are slowing down of global trade and shift in importing patterns of global economies. So far as the fall in Indian exports to China is concerned, the biggest reason is the sharp decline in one important commodity group i.e. iron ores. Due to the substantial fall in Chinese steel production, its global demand for this commodity has reduced significantly. Iron and Steel Association of China has predicted that it will probably contract further in the years to come. Moreover, like other industrial countries, China is getting more competitive and moves up the value chain. More of the inputs, going into final products, are now being sourced from inside the country than from outside. This may be the other reason for the decline in Chinese demand for Indian goods.

During the study period, Indian exports to China grew at a much faster rate as compared to their global trade. The same has been experienced during the first two sub-periods of the study. However, in the last sub-period i.e. from 2010-11 to 2015-16, the growth of India's exports to China remained negative. The *composition* of Indian exports to China has also undergone substantial changes. During the first decade of the present century, ores, slag and ash dominated the Indian exports to China. The reason for the sharp rise in exports of this commodity group was the heavy dependence of China's front-running steel industry on imports from India so that it could meet the growing demand for steel of its construction and defence industries. However, during the recent period, Chinese steel production has reduced significantly which has dampened Indian exports of ores, slag and ash (Singla, 2015). Moreover, the excessive exports of this commodity group may not be considered desirable for India in the long run as it falls in the category of natural resource-based products which are exhaustible. It is interesting to note that during recent times three commodity groups namely cotton; copper; and organic chemicals have made their presence realised as their share in India's total exports to China remained 40.77 per cent during 2015-16. The share of other commodity groups remained low and fluctuating.

The analysis of export instability reveals that India's export earnings from China were subject to strong variations. However, for the selected commodities, China's destabilisation effect was stronger during the first sub-period as compared to the second sub-period. One common aspect during both the sub-periods was that the instability in the value of exports was more due to the instability in the volume of the commodities exported rather than due to the fluctuations in unit values obtained. Hence, there is an immediate need to examine the demand and supply aspects of the commodities exported to China and the remedial measure should be adopted. Further, as all the commodities and markets do not contribute equally to the export instability, there is a need for disaggregate studies, both commodity-wise and market-wise. The commodities and markets with higher instabilities must be identified. The over-dependence on higher markets or commodities can prove very harmful. Attempts can also be made to explore the possibilities of shifting the exports from higher instable commodities and markets to lower ones. So, there is a need for commodity as well as market-specific policies. The commodities exported to China with stable export proceeds must be encouraged to sustain the long run export earnings.

Refernces

Bajpai, K. P., & Mattoo, A. (2000). *The Peacock and the Dragon: India-China relations in the 21st century*. Har Anand Pub.

Brar, J. S. (1996). *India and European Union: Issues in Economic Relations.* Vision & Venture.

Das, S. K., & Pant, M. (1989). On Export Diversification and Earnings Instability Theory and Evidence. *Indian Economic Journal, 36*(3), 65.

Debroy, B. (1989). China's external trade - A review. *Foreign Trade Review*, 24(1), 1–36.

Devkota, S. C. (2004). Causes of Export Instability in Nepal, International Trade 0410002. *Economics Working Paper Archive (EconWPA).*

Ganguli, B.N. (1956). *India's economic relations with the Far Eastern and Pacific countries in the present century.* Calcutta, Bombay and Madras: Orient Languages Pvt. Ltd.

Gill, S. S. (1983). *Political Economy of Indo-Soviet Relations, 1947-1980.* Rajesh.

ITPO. (2003). A strategy for enhanced economic cooperation between India and China. New Delhi: Trade Information Department, Indian Trade Promotion Organisation.

Kaur, N. (1993). *India's exports: an analysis of instability and performance.* Ph.D. Thesis (unpublished), Department of Business Management, Patiala: Punjabi University.

Lanceiri, E. (1987). Export instability and economic development: a reappraisal. In H.W. Singer, N. Hatti and R. Tondon (ed.). *International Commodity Policy-Part II.* New Delhi: Ashish Publishing House, 567-593.

Macbean, A.I. (1966). *Export instability and economic development.* London: George Allen & Unwin Ltd.

Savvidos, A. (1984). Export Instability and Economic Growth: Some New Evidence. *Economic Development and Cultural Change*, 32(3), 607-614.

Singh, S. (2005). *China-India economic engagement: Building mutual confidence.* CSH Occasional Paper, No. 10. New Delhi: Rajdhani Arts Press.

Singhal, K.C. and N. Kaur (1986). Destination Wise Export Instability in India. *Margin*, 18(3), 61-71.

Singla, S. K. (2015). An Analysis of India's Export Performance with China. Foreign Trade Review, 50(3), 219-230.

Sinha, D. (1999). *Export Instability, Investment and Economic Growth in Asian Countries: A Time Series Analysis.* Center Discussion Paper No. 799, Yale University: Economic Growth Centre.

The Hindu. (2016). *Who killed Indian exports.* April 21. www.euroasiapub.org

Yin, X. (2004). China's trade reforms and economic development. *China Report*, 40(4), 407–417.

7

An Analysis of Chinese Perspectives on Indian "Look East Policy"

Shubham Karmakar

Introduction

In 1991, to help the Indian economy in order to use foreign trade and attract foreign investment returning to normal track, India has implemented a "Look East Policy". With international Changes in the situation and the strengthening and development needs of India's national strength, 2003 The post-East Policy began to enter a new phase. The new stage of India the "Look East Policy" also has new interests and strategic adjustments. The whole need, especially in the relationship between India and ASEAN, is even more Development. At the same time, the "Look East Policy" and India-ASEAN relations, It also has multiple effects on China in its immediate vicinity (Bower 2011). This article tries to explore the relationship between India and ASEAN from the Chinese perspective. In order to balance regional power and avoid a situation of regional hegemony, "Look East Policy" is fundamental. Moreover, it's important to learn how China is perceiving this policy through scholarly articles.

In 2003, when the Indian Foreign Minister Yashwant Sinha announced that the "Look East Policy" had entered a new stage, India has consciously extended the "Look East Policy" that was originally implemented to the economic and trade level to politics, military and other fields, and as a long-term strategy to enhance its international influence. Its geographical scope covers ASEAN and further expands to Australia, even China and other East Asian countries. From this point of view, the new phase of the "Look East Policy" is different in depth and breadth from the previous. First, from policy to strategic height. Looking at the economic achievements in the pre-stage of the "Look East Policy", such as 1993-2003, the bilateral trade volume between India and ASEAN increased from 2.9 billion US dollars to 12.1 billion US dollars, with an annual growth rate of 11.2%; in 2003, ASEAN follows the EU and the US as India's third-largest trading partner. With the recovery of the Indian economy and the improvement of national power, India hopes to give more content on the basis of the economy, and the "Look East Policy" has to undertake new tasks. Former Indian Foreign Minister Ahmed said: "The "Look East Policy" is not only a foreign economic policy, but also a shift in India's interest appeal to a strategic direction." The new phase of "Look East Policy" was promoted to a strategic position and became a big Indian country. An important part of the strategy is an important practice for India's foreign strategic adjustment. During this period, the Indian government has been upgraded from a policy that mainly solves economic problems to a strategic plan that focuses comprehensively. The "Look East Policy" has also evolved from a tentative policy to a long-term strategy with clear objectives and plans.

Second, the expansion of strategic interest space. India is no longer content to define itself in South Asia and Southeast Asia. The extension of the concept of "East" in the new stage shows that it wants to cooperate not only with ASEAN, but also for India to extend to the wider Asia-Pacific region. India has begun to attach importance to cooperation with important Asia-Pacific countries such as China, Japan, South Korea and Australia. It also hopes to occupy a key position in Asia-Pacific affairs, and the "East Policy" plays a vital role in this process. As the Asia-Pacific region is increasingly becoming the main region for world development, India is bound to move forward with the tide of the times. Based on this, India's interest expansion path is clearly reflected and serves the implementation of the country's overall strategy (Muni and Chadha 2015).

Again, more emphasis is placed on political issues and security issues. In the new stage, India's interest demands are no longer limited to economic and trade fields, and demand in the political and security fields is stronger than in the previous stage. India is eager to become a world power, which is the goal that it has always pursued. The areas of politics and security are related to the further cooperation between India and ASEAN countries. The current non-traditional security issues such as terrorism and piracy are becoming increasingly prominent. India needs to cooperate with relevant regional organisations and countries such as ASEAN in a new situation and security environment.

Finally, start competition with China. In fact, India's "Look East Policy" has the intention to check and balance China, but at least from the current strength comparison, it is still not realistic. However, China and India are both ASEAN neighbours, and competition is inevitable.

Due to the good results of the "Look East Policy", successive Indian governments have maintained this policy, especially in 2014, the Modi government upgraded the "Act East Policy". "Intensification of depth and breadth." This shows that the eastward policy is consistent with India's current profit expectations, and the new phase of "Look East Policy" as an important foreign strategy of India must be continuously studied in depth.

Discussion

The comprehensive development of India-ASEAN relations under the "Look East Policy" in the new stage

The development of relations between India and ASEAN under the new stage of "Look East Policy" is based on economic cooperation, and promotes the strengthening of political, security, and social and cultural relations between the two sides. The promotion of bilateral relations between India and ASEAN countries strengthens overall cooperation between Indian and ASEAN.

Economic Cooperation

The fundamental task of the "Look East Policy" in the new stage is to develop the economy. Therefore, the establishment of liberalised trade arrangements and the promotion of bilateral trade is still the main theme of this stage. The bilateral trade between India and UK shows fluctuating trend (Kaur et al 2018). Against the background of rapid economic globalisation, India has more expectations for ASEAN with prominent geographical advantages and stronger economic vitality and hopes to achieve substantial growth in investment and trade with ASEAN.

First, it has stepped up the establishment of the India-ASEAN Free Trade Area. In order to strengthen the economic cooperation with ASEAN, India has agreed to establish a trade and investment zone for India and the ASEAN region, including free trade in goods, services and investment, with reference to the construction mechanism of the China-ASEAN Free Trade Area. Subsequently, the two parties signed the Agreement on Trade in Goods in August 2009, paving the way for the creation of the huge free trade zone of India-ASEAN (Sit 2013). The two parties also completed the signing of the Freedom of Service and Investment Agreement in January 2015. Since then, the construction of the India-ASEAN Free Trade Area has achieved initial success (Panda 2015).

Secondly, promote bilateral economic and trade relations. During the construction of the India-ASEAN Free Trade Area, India has negotiated trade with ASEAN countries one by one in order to reduce the difficulty of negotiating with ASEAN as a whole. For example, in the process of India's deepening of the ASEAN Economic Cooperation Circle, Singapore's role as a "leader" is very prominent, and it has always supported India to establish a closer relationship with ASEAN. Nowadays, Singapore, Thailand, Malaysia and other countries have become an important trade and investment partners of India. Before that, India's economic trade and assistance to Myanmar, Vietnam, Laos and other countries will help eliminate mutual doubts and gradually win the ASEAN's Support and trust. At the same time, the continued advancement of the free trade zone has also created a broad platform for the building of economic and trade relations between India and ASEAN countries (Zhu Xiong-gun 2015).

Thirdly, in order to strengthen the connection between India and the ASEAN region. ASEAN requires the completion of the construction of the Inmartai three-way expressway as soon as possible and the expansion of cooperation with Laos and Cambodia. At the same time, develop a new Indian-Malaysia-Laos-Vietnam-Myanmar highway to improve the physical connection between India and ASEAN. In addition to land transportation, India and ASEAN also cooperate closely in the field of shipping and shipping to facilitate the flow of goods and personnel exchanges between each other (Kishimoto 2017).

Fourthly, strengthening the regional connectivity between India and ASEAN can also make up for the weak links in the northeastern part of India and the less developed regions of ASEAN. The northeastern part of India is bordered by Myanmar. It is a land passage and shortcut that connects Southeast Asia, but it has not been fully developed. ASEAN also urgently needs to establish internal and external transportation networks to promote the development of remote and underdeveloped areas such as Myanmar, Vietnam and Cambodia.

The advancement of infrastructure construction now brings new opportunities for investment and trade and tourism in India and ASEAN. According to statistics, in 2013, there were 2.95 million trips from India to ASEAN countries, and ASEAN received direct investment from India at 2.1 billion U.S. dollars. The bilateral trade volume between India and ASEAN has exceeded 100 billion U.S. dollars in 2015. The new phase of "eastward policy" still regards the deepening of economic cooperation between India and ASEAN as the core link, and the degree of regional economic cooperation integration between the two sides is gradually deepening (Wang 2017).

Political Cooperation

ASEAN is in the forefront of the Asia-Pacific region, and the evolution of India-ASEAN political and diplomatic relations will directly affect

India's future influence in the Asia-Pacific region. As a whole, ASEAN also hopes to maintain peace and stability in Southeast Asia and use India's expanding influence to enhance its political status and continue to guarantee its detached status in dialogue with other major powers. Moreover, some ASEAN countries have also taken advantage of the support of major powers to win opportunities to lead ASEAN affairs. In December 2005, ASEAN invited India to participate in the first East Asia Summit and established a "10+1" cooperation mechanism with India to integrate India into the process of regional cooperation (Laporta 2015).

The form of cooperation between India and ASEAN has always kept the multilateral and bilateral parallel. The exchange of visits between senior leaders of India and Southeast Asian countries has become an important way for both sides to strengthen political understanding and trust. At present, India has established strategic partnerships with Indonesia, Vietnam and Singapore. The level of bilateral relations has gradually enriched, and India's political image in the ASEAN region has also improved significantly. ASEAN is a coalition of small and medium-sized countries, and most of them are members of non-aligned organisations. The continuous improvement of the level of bilateral relations with ASEAN countries is conducive to maintaining the status of Indian non-aligned leaders. In November 2015, the 13th India-ASEAN Summit was held in Kuala Lumpur. During the meeting, ASEAN leaders expressed their welcome to India's "East Policy" and proposed that the "Eastward Policy" could be an important complement to the ASEAN Community. On the basis of existing cooperation, India and ASEAN continue to push bilateral cooperation to new heights through various forms.

Military security cooperation

The security situation in Asia today faces many challenges. Non-traditional security incidents are frequent, and terrorist activities are rampant. ASEAN and India are also deeply affected. In view of the common interests and goals, the two have coincided with the need to enhance military security cooperation; and the security and defense cooperation between India and ASEAN has a natural convenience in geography, making the cooperation between the two parties more targeted and practical.

1. Reduce the surrounding traditional security threats. There are separatist forces in northeastern India, and Myanmar is often a safe haven for these insurgents, and Cambodia is an important source of smuggling weapons for rebel groups. India needs to work closely with these governments to address such threats. In 2012, Myanmar's President Wu Dengsheng visited India and the two sides firmly affirmed their cooperation in strengthening the military in the field of combating terrorist insurrection. The frequent military linkages between India and its neighbors in Southeast Asia have promoted the effective development of military cooperation.
2. Jointly address non-traditional security issues. First of all, counter-terrorism has become an urgent task. After the "9.11 incident", terrorist forces spread rapidly around the world, and India and Southeast Asian countries also became disaster areas with frequent terrorist activities. In 2015, 159 Indonesian nationals and 59 Malaysian nationals joined the Islamic State Organisation. Terrorism is also the primary factor affecting India's domestic security, and terrorist organisations in the Middle East, South Asia and Southeast Asia are echoing and threatening India. Similarly, terrorism in countries such as Indonesia, Malaysia, and the Philippines poses a security threat to ASEAN today. The anti-terrorism cooperation between India and ASEAN is based on a solid foundation of mutual benefit. The joint anti-terrorism exercise is the normal cooperation between the two sides. In March 2016, India launched a joint exercise with Indonesia to deal with the threat of terrorists. This model brings together many anti-terrorism experiences and strengthens the counter-terrorism power.

Second, counter pirates and ensure the safety of maritime affairs. The Malacca Strait in Southeast Asia is a frequent area of piracy. According to statistics, there were 212 piracy cases in the Straits of Malacca from 2000 to 2012. Ships were missing and 14 were robbed. The number of people killed was 7 and the number of detainees reached 248. Serious casualties and property damage. India and most of the ASEAN countries' energy and trade transportation rely heavily on the Straits of Malacca. In response to this problem, India and ASEAN have been trying to maintain communication and navigation safety in the Malacca channel and the Indian Ocean through effective military cooperation. India's security defense cooperation with Indonesia, Malaysia and Singapore can consolidate control of the Indian Ocean, and of course its self-interest in maintaining the status of a superpower in the South Asian subcontinent (Edwards 2015).

In addition to the Malacca waters, other Southeast Asian waters are also areas of piracy. According to the International Maritime Bureau, there were 178 maritime attacks in Southeast Asia in 2015, and according to the New York Times on September 18, 2016, Southeast Asia has replaced Africa as the most pirate region in the world (Shira *et al.* 2017). In order to respond to this situation, frequent maritime joint exercises, joint patrols, and regular docking of warships at ports in both sides have become the regular content of India-ASEAN to maintain maritime security. In 2016, India and Thailand conducted joint patrols in the Andaman waters to strengthen coordination and counterattack crimes at sea.

Social and Cultural cooperation

India has a long history and cultural ties with Southeast Asia, with a large population of Indians spread across ASEAN countries. The social and cultural cooperation between India and ASEAN mainly includes two levels, national and civil, including natural disaster management, environmental climate change and biodiversity, and health, education, culture and personnel exchange.

First, at the national level, India provided $1 million to Indonesia in December 2004 during the tsunami, moreover emergency supplies and dispatched naval fleets to coordinate rescue operations by the Indonesian military. The connection between Singapore and India is clearly marked. In May 2015, the Indian Cultural Center in Singapore's Little India District was officially unveiled. The establishment of the Cultural Center not only preserves the cultural wealth brought by Indian immigrants, but also further spreads the traditional culture of India.

Second, at the civilian level, India assisted the ASEAN Entrepreneurship Center in carrying out projects to help ASEAN organise English language training in Cambodia, Malaysia, Laos, Vietnam, Indonesia and other countries. Thc two sides established the ASEAN-India Student Exchange Program and the India-ASEAN Media Exchange Program. In fact, through a profound historical and cultural connection, it is easier for India and ASEAN and the public on both sides to understand each other's intentions so that the Indian-ASEAN regional society can achieve the effect of resonance (Billington 2017).

Thirdly, the potential test of India-ASEAN relations to China in the new stage, signifies the common interests of India and ASEAN have deepened the relationship between the two sides and have formed a situation in which the economy, politics and military are linked together. In fact, India-ASEAN cooperation also involves China, which will naturally have an impact on China's external environment. Since China has always been a vital partner of India and ASEAN, it is possible to prejudge the possible adverse effects of India-ASEAN cooperation on China, and it is beneficial to take effective measures early and turn crisis into opportunity.

Perception of each other in relation to ASEAN

China's perception of threat

India vis-à-vis the rest of the world are anxious about China's activities in South Asia. It is worried that India's status and strategic space in South Asia will be challenged, but India alone cannot suppress China. Thus, the strength of the joint ASEAN countries has become the ideal choice. And some ASEAN countries also bear the psychological cognition of China's "threat", which coincides with the Indian perception. For example, the US National Interest magazine said that India and Vietnam are responding to China through more active military cooperation. The bilateral relationship between India and Vietnam is even closer than that of the Nehru and Ho Chi Minh periods. In June 2016, India proposed the sale of the supersonic missile "Brahmos" cruise missile to Vietnam, which was counterproductive to China (Wang 2017).

In addition, India has also strengthened its naval capacity building with important coastal countries such as Indonesia and Australia to have better control of the Indian Ocean. At the same time, India's support for military production and defense construction in ASEAN countries is still sufficient to undermine its influence in South Asia and Southeast Asia. This will continue to affect China's proactive participation in South Asia and Southeast Asia, and even undermine China's legitimate interests (Wang 2017).

China's perception on India regarding South China Sea

The insufficiency of the South China Sea issue and even the intensification of a certain period of time cannot be separated from the involvement, provocation and promotion of countries outside the region. As early as April 19, 2000, the "Indian Express" once declared: "Ranging from the north of the Arabian Sea to the South China Sea, but wherever its eyes are, the Indian Navy wants to be on it" (Wouters et al. 2013). Of course, for various reasons, India did not use force to intervene in the South China Sea. However, India is still frequently seen in the South China Sea region. The first is to covet the rich oil and gas resources of the South China Sea. For example, in October 2011, the Indian Oil and Gas Company signed an agreement with the Vietnam National Oil and Gas Group to jointly develop offshore oil and gas resources in the South China Sea.

Secondly, India's involvement in the South China Sea issue can participate in the affairs of the international focus area, demonstrating its international influence. At the same time, some ASEAN countries intend to draw on Indian power and use its influence to contain China. Despite this, India's official statement is: Call on all parties to exercise restraint and strive to maintain stability and peace in the South China Sea. However, India's move still requires more research to avoid unnecessary embarrassment for China's related affairs.

Counter argument: India-ASEAN Relations Provide New Opportunities for China under the "Look East Policy" in the New Stage

At present, the closeness of the relations between countries in the world has reached a new height. Even if the parties have differences on some specific issues, it does not hinder cooperation. Seeking common ground while reserving differences is the most ideal form. Although China and India have a small number of conflicts of interest prior to the Covid-19 era, they are still essentially close-knit partners. The implementation of the "eastward policy" in the new stage can also be regarded as an important opportunity for China and India to strengthen cooperation. The deepening of India-ASEAN relations has improved the common interests of Asian countries and is conducive to building a community of Asian destiny.

(1) The successful experience of India's "eastward policy" has provided reference to China. Since India implemented the "eastward policy", it has achieved fruitful results and is gradually realizing its dream of a big country. The success of the "eastward policy" has its inevitable elements to be materialised, and China can learn valuable experience to promote its progress in foreign exchanges.

First of all, India has expanded its relationship with ASEAN with historical and cultural ties and gained high recognition. China can also tap the links and advantages at the cultural level. Ancient China has different degrees of connection with the cultures of Southeast Asian countries. This is the traditional basis for the friendship between China and ASEAN. Chinese overseas Chinese are valuable and unique resource advantage for the important role of connecting China and Southeast Asia. According to statistics, from 2007 to 2008, the total number of Chinese overseas Chinese was 45.43 million, of which 33.86 million were from ASEAN, accounting for 73.5% of the world's 45.43 million overseas Chinese (Chabal 2013). In terms of willingness and ability, Chinese overseas Chinese are an important driving force for cooperation between China and Southeast Asia. State-level departments such as the Overseas Chinese Affairs Office of the State Council and non-Chinese Chinese and overseas Chinese social organisations could actively establish contacts with overseas Chinese in Southeast Asia and find effective ways and means to help China-ASEAN cooperation. At the same time, China needs to rationally play the role of domestic universities with programs to train Southeast Asian students, further promote exchanges between the two sides, create a friendly and trusting atmosphere, and consolidate the foundation for future cooperation and development. Most of the aforementioned steps are gradually being covered under the China's Belt and Road Initiative.

Secondly, the military cooperation between India and ASEAN countries has played a key role and invites China's attention. The main form of military cooperation between India and ASEAN countries is frequent military exchanges and joint military exercises. However, cooperation between China and ASEAN in this regard needs to be improved. China should take the initiative to increase exchanges with the ASEAN military, such as the January 2016 Chinese Navy 152 fleet to promote friendly visits to Indonesia and other activities should be promoted. In addition, the current level of China's military technology and military manufacturing industry is advancing by leaps and bounds, and it can also encourage the export of military products to Southeast Asia. It can meet the needs of ASEAN countries for the diversification of military equipment selection, and also increase the channels and links with relevant countries.

(2) Regional economic cooperation with ASEAN as the axis ushered in a major opportunity In 2014, the Modi government focused on the "Eastward Action Policy", indicating that the "Look East Policy" in the

new stage highlights Southeast Asia as a breakthrough and integrates the Asia-Pacific region. The strategy entered into a stage of substantive development. In response to the new international situation, India has made substantial adjustments in its Asia-Pacific strategy, fully participating in Asia-Pacific affairs, expanding relations with other major powers, and thus creating favorable external conditions for its own development from political, economic, and military security aspects (Woertz 2007). In 2016, the China-ASEAN Free Trade Area has entered a stage of consolidation and improvement and has strengthened its confidence in establishing a huge free market of China, India and ASEAN with ASEAN as its axis. At present, the social and economic development of India and some ASEAN countries are at the stage of labor-intensive industries. China is undergoing industrial adjustment, and some enterprises that are in line with the national conditions of India and ASEAN countries can be transferred to achieve a win-win situation and even a win-win effect. Affected by factors such as rising labor costs, China's traditional manufacturing needs to be transformed, while India and ASEAN countries can provide enough raw materials and low-cost labor. For example, Cambodia has absorbed a large number of garment factories from China in recent years, which has increased the income of Cambodian local people and solved employment difficulties. In addition, China has a strong capital reserve, while India and ASEAN have insufficient infrastructure, and China's capital can directly ease the pressure on India and ASEAN. In January 2017, Chinese companies invested in the construction of the largest power station project in Indonesia, with a total investment of 2 billion US dollars would have been completed in 2020. However, due to the outbreak of Covid-19 pandemic, many countries renegotiated their deals, therefore the deals might be canceled or the scale be limited (Baxter 2021). The "going out strategy" of Chinese enterprises is in line with the needs of the current economic development stages of India and ASEAN countries. As the consumption power of India and ASEAN increases, Chinese companies will enter the local production and sell products on the spot, which will also gain a broader market space.

(3) China-India-ASEAN tripartite joint construction of a rational regional pattern

China and India are accelerating development today. After the official establishment of the ASEAN Community in December 2015, ASEAN has become a force to be reckoned with in the Asia-Pacific region. The increasing influence of the three will help build a more equitable and reasonable Asia-Pacific region. First of all, the rise of India is not in contradiction with China. India plays an important role in the Asia-Pacific region, which is beneficial to balancing the strength of Western developed countries led by the United States. Although India's "eastward policy" and US "return to Asia-Pacific policy" have overlapping interests, the United States hopes to support India to contain China. However, India cannot only rely on the United States. Although China and India still have differences on certain issues, in the final analysis, cooperation is the mainstream. At the G20 summit in September 2016, President Xi Jinping and Prime Minister Modi made an accurate definition of Sino-Indian relations: The Chinese side stated that it should grasp the general direction of China-India relations, strengthen communication on major issues involving common interests, and continue to improve together. The global economic governance has made a major contribution while the Indian side said that China and India are in similar positions in international affairs, and Asian countries can work together to meet the Asian century.

Secondly, ASEAN has made outstanding contributions to the construction of regional patterns. The ASEAN countries are committed to internal integration and use their overall strength to fight for the right to speak on the international political arena. This behavior is itself changing the power structure of the Asia-Pacific region. At the same time, ASEAN has created many regional cooperation mechanisms and is working with other countries to move towards a just and democratic direction to change the power of unreasonable international and regional patterns. In February 2017, the 17th round of the Regional Meeting Economic Partnership Agreement (RECP) was launched. The 10 ASEAN countries and 6 dialogue partners (China, Japan, India, Australia, Korea, and New) have been engaged in economic and technological cooperation and SMEs. There is consensus in both areas, and most countries want to accelerate the negotiations. The promotion of RECP will bring together Asia-Pacific countries to work together to build a diversified and dynamic free trade zone, and ultimately share fruitful results.

(4) India-ASEAN is paying more attention to long-term interests and is conducive to China's resolution of the crisis

When both India and ASEAN are considering maintaining a stable economic cooperation relationship with China, this will help to deal with differences with China as calmly and sensibly as possible on political and security issues and provide a solid social foundation for resolving conflicts. On July 12, 2016, the announcement of the results of the so-called "South China Sea Arbitration Case" triggered intense discussions among countries around the world; Indian side stated that the situation should be resolved through consultation and negotiation. The arbitration, except for the Philippines and Vietnam, welcomed by the rest of the ASEAN countries. From this point of view, China's persistent and diligent work in the field of international politics is gradually realizing the expectation of building a friendly and good-will revival of the external environment.

Conclusion

The "Look East Policy" in the new stage has become an important cornerstone of India's Asia-Pacific strategy and the dream of realizing a big country. Its strategic intention is not only to develop economic relations with ASEAN, but also to use the power of ASEAN to go to a larger world stage and gain more realism. ASEAN is willing to accept India's "eastward policy", it is also a consideration based on its own interests. It also aims to seek more opportunities and voice by using the checks and balances of major powers to maintain stability in Southeast Asia. As India and ASEAN have doubts about China's development, India's "look east policy" has the possibility, jointly ASEAN, has the potential to adjust China's influence. But we should also recognise that India's "look east policy" also brings many opportunities for China. Both China and India need a peaceful and stable external environment to achieve development. The two countries have a common understanding on global climate change and building a world-wide economic order. They can fully cooperate and achieve common development. Therefore, only India and ASEAN and China can strengthen cooperation and mutual tolerance, and truly form stable regional development and close cooperation between countries, which can help Asia to prosper in the future and contribute to world development and prosperity.

References

Baxter, T. (2021) "2020: a dismal for coal power", *China Dialogue*, available at https://chinadialogue.net/en/energy/2020-a-dismal-year-for-coal-power/, last visited on 23/02/2021

Bhatia, S.K., Bhardwaj, M., & Kaur, P. (2018). An Empercial Analysis of India - UK Bilateral Trade.

Billington, M. (2017). "A hub for the Maritime Silk Road", *Executive Intelligence Review*, 44(4).

Bower, E. (2011). "Enter the Elephant: India is Part of Asia". *Southeast Asia from the Corner of 18th and K Streets*, *2*(2). Accessed from at csis.org/publication/enter-india-part-asia.on March 22, 2018.

Cao Wenzhe and Huang Weizi. (2015) "Analysis of the Thailand Kra Canal Project under the Vision of China's "Maritime Power" Strategy", The institute of International Studies, School of Law & Political Science, Ocean University.

Chabal, P. (ed.) (2013). India, SCO and the Evolving Regional Multilateral Order: Explaining New Delhi's Regional Vision, *The SCO's Impact on Region-Building in Asia*, L'impact de l'OCS sur la construction de l'Asie, Paris: LGDJ.

Edward, N.G. (2015). The rise of Chinese FDI into ASEAN, *Nikko Asset Management*.

Kishimoto, M. (2017). "Laos merely a bystander as China pushes Belt and Road ambitions", *Nikkei Asian Review*.

Laporta, L. C. (2015). "The Maritime Silk Road: China and the ASEAN", *ESCI*.

Muni, S.D. and Chadha, V. (eds.) (2015). "India in East Asia: Reviewing the Role of a Security Provider", *Asian Strategic Review 2015: India As A Security Provider*, New Delhi: Pentagon Press and IDSA, 213-229.

Panda, J. P. (2015). "Alignment Minus Alliance: India's China Quandary on Alternative Institution Building". *Georgetown Journal of Asian Affairs,* 2(1), 21-30.

Shira, D. and Associates (2017). "Kra Canal project revisited as part of China's Maritime Silk Road", *ASEAN Briefing.*

Sit, F. S. (ed.) (2013). "Deliberating a 'Cross-Regional' Perspective: China, India and the Emerging World Order", *China-India Cooperation Prospects, Singapore*: Enrich Professional Publishing, 241-258.

Wang, G. (2017). "Zhong Mei Nan Hai Bo Yi Yu" [Sino-US game in the South China Sea and 'the Belt and Road Initiative' in ASEAN], *Around South East Asia*, vol. 5.

Woertz, E. (ed.) (2007). "India's Modi-fied Africa Policy: A Non-China Centric Advance", *Re-configuration of the Global South: Africa and Latin America in the 'Asian Century'*, London and New York: Routledge.

Wouters, T., Defraigne, P., and Defraigne, J. C. (eds) (2013). "BRICs, China and the emerging world order: is the PRC writing a new global script?", China, the *European Union and Global Governance*, UK: Edward Elgar, 311-324.

Zhu Xiong-gun. (2014). "The Influences and Countermeasures from the Changes of the Situation of Mynamar to the Safety of China-Myanmar Oil-gas Pipeline", *Institute of International Studies, Yunnan University.*

Further Readings (Not Cited)

Dixit, N.J. (2001) "India' Foreign Policy and its Neighbour". New Delhi: Gyan Publishing House.

Ghiasy, R., Fei Su and Saalman, L. (2018). "The 21st Century Maritime Silk Road; Security Implications and ways forward for the European Union", Stockholm International Peace Research Institute.

Heide, D., Hopper, T., Scheuer, S., Stratmann, K. (2018). "EU ambassadors band together against Silk Road, Handelsblatt Global.

Hong, Z. (2007). "India and China: Rivals or Partners in Southeast Asia?" Contemporary Southeast Asia, 29(1), 121-142. Retrieved from www.jstor.org/stable/25798817.

Li Yuan-yuan. (2013). Analysis on the Development of India's "Look East" Policy and its Impact on China, School of International Studies, Peking University, Beijing, 100072, China, 许昌学院报

Liu Xiaojuan. (2007). "Analysis of India's" "Eastward Policy". Sichuan, China: Sichuan University Press.

Miglani, S. (2018). "Asian giants China and India flex muscles over tiny Maldives", Reuters.

Panda, J.P. (2014). *China's Tryst with the IORA: Factoring India and the Indian Ocean.* Strategic Analysis.

Panda, J. P. (2015) "Future of India-China Boundary: Leadership Holds the Key?", Strategic Analysis, 39(3), 278-292.

Panda, J. P. (2016). "Institutionalizing the African Reach: Reviewing China's and India's Multilateral Drive", Journal of Asian and African Studies.

Panda, J. P. (2016). Narendra Modi's China policy: between pragmatism and power parity, Journal of Asian Public Policy, 9:2, 185-197.

Scot, D. (2007) "Strategic Imperatives of India as an Emerging Player in Pacific Asia". International Studies, (2).

Shihai, S. and Jiang Yili. (2007). Research on South Asian International Foreign Relations after World War II. Beijing: Fang Zhi Publishing House.

Wan Daobin. (2011). "Comment on India's" Eastward Policy "after the Cold War". Xinjiang University.

Wang Chuanjian. (2007). "India's East Asian Cooperation Policy Viewed from the Implementation of "Eastward Strategy". Research on Nanyang Issues, (1).

Weimin, H. (2011). "India's, eastward policy" is not targeted at China", World News.

________. (2017). "Vietnam police halt anti-China protest over islands", Reuters.

________. (2016). China's Transition Under Xi Jinping, New Delhi: Pentagon Press.

________. (2017). India-China Relations: Politics of Resources, Identity and Authority in a Multipolar World Order, London & New York: Routledge.

PART III

Measuring Value Chain and Trade Relations between India-East Asia

8

India's Participation in Global Value Chain with Selected East Asian Countries

Exploring the Facts

Sandeep Kaur, Manpreet Kaur & Harpreet Singh

Introduction

Global Value Chain (GVC) is more prominent in the integration of services and goods at world level. It has increased the interconnectedness of economies due to growing specialisation in specific activities in the industries. GVC gives opportunity at an earlier stage of development if there is competitive cost advantage for e.g. low labour cost. GVCis especially important for low-income countries where most of the firms are SMEs and they improve their capabilities. (Cusolito et al. 2016) GVC encourages upward movement by rewarding skills, learning, and innovation. GVC participation has to pay big dividends of overcoming obstacles developing economies with the fastest growing GVC participation have gross domestic product per capita growth rates more than 2 per cent higher the average (Cusolito et al. 2016).

According to the UNCTAD report, 2013 Global Value Chain was made a significant contribution to international development. There is a contribution of 30 per cent of value added trade in GDP of developing countries while it is 18 per cent for developed countries. (https://en.wikipedia.org/wiki/Global_value_chain). GVC is especially important for low-income countries where most of the firms are SMEs and they improve their capabilities. GVC encourages upward movement by rewarding skills, learning, and innovation. Global Value Chain is playing an important role in economic growth links in developing countries. In developing countries, GVC builds productive capacities through technology dissemination and skill building (Chains, 2013). Keeping in view of its significance, the present paper is an attempt to study the growth and performance of the Global value chain for the period of 1990-2018.

In this paper, the study also attempts to understand where India stands in the global value chain for the particular industry i.e. electrical and machinery industry. The electronics industry largely contributes to India's merchandise imports. There is a widening gap between the country's electronics hardware demand and its domestic production capabilities even after two decades of trade liberalisation (Francis 2016 and Saripalle 2015).

The motivation behind choosing the electrical and machinery industry is recognizing its importance in technologically intensive sector, the Indian government has identified it as one of the champion sectors under the Make-in-India program. In the era of the splintered production process, it is important for a country to not only be part of the global value chain which enables a country to benefit from the spillover effect but upgrade and move to higher value-adding activities to achieve sustained economic growth and development. Currently, India heavily imports dependent in this particular sector and existing literature states the reason for this is the signing of Information Technology Agreement (ITA-I) in 1995 where India committed to the removal of all customs duties by 2005 (Dash & Chanda, 2017).

The study is focused on the

i. To study the growth and performance of India's Global Value Chain for the period of 1990 to 2018
ii. To analyse India 's Inter-Country Input-Output (ICIO) table for understanding the content of domestic and foreign value-added overall and particularly Electrical and Machinery industry

iii. To examine overall India's GVC forward and backward participation index and particularly Electrical and Machinery industry

Review of Literature

There is not vast literature on the current theme of the study. But still, an attempt has been made to understand the role of GVC in Asia. Banga (2016) has also investigated the impact of the Global Value Chain on employment in India. The study evaluates that how increasing Foreign Value Added in output through Foreign Value Added in exports to backward linkages and Domestic Value Added in exports of intermediate goods affects the employment growth by forwarding linkages. The study covers three sectors manufacturing, services, and agricultural sectors and applies the methodology of fixed effects of the generalised method of moments during 1995-2011. The study examines how is the impact on employment growth in the industry-level of participation in the Global Value Chain. The result shows that higher backward linkages have negatively influenced employment growth. But higher forward linkages did not have any statistically significant impact on employment. Kiyota et al., (2017) explored the competitiveness of the global value chain in Asian countries. The study examines the competitiveness of industries in six Asian countries China, India, Indonesia, Japan, South Korea, and Taiwan. The study has used the methodology of World Input-Output Database tables from 1995 to 2011. The study measured competitiveness by the value-added industries contribution to the production of final goods, which they refer to as global value chain income, rather than by gross exports. They find that GVC income in Asian countries presents a different picture in European countries. Koponen (2012) has examined to better precisely the creation and distribution of value in the level of an individual product of global value chain in the machinery industry. The study defines organisational as the geographical distribution of the value chain. The methodology aimed at gathering data for accurate comparisons of different product sizes locations of production as well as regions of sales. The study provides a great value distribution in the machinery industry through the global value chain, which has introduced the product, production, sales of different scenarios. The study suggests that the global economies of companies are becoming complex in different webs and networks. Wang et al. (2016) highlighted the characteristics of the global value chain. The study analyses the extent of both outsourcing and off shoring varies by sectors and countries. The objective of the study developed a set of country sector level measures of global value chains regarding average production length, the intensity of participation and relative upstream positions on a production network. The study found that distinguish production activities are done inside a country and cross borders once or multiple times.

Data Methodology

This paper is entirely based on secondary data analysis. Secondary data on trade-in value added is available for India with China, Indonesia and South Korea; it studies the overall and bilateral trends and patterns in trade which gives the information on trade-in value-added. This paper has used the euro database and WIOD, TIVA data source. In this paper, the input-output model has been used, which was developed by Leontief (1951). The study has tried to bridge the current divergence between input-output and value distribution approaches to Global Value Chain analysis. The study has also represented the backward and forward linkages of interrelating countries on the behalf based on the input-output econometric analysis. The study has evaluated out of vertical specialisation of international trade domestic and foreign contents in a country's gross exports, the development of value-chain in a global production network. The study has been measured from the OECD inter-country input-output (ICIO) database (TIVA, 2016). The analysis has been carried at the aggregate level. The study has used the following selected indicators of the world ICIO table.

Table 8.1: List of Indicators (Decomposition of Gross Exports)

	Gross Exports (Goods and Services)	E*	E* (1+9)
1.	DV indirect final goods exports	DVA_FIN	DVA
2.	DV in intermediates exports absorbed by direct importers	DVA_INT	
3.	DV in intermediates re-exported	DVA_INT rex	
4.	DV in intermediates that returns via final imports	RDV_G	RDV
5.	DV in intermediates that returns via intermediate imports	RDV_G	
6.	Double counted intermediate exports produced at home	DDC	PDC
7.	FV in final goods exports	FVA_FIN	FVA
8.	FV in intermediate goods exports	FVA_INT	
9.	Double counted intermediate exports produced abroad	FDC	
10.	DV in intermediates re-exported		FL
11.	Global Value Chain (GVC)		FVA+FL
12.	Vertical Specialisation	VS	VS*(5+6+7+8)

Source: Koopman et al., 2014.

GVC participation index can be computed by the sum of forward and backward linkages, If the forward linkages are larger than backward linkages, it implies that the country is positioned upstream in the global value chain and provides raw material or intermediate goods to downstream countries. If the forward linkage is less than backward linkage, this implies that the country is positioned downstream in the global value chain while using intermediate inputs from upstream countries.

Evolution of GVCs

According to UNCTAD-Eora Global Value Chain Database, "GVCs are coordinated by multinational enterprises (MNEs) investing in productive assets worldwide and trading inputs and outputs intra-firm, at arm's length or through their network of non-equity mode (NEM) partners." "According to OECD (TIVA), where the different stages of the international trade, production and investment process are increasingly organised and located across different countries, so-called global value chain."Table 8.2 illustrates India's performance of Global Value Chain for the period of 1990-2018. World Global Value Chain has increased the US$3662.15 million to the US$ 21269.31million and its percentage share has increased from 1.10% to 6.39% during 1990 to 2018. On the other side, India's Global Value Chain has increased the US$ 22.43 million to the US$ 412.32 million while its percentage share increased from 0.48% to 8.75% from 1990 to 2018.

Table 8.3 shows for World and India's Top Lead total Export Industries in value addition during from the period 1990-2015. The industries include Agriculture, Mining and Quarrying, Food & Beverages, Textiles and Wearing Apparel, Wood and Paper, Petroleum, Chemical and Non-Metallic Mineral Products, Metal Products, Electrical and Machinery, Transport Equipment, Other Manufacturing, Recycling in the Electrical and Machinery, World Export has the highest share in value-added contribution in exports of India i.e. 23.40% and India has also the highest share i.e. 22.36% in the same industry during 1990 to 2015.

Figure 8.1: Percentage Share of Industry-Wise Value Added Contribution in Exports

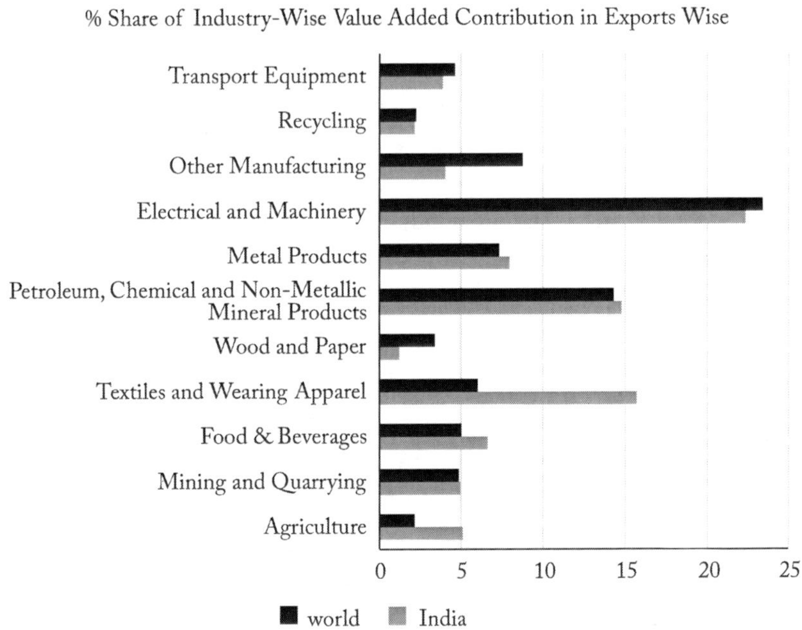

Table 8.2: India's Performance in Global Value Chain (1990-2018)

Year	World GVC (US$ Million)	% Share	India GVC (US$ Million)	% Share
1991	3662.15	1.10	22.43	0.48
1995	5344.72	1.61	38.46	0.82
2000	6446.61	1.94	59.47	1.26
2001	6370.91	1.92	59.82	1.27
2005	10712.49	3.22	125.77	2.67
2010	17593.75	5.29	282.51	5.99
2011	19477.23	5.85	317.29	6.73
2015	19276.86	5.79	333.20	7.07
2016	19701.42	5.92	363.87	7.72
2017	20503.36	6.16	385.94	8.19
2018	21269.31	6.39	412.32	8.75
Total 1991-2018	**332678.00**	**4.11***	**4712.85**	**4.63***

Source: UNCTAD-Eora Global Value Chain Database, 2019*Average.

Table 8.3: Industry-Wise Value Added Contribution in Exports of India and the world (1990-2015)

S. No.	Industries	Total World (US$ Million)	%	Indian Value (US$ Million)	%
1.	Agriculture	7277.11	2.17	256.76	5.11
2.	Mining and Quarrying	16281.38	4.85	248.48	4.94
3.	Food & Beverages	16879.40	5.03	333.53	6.63
4.	Textiles and Wearing Apparel	20205.10	6.02	791.01	15.74
5.	Wood and Paper	11481.53	3.42	61.91	1.23
6.	Petroleum, Chemical and Non-Metallic Mineral Products	48062.05	14.32	1124.04	14.80
7.	Metal Products	24678.31	7.35	401.78	7.99
8.	Electrical and Machinery	78548.44	23.40	744.17	22.36
9.	Transport Equipment	29466.00	8.78	195.91	3.90
10.	Other Manufacturing	7584.44	2.26	203.60	4.05
11.	Recycling	1031.06	0.31	109.15	2.17
12	**Total Industries**			**5026.83**	

Source: UNCTAD-Eora Global Value Chain Database, 2019.

Source: Authors' Calculation from the Eora database, 2019.

Measurement of Global Value Chain Indicators

The study focuses on a macro-economic approach to analyse various global value chain indicators.

India's Decomposition of Gross Exports

The gross exports[1] of India at the aggregate level is decomposed using Koopman et al., (2014) for the period 2000 to 2014 (as presented in Table 8.4). Tracing the value-added suggests the following, first, though an overall increase in gross exports is observed, the study notices falling domestic value-added (DVA) from 90 per cent in 2000 to 78 per cent in 2014 while foreign value added (FVA) increased from 10 per cent in 2000 to 21 per cent in 2014 (Figure 8.2). In other words, on an average over the period 2000 to 2014, Indian gross exports comprise 80 per cent of domestic content and 21 per cent of foreign content. The remaining 0.42 per cent of gross exports is due to domestic intermediate exports that finally return home (4.82 per cent) and pure double-counted intermediate exports produced at home (0.11 per cent).

The table 8.5 represents global value chain [2]participation index of India using the forward and backward linkages extracted from gross exports. The linkages (both forward and backward) and GVC participation as a share of gross exports are presented in Table 8.5. The trends indicate the increased GVC participation of India over the period 1995 to 2014, with minor increasing forward linkages from

---

[1] **Gross Exports (E*),** DVA is a DV indirect final goods exports DVA_FIN +DV in intermediates exports absorbed by direct importers DVA_INT +DV in intermediates exports absorbed by direct importers DVA_INTrex, RDV is DV in intermediates that returns via final imports RDV_G+ DV in intermediates that returns via intermediate imports RDV_G, PDC=Double counted intermediate exports produced at home, FDC=Double counted intermediate exports produced abroad, FVA is a FV in final goods exports+ FV in intermediate goods exports, FL=DV in intermediates re-exported.

[2] Forward participation index shows the share of exported goods and services used as imported inputs in producing the importing country's exports. Backward participation index measures the value of imported inputs in the overall exports of a country for the particular industry.

Table 8.4: Decomposing India's Gross Exports (%) at aggregate level

Year	DVA	RDV	PDC	FDC	FVA	FL	GVC=FVA+FL
1995	90.54	0.11	0.01	1.31	9.33	6.29	15.62
1996	90.28	0.11	0.01	1.42	9.6	6.38	15.98
1997	90.13	0.14	0.01	1.5	9.71	6.74	16.45
1998	90.15	0.16	0.01	1.55	9.69	7.28	16.97
1999	89.34	0.18	0.02	1.81	10.47	7.66	18.13
2000	88.55	0.16	0.02	2.14	11.27	8.01	19.28
2001	87.29	0.2	0.02	2.43	12.49	7.95	20.44
2002	87.1	0.2	0.02	2.37	12.68	7.8	20.48
2003	86.43	0.22	0.03	2.58	13.33	7.96	21.29
2004	83.93	0.28	0.04	3.22	15.74	8.18	23.92
2005	82.18	0.33	0.05	3.57	17.45	7.91	25.36
2006	80.1	0.35	0.06	4.2	19.49	7.8	27.29
2007	80.45	0.4	0.07	4.25	19.08	7.99	27.07
2008	76.99	0.4	0.08	4.98	22.53	7.47	30.0
2009	78.58	0.43	0.08	4.13	20.91	6.99	27.9
2010	77.16	0.49	0.1	4.71	22.24	7.26	29.5
2011	75.35	0.52	0.1	5.29	24.03	7.3	31.33
2012	78.42	0.51	0.11	5.11	20.95	6.77	27.72
2013	78.26	0.45	0.12	5.34	21.17	6.9	28.07
2014	78.87	0.42	0.11	4.82	20.61	6.75	27.36
Average	83.51	0.30	0.05	3.34	16.14	7.37	23.51

Source: Authors' calculation using TIVA and WIOD database.

Figure 8.2: Percentage of Gross Exports

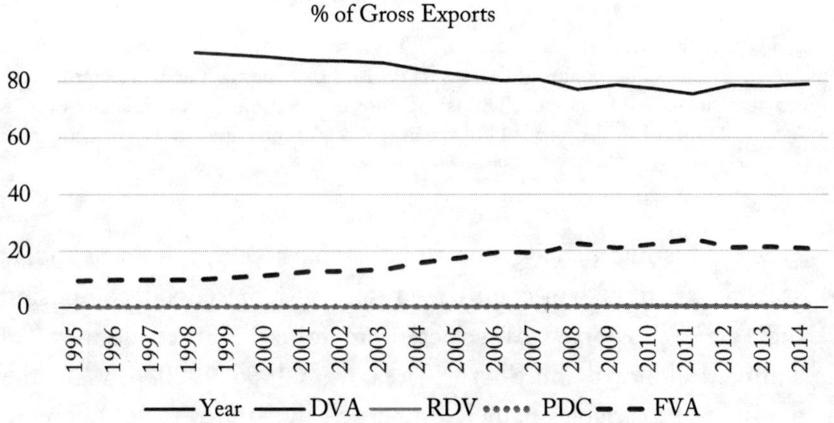

Source: Authors' calculation using TIVA and WIOD database.

6.29 per cent to 6.75 per cent and sufficient increasing backward linkage from 9.33 per cent to 20.6 per cent (Figure 8.3). The backward linkages are greater than the forward indicate that India is on the downstream part of the value chain or a supplier of intermediate inputs. The indicators also suggest that on average about 27.36 per cent of gross exports are sustained due to participation in GVCs of which 6.75 per cent is due to forward linkage and 20.61 per cent is due to backward linkages.

Table 8.5: India's Backward and Forward Linkages (1995 to 2014)

Year	Backward Linkages	Forward Linkages	GVC
1995	9.33	6.29	15.62
2000	11.27	8.01	19.28
2001	12.49	7.95	20.44
2005	17.45	7.91	25.36
2006	19.49	7.8	27.29
2010	22.24	7.26	29.5
2011	24.03	7.3	31.33
2012	20.95	6.77	27.72
2013	21.17	6.9	28.07
2014	20.61	6.75	27.36

Source: TIVA and WIOD database.

Note: DVA is the domestic value added; FVA is the foreign value added or backward linkage in global value chains (GVCs); RDV is the domestic value of intermediate exports that finally return home. PDC is the pure double counted intermediate exports produced at home. FL is the forward linkage in GVCs. All the values are as a percentage of gross exports.

The study's main analysis on the bilateral decomposition of India's gross exports with Asian countries. Table 8.6 represents decomposing of India's gross exports with selected emerging Asian economies (%) i.e. China, Indonesia, and South Korea, from 1995 to 2014. With the help of relevant variables namely domestic value-added (DVA), foreign value added (FVA), double-counted intermediate exports produced at

Figure 8.3: India's % GVC Participation Index

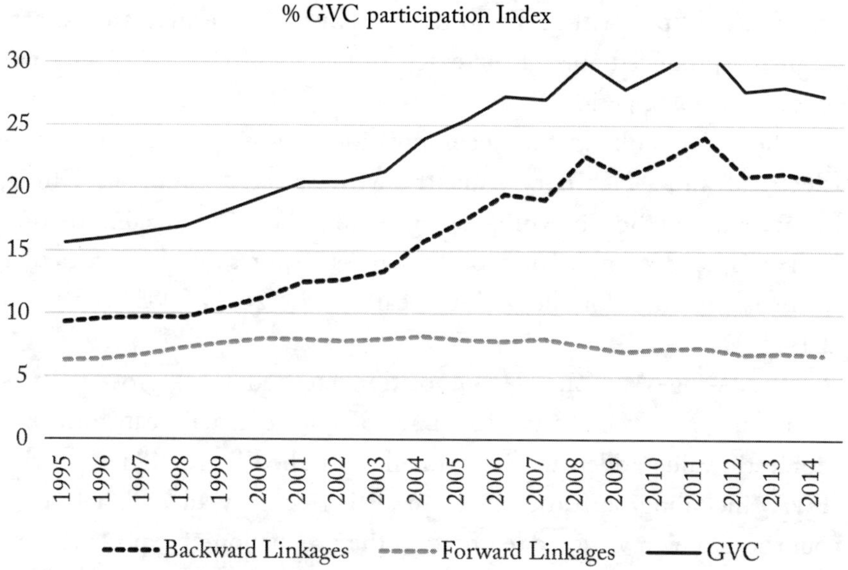

Source: TIVA and WIOD databse.

home (DDC), double-counted intermediate exports originally produced abroad (FDC), the study tries to find out the performance of India with these economies.

The domestic value-added share in gross exports of India with China has declined from 90.72% to 84.36% during 1995-2014. However, India's double-counted intermediate exports share with China produced at home increased marginally. Alternatively, its foreign value-added percentage share grew up from 5.83% to 12.51% and also double-counted intermediate exports originally produced abroad declined marginally from 3.41 % to 3.07% for the same period. On the other hand, India with Indonesia domestic value-added i.e. 11 per cent declined from 1995 to 2014, but foreign value added has grown. India's domestic value added's percentage share in gross exports with Korea has declined from 87.96 per cent to 67.24 per cent for the same period. However, double-counted intermediate exports' share has increased. On the other hand, its foreign value-added percentage grew up from 9.1 per cent to 17.49 per cent and also double-counted intermediate exports originally produced abroad increased from 2.92 per cent to 14.43 per cent for the same period.

The study looks at the decomposition of gross exports of India's Electrical and Machinery Industry with selected countries China, Indonesia, and South Korea using Wang-Wei-Zhu decomposition (2018). The decomposition of the gross exports of this particular sector is provided for the various years: 1995, 2000, 2005, 2010 and 2014.

The Wang-Wei-Zhu decomposition method splits gross exports at the bilateral level of a particular sector into four main categories i.e. "domestic value added which is finally absorbed by foreign countries (DVA) including both the direct importing country and other foreign countries, foreign value-added used in the production of exports (FVA), return value added (RDV) is the portion of domestic value-added which is initially exported but at the end returns home embedded in the imports from abroad and consumed domestically, and purely double-counted terms (PDC) is the term that accounts for the back and forth intermediate goods trade". (Wang-Wei-Zhu, 2018). These different components of gross exports provide valuable information regarding the cross-country production sharing processes. Table 8.7 represents India's Bilateral Decomposition with Asian Countries in Specific Electrical and Machinery Industry. India's domestic value-added (DVA) with China has the highest content i.e. 84.09 per cent followed by Korea (83.91 percent) and Indonesia (83.5 percent). But foreign value added (FVA) has a share of 16 per cent in all countries. Similar, Return Value Added (RDV) has a higher share in Indonesia (0.62%) Korea (0.29%) and China (0.17%). On the other side, the percentage in purely double counted (PDC) has a share of 0.17%, 0.06% and 0.03% in Indonesia, Korea and China respectively. Both domestic value-added and foreign value-added components of gross exports follow the same direction. But Forward Linkages (FL) of India with Korea found the highest i.e. 8.54 percent, while China and Indonesia have nearly 4 per cent share in forward linkages. This may be

Table 8.6: Bilateral Decomposing of India's Gross Exports with Asian Economies (%)

		China	Indonesia	Korea
YEAR	Indicators	%	%	%
1995	DVA	90.72	89.26	87.96
	DDC	0.04	0.01	0.02
	FVA	5.83	9.48	9.1
	FDC	3.41	1.25	2.92
2000	DVA	90.48	84.5	85.63
	DDC	0.03	0.02	0.02
	FVA	5.98	11.51	10.33
	FDC	3.52	3.99	4.03
2005	DVA	86.95	83.37	74.32
	DDC	0.12	0.05	0.06
	FVA	7.46	13.7	16.82
	FDC	5.48	2.93	8.8
2010	DVA	84.12	78.2	67.62
	DDC	0.18	0.08	0.17
	FVA	10.21	19.36	18.46
	FDC	5.48	2.43	13.74
2014	DVA	84.36	78.2	67.94
	DDC	0.05	0.08	0.14
	FVA	12.51	19.36	17.49
	FDC	3.07	2.43	14.43

Source: Author compiled from WIOD and TIVA, 2019.
Note: DVA is the domestic value added; FVA is the foreign value-added, DDC is double counted intermediate exports produced at home. FDC is double-counted intermediate exports originally produced abroad. All the values are in percentage of gross exports.

the result of the Indian government's National Electronic policy (2012) aiming for boosting domestic manufacturing and improving India's global market share.

Table 8.7: Indian Electrical and Machinery Industry's Bilateral Sectoral Decomposition with Selected Asian countries (average of 1995-2014)

Indicators	China	Indonesia	Korea
DVA	84.09	83.5	83.91
FVA	15.72	15.74	15.73
RDV	0.17	0.62	0.29
PDC	0.03	0.17	0.06
FL	4.31	4.02	8.54

Source: Author compiled from WIOD, 2019.

Vertical Specialisation of Electrical and Machinery Industry

"Vertical Specialisation (VS) is a summary statistic to measure international production sharing widely used in the literature (e.g., Hummels et al. (2001) and Antras (2013)). However, as shown by the figure (below) of gross export decomposition, there are different components within VS[3], and each has a distinct economic meaning and describes various types of cross-country production sharing arrangement." (www.nber.org).

For instance, "a high share of foreign value-added in India's final goods exports (FVA_FIN) may mean that India mainly involves in final assembling actions based on imported parts and participates in cross-country production distributing on the low end of a global value chain. While a growing foreign value-added share in India's intermediate exports (FVA_INT) might imply that India is improving its industry to start manufacturing intermediate goods for other countries, primarily when considerable of these goods are shipped to third countries for final goods production." (www.nber.org) The latter is an indication that the country is no longer at the bottom of the GVCs (Gereffi, 2014). "Pure double counting terms in a country's exports (PDC) can only occur when there is back and forth trade of intermediate products. An increasing weight of

[3] Vertical Specialisation (VS) Index proposed by Hummels, Ishii, and Yi (2001) provide a method of measuring vertical specialisation. "It refers to imported goods that are used as inputs to produce a country's export goods".

Figure 8.4: Indian Electrical and Machinery Industry's Bilateral Sectoral Decomposition with selected Asian countries

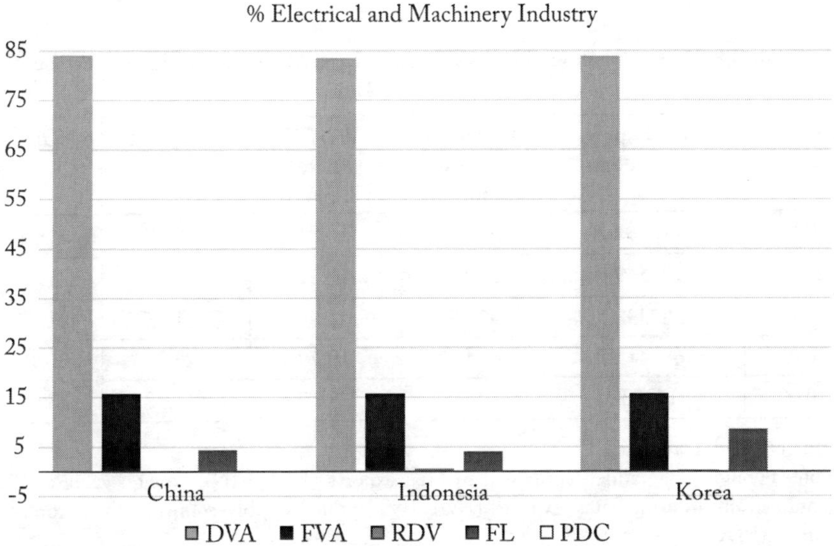

Source: Author compiled from WIOD, 2019.

PDC share in VS indicates the deepening of cross-country production sharing. Intermediate goods have to cross national borders multiple times before they are applied in final goods production. Hence, understanding the relative significance of these parts and their dynamic course over time in a country's total VS can help us to assess the extent and pattern of cross-country production sharing and discover the significant drivers of the general increase of VS in a country's gross exports during the last two decades" (Wang et. al. 2014). As shown in Table 8.8, the gross exports of India's Electrical and Machinery Equipments (TIVA sector 27) have increased from the US $ 71628.52 million to the US $ 1435380 million from 1995 to 2014. Vertical specialisation percentage share in gross exports has increased from 21 per cent in 1995 to 46 per cent in 2010. But after that, it has tremendously decreased and reached 20 per cent in 2014. This is due to decrease in the share of all the components i.e. Foreign value added contained in final exports (FVA_FIN), Foreign value added contained in intermediates exports (FVA_INT), Pure double-counting from foreign sources (PDC)

Table 8.8: Decomposition of India's Electrical and Machinery Industry Vertical Specialisation Index

Year	Gross Exports (US$ Million)	VS Share (in gross exports)	FVA_FIN Share (% of VS)	FVA_INT Share (% of VS)	PDC
1995	71628.52	20.51	10.81	9.69	9.7
2000	124549.9	23.41	12.31	11.09	11.1
2005	382338.3	43.45	21.99	21.43	21.45
2010	683415.1	45.93	19.79	26.09	26.13
2014	1435380	19.58	5.59	13.78	13.94

Source: TIVA Database

Note: Foreign value added contained in final exports (FVA_FIN), Foreign value added contained in intermediates exports (FVA_INT), Pure double-counting from foreign sources (PDC).

Figure 8.5: Vertical Specialisation Index

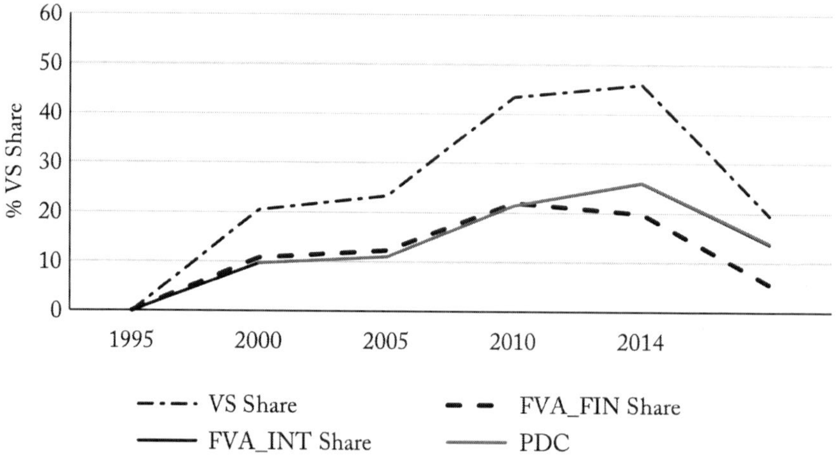

Source: TIVA Database.

Conclusion

The performance of the global value chain of India shows that India's Global Value Chain participation has increased the US$ 22.43 million to the US$ 412.32 million while its percentage share increased from 0.48% to 8.75% during 1990 to 2018. Domestic Value Added (DVA) in the gross exports of India is high in 2000 and shows a decrease in 2005 and 2010. However, it showed an increase in 2014. This may be due to the National Policy on Electronics (2012). But, India is still in the downstream segment of GVC participation. In Electrical and Machinery, India has the highest share of value addition in exports with 22.36% during the study period. India's Electrical and Machinery Industry Bilateral Sectoral Decomposition with China, Indonesia and South Korea has shown the growth of domestic value-added (DVA) and foreign value added (FVA) in exports. But forward linkages (FL) of India with Korea has highly increased as compared to China and Indonesia. The paper found that the VS structure information is very attractive in India's electrical and machinery industry. Based on the above analysis, this paper found that India has the potential to become an overall global value chain and also in a particular industry. The policy which promotes domestic electronics and components production should be formulated to increase India's participation in GVC's by increasing forward linkages in the domestic value chain. Poor trade infrastructure has reduced India's GVC participation in this sector. Thus, there is a necessity to introduce a policy package for attracting investment to improve the infrastructure of the nation (Veeramani, & Dhir, 2017).

This study suggests that MSMEs can play an important role in exploring new market opportunities and therefore, their participation should be considered as the most important in the global value chain and special packages must be announced for increasing their contribution in GVC.

Make in India initiative will make this sector as a globally renowned.

References

Antras, P. (2013). Firms, contracts, and global production. CREI Lectures in Macroeconomics, manuscrito en la página web del autor.

Aw, B. Y., and Hwang, A. R. M. (1995). Productivity and the export market: A firm-level analysis. *Journal of development economics, 47*(2), 313-332.

Baldwin, R. E. (2006). Globalisation: the Great Unbundling (s). Helsinki: Economic Council of Finland.

Bernard, A. B., Jensen, J. B., and Lawrence, R. Z. (1995). Exporters, jobs, and wages in US manufacturing: 1976-1987. *Brookings papers on economic activity. Microeconomics, 1995*, 67-119.

Chains, G. V. (2013). Development: Investment and value added trade in the global economy. In United Nations Conference On Trade And Development (UNCTAD).

Clerides, S. K., Lach, S., and Tybout, J. R. (1998). Is learning by exporting important? Micro-dynamic evidence from Colombia, Mexico, and Morocco. *The quarterly journal of economics, 113*(3), 903-947.

Cusolito, A. P., Safadi, R., and Taglioni, D. (2016). Inclusive global value chains: Policy options for small and medium enterprises and low-income countries. *World Bank Publications.*

Dash, A. and Chanda, R. (2017). Indian firms in Electronics Global Value Chains: Sectoral Analysis, CWS Working paper, 41.

Ernst, D. (2014). Upgrading India's electronics manufacturing industry: regulatory reform and industrial policy. *East-West Center Special Study.*

Francis, Smitha. (2015). An Analysis of India's Merchandise Export Performance during 1999–2013: Existing Competencies and Emerging Policy Challenges," report submitted to the Department of Commerce, Ministry of Commerce and Industry, Government of India, New Delhi.

Francis, S. (2018). India's electronics manufacturing sector. Economic and Political Weekly, 53(34), 113.

Gereffi, G. (2014). Global value chains in a post-Washington Consensus world. Review of international political economy, 21(1), 9-37.

Grossman, G. M., and Rossi-Hansberg, E. (2008). Trading Tasks: A Simple Theory of Offshoring. *American Economic Review* 98(5), 1978–97.

Grubel H.G. and Lloyd, P. (1975). *Intra-Industry Trade: The Theory and Measurement of International Trade in Differentiated Products.* London: MacMillan.

Hummels, D., Ishii, J., and Yi, K. M. (2001). The nature and growth of vertical specialization in world trade. *Journal of international Economics, 54*(1), 75-96.

Jones, R., and Kierzkowski, H. (1990). The role of services in production and international trade: A theoretical framework. *The Political Economy of International Trade*, edited by R. Jones and A. Krueger. Oxford, U.K.: Basil Blackwell, pp. 31–48.

Saripalle, M. (2015). Tamil Nadu's Electronics Industry: Lessons for 'Make in India'. Economic and Political Weekly, 99-103.

Wang, Z., Wei, S. J., & Zhu, K. (2013). Quantifying international production sharing at the bilateral and sector levels (Now 1967). National Bureau of Economic Research.

https://en.wikipedia.org/wiki/Global_value_chain.

9

External Barriers to India's Agricultural Exports during WTO Regime

Manpreet Singh & Paramjit Nanda

Introduction

Agriculture and associated exercises stay the significant wellspring of vocation for almost 50% of the Indian populace. The agriculture and associated exercises have contributed 17.4 per cent of the Gross Value Added (GVA) of India in 2016-17 (Economic Survey, 2017-18). About more than fifty per cent of the population are dependent on agriculture for livelihood. Also the growth of other sectors are dependent on agriculture. (Tripathi and Prasad, 2009). "Therefore, a vibrant agricultural sector is crucial for reducing poverty through economic growth" (Ingco and Nash, 2004).

Agribusiness exchange assumes an indispensable part in the monetary advancement of a country. Indian agrarian/agricultural and prepared food varieties are sent out to in excess of 100 nations, fundamentally in the Middle East, Southeast Asia, SAARC nations, EU and the United States. The agribusiness area additionally appreciates a significant status in the reciprocal or provincial exchange plans and with regards to WTO dealings. Agricultural exports potentially contribute to foreign exchange earnings for India. Expanding export opportunities also mean bigger markets and a higher value for production.

"During the period 1945-1994, international trade policies had been governed by an international treaty known as the General Agreement on

Tariffs and Trade (GATT)" (Krugman and Obstfeld, 2016, p. 7). NTB (Non-Tariff Barriers) is a part of WTO agreements which play a paramount role in deciding the direction of exports.

"Non-Tariff measures are those, other than normal tariffs, that have the effect of restricting trade between nations. The prominence of NTBs has increased after the abolition of quotas or a significant reduction in tariffs due to continued intervention of WTO after 1995. Hence it is not surprising that the developed countries with relatively lower tariffs are more prolific users of NTMs/NTBs especially to keep out low-cost products from developing countries" (Krishnan, 2016, p. 144).

To promote agricultural exports of India, various policy measures have been undertaken at the domestic and international level. At the international level, Agreement of Agriculture (AOA) was prepared during the Uruguay Round i.e. on January 1, 1995. The AOA is an international treaty of WTO. It emphasizes on the free and market-oriented trading system in agricultural trade. It depends upon three aspects or pillars namely; market access, domestic support and export subsidies. However, over the recent couple of years, India's exports have begun declining. In the worldwide situation of high protectionism, Indian exports encountered a negative growth rate in 2014-15 (i.e. -0.4 percent) and 2015-16 (i.e. -9.5 per cent). Indian imports also encountered a negative growth rate in 2015-16 (i.e. -9.0 percent). India is the second-biggest maker of agricultural items and agribusiness is the source of livelihood for 50% of the Indian populace. In 2016, India's share of agricultural exports in world exports and imports was 2.1 and 1.8 per cent respectively (the share is very low). India's agricultural exports also declined from $36 billion in FY13 to $30 billion in FY17 (GOI, 2018), which has raised worries among the policymakers.

In this context, the paper tries to find out external barriers in the form of non-tariff restrictions imposed on Indian agricultural exports by major countries namely USA, Russia, China, Japan, Australia, New Zealand, Iran, UAE, UK, EU, Bangladesh and Indonesia. For this purpose, the paper has been separated into three sections. The first section focuses on the growth and structural changes in the direction of agricultural exports to these nations; the second section highlights various non-tariff barriers; the third section discusses the conclusions and policy implications.

Review of Literature

Goyal and Mukharji et al. (2017) investigated food safety issues of Indian exports by using secondary data and tried to identify food safety restrictions faced by Indian exports in major export markets. It was found that the Indian share of fresh and prepared food items declined from 12.02 per cent in total Indian exports from 2012-13 to 11 per cent in 2016-17. The study revealed that from April 1, 2005, to May 31, 2017, total 2240 notifications raised by European Union in RASFF portal against India. The most elevated no. of interceptions raised against India for the presence of the unsafe life form in the plant and produce sent out when contrasted with other developing country exporters to the EU. The interceptions for India during that period were 1324 when contrasted with 452 for Brazil, 422 for Vietnam, 114 for Turkey and 602 for China. The majority of the warnings raised against India because of the presence of higher endorsed levels of pesticide residue.

Saqib and Teneja (2005) concentrated on non-tariff restrictions and India's exports to ASEAN and Sri Lanka. It was observed that since 1997-98 India's exports to ASEAN (six significant nations) expanded from the US $ 2410 million to the US $ 4518 in 2002-03. However, the share of exports to ASEAN nations in total Indian exports expanded from 6.9 per cent in 1997-98 to 8.6 per cent in 2002-03. The different non-tariff restrictions faced by Indian exports are imported policy restrictions, standards, testing, labeling and certification requirements, anti-dumping and countervailing measures, export subsidies and domestic support and government procurement. In 2002-03, 26 per cent of the total items exported to Thailand faced non-tariff barriers, followed by 14 per cent to Singapore and 12 per cent Malasia.

Krishnan (2016) analysed the effect of Non-Tariff restrictions on Indian exports using panel data having a time series component of 12 years (2001-2012) and cross-section composed of three countries for various parameters. To find the impact of non-tariff barriers regression and factor analysis have been used. It was found that a 1 per cent expansion in no. of export consignment rejections leads to 0.12 per cent decline in total export value to these countries. It was found that the rate of rejection of food products was very high compared to other categories like cosmetics, drugs and antibiotics etc.

Deb (2007) attempted to analyse non-tariff restrictions in agricultural trade and their issues and implications for least developed nations. It was observed that the most elevated non-tariff measures faced by LDCs for export of agricultural commodities by Developed Countries, Middle East and North Africa, followed by manufacturer products. In the case of minerals and fuel products very less NTMs used. It was found that Bangladesh faced the highest non-tariff measures from the EU (i.e. 93.40 per cent) followed by USA (90.90 per cent) and Japan (63.40 per cent) respectively.

Ferrier (2017) investigated the effect of Non-Tariff restrictions on Agricultural Trade. It was found that Japan put minimum restrictions on agricultural exports out of the developed countries. It was found that from 1995-2015 maximum i.e. 32 per cent SPS STCs were related to animal disease followed by customs and certification, i.e. 15 per cent and 16 per cent related to conformity and risk assessment, 11 per cent to tolerances and plant pests each.

Database and Methodology

Secondary data have been utilised for the current study. The data have been taken from Economic Survey (Various Issues), World Trade Statistical Review, APEDA and EUROPHYT. The 12 major countries selected to find the growth and structural change of Indian exports. The percentage share and Compound Annual Growth Rate (CAGR) has been calculated to analyse the data.

Results and Discussions

Agricultural Exports Share in India's Agricultural GDP

Table 9.1 shows that Indian farming exports expanded from Rs. 6317 crore in 1990-91 to Rs. 228001 crore in 2016-17 (i.e. expanded by 36.09 times) and agricultural GDP expanded from Rs. 164575 crore to Rs. 2674006 crore (i.e. expanded by 16.24 times) during a similar period. In the event of share of agricultural exports in agricultural GDP, share expanded from 4 per cent in 1990-91 to 7 per cent in 1995-96 and diminished to 6 per cent in 2000-01 and 2005-06 and again expanded to 7 per cent in 2010-11 and to 9 per cent in 2016-17, showing better performance during Post-WTO period.

Table 9.1: Agricultural Exports Share in India's Agricultural GDP

Year	India's Agricultural Exports (Rs. Crore)	India's Agricultural GDP (Rs. Crore)	Share of Agricultural Exports in Agricultural GDP (Percentage)
1990-91	6317	164575	4
1995-96	21138	312413	7
2000-01	28582	495271	6
2005-06	46703	720168	6
2010-11	111393	1524552	7
2015-16	216369	2471800	9
2016-17	228001	2674006	9

Source: Government of India, Economic Survey, Various Issues.

India's Share in World Agricultural Exports/Imports

Table 9.2 mirrors that in spite of the increment in the portion of India's agricultural exports and imports in world trade, the share is discovered to be very low. The portion of India's agrarian exports in world exports of agricultural items expanded from 1.1 per cent in 2000 to 2.3 per cent in 2017, while imports share expanded from 0.7 per cent in 2000 to 1.9 per cent in 2017.

Table 9.2: India's Share in World Agricultural Exports/Imports (Percentage)

Year	Share in World Agricultural Exports	Share in World Agricultural Imports
2000	1.1	0.7
2005	1.2	0.8
2010	1.7	1.3
2017	2.3	1.9

Source: World Trade Statistical Review, WTO, 2018.

Country-wise Growth of India's Agricultural Exports

Table 9.3 shows the country-wise compound annual growth rate of agrarian exports. During Pre-WTO period (1987-88 to 1995-96) farming exports to Indonesia encountered the most elevated growth rate (i.e. 168.51 percent) followed by China (53.43 percent) and Bangladesh (33.36 percent) respectively, though exports to Russia and New Zealand experienced negative growth rates (i.e. -10.1 per cent and -1.73 per cent respectively).

In case of Post-WTO period (1996-97 to 2017-18), all countries experienced positive growth rate. The countries namely Iran, China, New Zealand, Australia, Russia, USA, Indonesia, UAE and EU experienced double-digit growth rate. Exports to Japan and Bangladesh experienced the lowest growth rate (i.e. 6.5 per cent and 8.72 per cent respectively).

The sub-period analysis of Post-WTO period reveals that during Post-WTO Period I (1996-97 to 2006-07) exports to China, New Zealand, Bangladesh, Indonesia and Japan experienced double-digit growth rate and exports to Russia experienced negative growth rate (-4.54 per cent) during that period. During Post-WTO Period II (2007-08 to 2017-18) Iran, Russia, Australia, USA, New Zealand, Iran and Indonesia experienced double-digit growth rate, while exports to Bangladesh and UAE experienced a negative growth rate.

Comparative analysis of Pre and Post-WTO period reveals that Russia, Japan, USA, Australia, New Zealand, Iran and UAE experienced an increase in their growth rates during Post-WTO period, while

Indonesia, China, Bangladesh, EU and UK experienced a decline in their growth rate of exports.

Comparative analysis of Post-WTO Period I and II reveals that exports to Russia, USA, Iran, UK and EU experienced an increase in their growth rates during II period, while exports to China, Japan, Australia, New Zealand, Bangladesh, Indonesia and UAE experienced a decline in their growth rates during II period.

Table 9.3: Country-wise Growth of India's Agricultural Exports

Period	Pre-WTO Period (1987-88 to 1995-96)	Post-WTO Period (1996-97 to 2017-18)	Post-WTO Period I (1996-97 to 2006-07)	Post-WTO Period II (2007-08 to 2017-18)
Russia	-10.1	11.51	-4.54	19.85
China	53.43	19.36	24.34	4.78
Japan	3.87	6.5	10.42	4.52
USA	6.71	15.86	6.77	12.92
Australia	11.02	18.22	15.16	13.49
New Zealand	-1.73	18.92	16.51	15.91
Bangladesh	33.36	8.72	15.28	3.36
Indonesia	168.51	15.58	12.73	12.18
Iran	8.8	29.24	1.59	21.89
UAE	12.74	14.62	8.91	4.47
UK	12.43	9.15	6.56	7.38
EU	14.74	10.29	7.38	8.53

Source: Based on Data given in India's Export Statistics, APEDA.

Composition and Structural Change in Direction of India's Agricultural Exports

Table 9.4 shows the composition and structural change in the direction of agricultural exports. The table reveals that countries constituting major share in India's agricultural exports consistently decreased their share from 57.08 per cent in 1987-88 to 51.01 per cent in 2003-04 and 36.41 per cent in 2017-18. Country-wise analysis reveals that as compared to 1987-88 in 2017-18 share of 6 countries increased and of 6 countries decreased in India's total agricultural exports. The highest decline has been experienced in case of exports to Russia (i.e. share reduced from 16.7 per cent in 1987-88 to 1.23 per cent in 2017-18), followed by USA (from 10.24 to 6.15 per cent) and UAE (from 11.86 to 7.17 per cent). The highest increase in share is experienced by exports to Bangladesh (i.e. from 1.81 per cent in 1987-88 to 5.44 per cent in 2017-18), followed by Iran (from 3.3 to 5.43 per cent) and Indonesia (from negligible to 2.23 per cent).

Table 9.4: Composition and Structural Change in Direction of India's Agricultural Exports (Percentage)

Year	1987-88	1995-96	2003-04	2011-12	2017-18
Russia	16.7	2.5	0.81	0.8	1.23
China	0.03	0.26	0.4	1.8	0.39
Japan	0.98	0.56	0.76	0.28	0.26
USA	10.24	4.1	5.82	17.66	6.15
Australia	0.06	0.27	0.44	0.75	0.77
New Zealand	0.06	0.03	0.1	0.09	0.16
Bangladesh	1.81	14.1	18.61	2.88	5.44
Indonesia	0	12.91	4.75	4.59	2.23
Iran	3.3	1.42	0.55	4.12	5.43
UAE	11.86	8.82	7.92	8.06	7.17
UK	5.49	3.5	3.67	2.03	2.24
EU	6.26	6.25	7.19	4.68	4.94
Total	57.08	54.72	51.01	47.74	36.41

Source: Calculated from India's Export Statistics, APEDA.

Thus at the world level, there are growing concerns regarding rising anti-globalisation and trade-restrictive measures. With the Brexit referendum, people see trade, movement of people and multilateral commitments with doubt and becoming wary of the benefits of globalisation (GoI, 2016-17). Thus, there are new limitations on visas and the danger of a reaction against the movement of people.

There is a quick expansion in last couple of years many trade-restrictive measures including a few types of non-tariff barriers (NTB's). As per the WTO Seventh Monitoring Report on G-20 trade measures, a total of 42 new trade-prohibitive measures were executed by G-20 economies (during 2016-17), amounting to the monthly average of six measures (though the number was seven during 2009-15). The share of world imports covered by these import-restrictive measures since October 2008 was 5 per cent and share of G-20 imports covered was 6.5 per cent in 2016. From October 2016-May 2017, trade coverage of these measures affecting imports was 0.37 per cent of the value of G-20 imports or 0.29 per cent of the value of world merchandise imports. Many studies have already shown that developed countries are using these measures as a means to impede trade from developing countries (Markus and John (2001); Alovi and Kenny (2005); Deb, U.K. (2007); Shinoj et al. (2009); K. Vijith (2016); CATR (2019)). In the year 2013 alone, around 62 per cent of total consignments were rejected consisting of food products. Bachetta and Bora (2001) revealed the prevalence of non-tariff restrictions faced by LDCs for their agrarian items in Table 9.5.

Table 9.5 clearly shows that developed countries and Quad countries (USA, Japan, Canada and Australia) have a elevated prevalence of NTMs, than other countries.

In India however there is a responsibility of the public authority to promote exports of fresh and prepared food items in India, but at a worldwide level agricultural trade faces several tariff and non-tariff restrictions. The WTO information on notifications shows the expanded utilisation of non-tariff restrictions as Sanitary and Phyto-Sanitary (SPS) measures by WTO member nations since the mid-1990s, in this way going about as a barrier to trade for Indian exports. Border rejections as a percentage of total notifications raised are most elevated for India when contrasted with other developing countries. Destruction of consignments was likewise most elevated for India. India likewise had the most elevated number of interceptions raised for the presence of the unsafe organic entity in the plant and produce imported as a contrast

Table 9.5: Frequency of Non-Tariff Measures (NTMs) faced by LDCs for Exports of Agricultural Commodities

Sr. No.	Commodities	Developed Countries	South Asia	The Middle East + North Africa	Latin America + Caribbean	Europe + Central Asia	East Asia + Pacific	Sub Sahara Africa	Quad
1	Agricultural and Fishery Products	48.24	14.87	57.69	34.24	32.93	24.42	18.58	41.98
2	Crustaceans (live)	58.64	8.33	75.00	30.98	43.56	22.22	20.00	50.00
3	Other Fish	64.49	14.07	75.16	30.96	43.85	22.87	20.28	55.43
4	Edible Fruits and Nuts	53.95	19.21	54.61	37.09	32.36	24.21	28.20	54.67
5	Coffee and Substitutes with Coffee	32.26	17.86	44.64	28.10	20.36	26.19	18.18	21.43
6	Oilseeds and Miscellaneous Grains, Seeds and Fruits	53.93	14.20	68.55	40.75	38.49	28.71	25.12	37.43

Source: Bacchetta and Bora (2001).

to other developing nation exporters to the EU. The interceptions for India during the period i.e. between 2005 and 2017 were 1352 vis-à-vis 922 for Vietnam, 602 for China, 452 for Brazil and 114 for Turkey. Table depicting the notifications rose by the EU shows that most of the concerns were raised during 2012-13.

Table 9.6: Number of Notifications Raised by EU

Year	Notifications
2012	263
2014	183
2015	267
2016	189
2017	183

Source: EUROPHYT.

Food products are facing non-tariff barriers in various forms. To export food products to the USA, comprehensive labeling prerequisite are essential with considerable product and content explanation. Export of paper items to the USA needs unscientific quarantine restrictions, custom, surcharges, eco-labeling requirements and compliance with SPS standards. NTBs include import bans, unjustified SPS measures, employment law, unreasonable packaging, labeling and other requirements, additional trade requirements like the certificate of origin, certificate of authenticity etc. NTB in the USA on agrarian items are as import licenses, import quotas and export endowments. The USA forces import licenses on fish, tobacco and vegetables, import quota on sugar and tobacco and gives export endowments on vegetables, rice, maize and wheat.

Japan forces tariff quota, state exchanging and state procurement chiefly on the tobacco, raw sugar and cereal items. Thailand's major NTBs are associated with import licenses, technical measures and amount controls. In terms of specific products, Table 9.7 shows ban or rejection because of issues associated to health and food security standards. It was found that most of the agricultural product rejected due to excess residue of pesticides and chemicals.

Table 9.7: India's Major Agricultural Exports Rejections

Sr. No.	Commodities	Market	Reasons for Rejections
1	Green Beans	US	Rejection
2	Peanut & Peanut Products	EU & Vietnam	Contamination (Aflatoxin) during storage, processing and while packaging
3	Mangoes	EU	Fruit flies
4	Indian Chillies	US, Saudi Arabia, Bhutan	The higher level of Chemical Residues
5	Vegetables	Developed Countries	Excess use of (i) Fertilisers & Pesticides (ii) Lack of Good Agricultural Practices (iii) Use of Banned Pesticides in U.S., E.U. & Japan
6	Shrimps	US	A higher level of chemicals & residues pest infestation
7	Vegetables (Including Egg Plans)	EU	
8	Rice	Iran, China	
9	Green Pepper	Saudi Arabia, Bhutan	
10	Table Grapes	US, Vietnam	
11	Obra	EU, Saudi Arabia	
12	Curry Leaves	Japan, Bhutan	

Source: EUROPHYT and Various Other Sources.

Thus the imposition of non-tariff barriers is a matter of serious concern for exporters and farmers as there are financial losses to them in the short term. In the long term, they will lose their market share in other countries. Further, compulsory inspection and audit of Indian agricultural exports in the US by USFDA will increase the cost of compliance, thereby hurting Indian farm exports. Farmers have the most difficulty in complying with the issues related to pesticides.

However, the country should view, these barriers as an opportunity to upgrade the quality standard and market sophistication (Jong Wanich, 2009). There is a need to do the following measures.

1. The government should make some restorative moves right away.
2. The pesticides and synthetic compounds that are restricted in developed nations ought to be eliminated and not subsidised.
3. State agriculture division should work with agriculture institutes and universities to prepare farmers to adopt GAP (Good Agricultural Practices).
4. The focal government ought to have a thorough approach for safe agribusiness and advance horticulture cultivating with plainly spreading out their vision plan.
5. The central government ought to give complete policy for safe agriculture and encourage agriculture by clearly laying out their vision plan.
6. There is a need for preparing of exporters, little and medium processors and other store network specialists through projects, such as the India-EU capacity building Initiative from the Trade and Development (CITD) project to update their insight about prerequisites of the importing nations.
7. Retailers from developed countries should be invited to work closely with Indian farmers.
8. Export incentives should be linked to quality and food safety standards.
9. There is a requirement for a friendly inter-governmental tie-up with importing nations to settle issues through two-way discussions and common acceptance of standards and procedures.
10. The Indian government and industrial bodies should work jointly in major export markets.
11. Awareness about quality parameters is highly needed up to the bottom level.
12. Harmonisation of technical standards must be encouraged.

At last, India needs a three-fold strategy to overcome this i.e. (a) enhancing the domestic level food quality and labeling standards (b) harmonisation of technical standards and (c) creating awareness regarding quality parameters.

References

Ansari, S.A. and Khan, W. (2015). India's Agriculture Trade Potential in Post-WTO Period, *Agriculture Economics Research Review,* 28, 93-100.

Bacchetta, M. and Bora, B. (2001). Post-Uruguay Round Market Access Barriers for Industrial Products, UNCTAD Policy Issues in International Trade and Commodities, Study Series No. 12. New York and Geneva, United Nations.

Byerlee, D., de Janvry, A., et. al. (2009). Agriculture for development: Toward a new paradigm, *Annual Review of Resource Economics*, 1(1), 15-35.

Deb, U.K. (2007). Non-Tariff Barriers in Agricultural Trade: Issues and implications for Least Developed Countries, Asia-Pacific Research and Training Network on Trade.

Economic Survey, Government of India, Various Issues.

Ferrier, P. (2017). Non-Tariff Measures and Agricultural Trade, Federal Reserve Bank of Chicago.

Goyal, M. and Mukharji, A. et. al. (2017). India's Exports of Food Products: Food Safety related Issues and Way Forward, ICRIER, WP No. 345, September 2017.

Ingco, M. and Nash, J. (2004). *Agriculture and the WTO: Creating a Trading System for Development*, World Bank/Oxford Univ. Press, Washington, DC.

Kour, S. and Bhau, P. (2013). Impact of WTO on Indian Agriculture during 1990-2004, Journal of Economic and Social Development, IX(1), ISSN 0973-886X.

Krishnan, K.V. (2016). Impact of Non-Tariff Barriers on Indian Exports; an Econometric Analysis, *Journal of Tropical Agriculture* 54 (2): 144-152, 2016.

Krugman, P.R. & Obstfeld, M. (2016). International Economics: Theory and Policy, Eighth Edition, Pearson Publication.

Nabi, T. and Dhami, J.K. (2013). Analysis of India's Agriculture Export Performance in Pre and Post-WTO Regime, *International Journal of Enhanced Research in Management and Computer Applications,* 2(4), 1-5, ISSN: 2319-7471.

Niranjan, S.K. (2016). WTO and Sugar Trade of India, Humanities and Social Science Reviews, 4(1), 41-48, ISSN: 2395-6518.

Rani, P. (2015). A Study of WTO and Agriculture Sector in India, *International Journal of Multidisciplinary Research and Development,* 2(9), 456-459, ISSN: 2349-4182.

Saqib, M. and Taneja, N. (2005). Non-Tariff Barriers and India's Exports: The case of ASEAN and Sri Lanka, ICRIER, WP No. 165.

Tripathi, A. and Prasad, A.R. (2009). Agricultural development in India since in determinants: A study onprogress, performance and determinants, *Journal of Emerging Knowledge on Emerging Markets*, 1(1), 63-92.

EUROPHYT, Various Reports.

10
Measuring the Concentration of India-East Asia Trade

Divya Vaid & Meenu

Introduction

India has trading relationships with all the major trading blocs and geographical regions of the world. Over the post-world war II period, maximum international trade was between European and North American nations, whereas developing countries trade was either with EU or U.S.A. and trade among developing countries was very small and limited. Since the 1970s, the trade blocs have been in operation and some important blocs appeared are: (1) North America and Central America, (2) the European Union plus much of its periphery, and (3) a new trade bloc comprised of the countries in East and Southeast (E&SE) Asia. The developing countries were not included in these blocs but still managed to expanded trade, with increased diversification in partners (countries/markets) and traded commodities (McDonald et al., 2008). Asian countries are expanded along with developed countries after the liberalisation period when Look east policy is initiated and Act East policy is introduced during the India-ASEAN Summit in 2014 to boost East Asia trade. The diversion of Look East into Act East policy brought speed in action towards East Asia which leads to a cordial relationship with the Republic of Korea (South Korea), Japan and the People's Republic of China. (Chakraborty 1 and Chakraborty 2, 2017)

Among East Asian Economies, China, Japan, Hong Kong and South Korea represented major economic cooperation to face globalisation challenges. Similarly, shifts in India's economic pattern have provided scope for trade with world economies, especially with East Asian Economies. Such kind of Cooperation between East Asia and India will provide advantage in terms of the Movement of goods, technology, ideas and human capital (Asher and Sen, 2005). India has a big opportunity to reap benefits in case of services that have major potential to grow in East Asia. India can have an advantage in terms of lower trade costs if it will be part of a Regional comprehensive partnership agreement.

India has no formal free trade agreement with China and Hong Kong so India needs innovative strategies to check out the rising imports from these East Asian economies. India needs to identify its export potential towards the developed and developing countries so it can work on trade agreement with such economies.

As part of Asian Economies, China contributed less than 5% share in India's exports whereas it contributed more than 10% in India's imports in 2014-15. Hong Kong has contributed around 4% in India's exports and around 1% in India's imports while South Korea recorded around 1% in India's exports and 3% in India's imports during 2014-15. Japan has recorded less than 3% share in India's exports and imports in 2014-15. The export and import between India and UK has been increasing which impact on Indian trade market (Kaur et al 2018). These economies are appearing to be a good opportunity for India if integration and agreement are executed efficiently.

In the present study, the direction of India's Foreign Trade to different countries with special emphasis on East Asian Countries, is divided into five major regions of the world such as:

1) Organisation of Economic Co-operation and Development (OECD) countries.
2) Organisation of Petroleum Export Countries (OPEC).
3) Eastern Europe.
4) Developing Countries.
5) Others/Unspecified Countries. (as per Reserve Bank of India database classification)

The present study is an attempt to analyse India's Trade with East Asia as a part of the region, namely Developing countries and other considered regions of the world. The present paper is divided into five sections. Section I covers the Review of Literature, Section II covers the data sources and methodology, Section III covers growth of India's exports and imports (Regions and East Asian Countries), Section IV includes structure and concentration of India's exports and imports (Regions and East Asian Countries). Section V includes analysis of India's concentrated exports and imports among East Asian countries (China, Hong Kong, South Korea and Japan). Lastly, Conclusion and Policy implications are provided according to the present study.

Objectives

The main objectives of the study are:

1) To examine the growth and structural changes in India - East Asia trade by analysing export destinations and import sources during 1991-92 to 2014-15.
2) To analyse the regions/countries concentration of India-East Asia trade (Export destinations and Import Sources) during the study period 1991-92 to 2014-15.
3) To identify the top five products exported to and imported from East Asian countries for selected years of the study period (1996-97, 2005-06 and 2014-15).

Review of Literature

This section is devoted to the reviewing of some of the studies concerned with the present paper. The studies reviewed are mainly based on the commodity composition and diversification of India's trade.

Michaely (1958) revealed that the majority of countries (i.e. 39) exports are more concentrated than their imports. Also, the exports of small countries are more geographically concentrated than exports of large countries for both developed and underdeveloped countries.

Murshed (2001) revealed that there exists a considerable rise in inter-regional trade within the region Asia. The GL indices for manufacturing as a whole with the rest of Asia increased between 1985 and 1992 for all the countries in this paper (i.e. 7) except South Korea and Hong Kong. East Asian economies have gained in manufacturing competitiveness.

Asian Development Outlook (2007) concluded that East and Southeast Asian regions have high concentration in case of exports. There has been intense growth in trade of intermediate products—especially in parts and components of electrical machinery and transportation equipment centered on the People Republic of China.

McDonald et al. (2008) concluded that Advanced Asian countries shifted its exports from the EU and the US towards countries within the region, whereas other member countries of Asia directed their exports towards EU and US. The Primary commodity-producing sectors expanded, whereas secondary and tertiary sectors have shown a decline.

Haraguchi and Rezonja (2009) concluded that among considered five East Asian countries, Malaysia, Thailand and Philippines have shown increase in foreign trade in harmony with their stage of development, country size and availability of natural resources as compared to the Republic of Korea and Indonesia.

Seshadri (2009) concluded that India's exports to developing countries have increased from 43.56% in 2000-01 to 58.16% in 2007-08, whereas the maximum of Indian imports. Sourced from developing countries went up to 61.18% in 2007-08. After the major shares recorded by U.S.A. and China, the Asian countries, U.A.E., Singapore and Saudi Arabia have recorded major shares during 2007-08.

Nayak and Kumra (2010) highlighted that India's export growth to the USA declined in the Post-reform period (1991-92 to 2006-07). The paper has shown a fall in exports to OECD and Eastern Europe but the rise in exports to OPEC and developing countries.

Veeramani (2012) examined India's growth rates of merchandise exports for the period 1993-94 to 2011-12. The paper shows India's export shifted in favour of emerging markets i.e. Asia and Africa.

Sahni (2014) studies India's exports for the pre-reform period (1980-81 to 1991-92) and the post-reform period (1992-93 to 2010-11). The developing countries have manifested exceptional performance during the pre-reform period due to higher exports to Asia, Africa and Latin America in comparison to OECD countries.

A study of both PHD Chamber (2015), and Kaur and Gopal (2016) revealed that the share of developed regions (EU and America) declined while the share of fastest-growing developing regions i.e. Asia is increased during the considered study period.

Database and Methodology

The present study has taken data from the following secondary sources-

(a) Handbook of statistics on Indian Economy.
(b) Annual publications, Reserve Bank of India, Government of India (Various Issues).
(c) DGFT, EXIM Databank.

Exports, Imports of India of 5 major regions with special reference to major East Asian countries from the period 1991-92 to 2014-15 are analysed with the help of (i) compound annual growth rates, (ii) percentage shares and (iii) concentration index. The methodology used for various types of analysis is explained as:

Growth Rates of India's Exports and Imports (Regions/Countries)

The compound growth rate has been calculated to analyse the growth of India's region/country-wise exports and imports under the study period (1991-92 to 2014-15). Growth rate implies the amount of increase that a variable has achieved within a specific period and context. The annual average growth rates are computed for studying the growth pattern of the direction of India- East Asia trade. Growth rates have been calculated by using an exponential function as follows:

$$Y_t = ab^t e^u$$

Transforming the above equation into the linear form:

$$\text{Log} = \log a + t \log b + u \log e$$

Where y_t = value of the dependent variable in the year t.

t = trend variable

u = disturbance term

a and b = constants

The growth rate(r) has been computed for the estimated value of the regression coefficient 'b' is follows as:

$$r\ (\%) = \{\text{antilog}\ (\log b)-1\}*100$$

OR

$$r\ (\%) = (\hat{b}-1)*100$$

The growth rate of India's destination-wise export and import (region/countries) are calculated for the whole study period 1991-92 to 2014-15 and for the sub-periods (a) 1991-92 to 2000-01 (b) 2001-02 to 2010-11 (c) 2011-12 to 2014-15.

Structure of India's Exports, Imports (Regions/Developing Countries)

The structural shift of Indian destination-wise foreign trade is calculated for exports and imports of various trading regions and Asian countries with the help of percentage shares calculated as follows:-

(A) At selected points of the study period (1991-92 to 2014-15): The shares of major regions and developing countries in India's Exports and Imports.

(B) Trade balance of Developing countries for selected years of the study period.

In the present study, the concentration ratio is measured which is based on the shares of individual element i.e. trading regions/Asian countries of India for each year of study period 1991-92 to 2014-15.

Let m denote the number of these trading partners and qit represents the export to or import from the ith partner region at time t. The sum of qit from 1 to m will be qt and the share of each country in export or import for year t, would be expressed as:

$$\text{Pit} = Qit/Qt$$

Pit = Percentage share of each trading partner in India's total trade

i = 1, 2, 3, _, _, _, _, _, m

And t= 1, 2, 3, _, _, _, T

In the present study, m is equal to 14 for country concentration. In the case of region-wise concentration, m is equal to 5 and period T is equal to 24. The concentration measure used in the present study is based on Pit i.e. calculated for each region/country at time t. The given measure of concentration considers only some of Pit's and the measure is known as concentration ratio (CR).

Concentration Ratio (CR): It is the total share of k region/countries that have the largest shares in export and import of a particular. It is denoted by CR(k) and calculated as:

$$CR(k) = \sum_{i=1}^{m} Pit \quad , k<m$$

The selection of k is arbitrary but in most cases, CR (4) and CR (8) are used. A low concentration ratio indicates that a country's trade portfolio comprises a great variety of trading countries and vice versa.

In the present paper, the region concentration is measured followed by country concentration with special reference to East Asian countries which are the part of Developing countries. Further, the paper also measured the product concentration (By using 2 digits HS Codes) for the major East Asian countries Such as People's Republic of China, Hong Kong, South Korea and Japan.

Growth Analysis of India's Exports and Imports

The present section is based on the analysis of growth performance of direction of India's exports and imports towards regions and east Asian countries for whole of the study period 1991-92 to 2014-15 and also, for the sub-periods 1991-92 to 2001, 2001-02 to 2010-11 and 2011-12 to 2014-15. For the study period (1991-92 to 2014-15), India's exports mainly to given regions/countries grew by 18%, whereas India's Imports from considered trading partners grew by 20.1%. During 2011-12 to 2014-15, India's Exports experienced the growth rate of 9.7% whereas India's Imports grew by 4.9% (i.e. less than the growth rate of Exports for considered four years). Since 1991-92 the growth rate of Imports has been consistently more than the growth rate of Exports, except for the sub-period 2011-12 to 2014-15.

Growth Analysis of India's Exports and Imports (Regions)

Table 10.1 shows the Annual Average Growth rate of Indian export. During the study period (1991-92 to 2014-15), the highest growth rate in India's total exports is registered by the region OPEC (22.9%)

followed by Developing countries (21.4%), others/Unspecified (19.9%) and OECD (14.6%) whereas Eastern Europe registered the least growth rate i.e. 8.4%. For the first decade i.e. 1991-92 to 2000-01, the highest growth is registered by Developing countries (21.3%) and the lowest growth is recorded by others/unspecified (2.5%). During second decade (2001-02 to 2010-11), the highest growth is registered by others/unspecified (34.9%) in place of Developing countries (23.2%) and lowest growth is recorded by Eastern Europe in India's total exports. During last four years of the study period (2011-12 to 2014-15), Developing countries registered the highest growth rate i.e. 12.1% followed by OECD (11.2%) while others/unspecified recorded negative growth rate (-19.5%) in India's total exports.

In Table 10.2 in case of Imports, the others/unspecified region recorded the highest growth rate for the whole of the study period (56.7%), for the years 1991-92 to 2000-01 (98.7%) and 2011-12 to 2014-15 (95.7%) whereas OPEC recorded the highest growth rate (60.2%) for the second decade of the study period (2001-02 to 2010-11). The lowest growth is registered by OECD region (16.1%) during 1991-92 to 2014-15 and second decade of the study period (22%) whereas Eastern Europe (9.7%) recorded the lowest growth for the first decade of the study period. During 2011-12 to 2014-15, the lowest and negative growth is registered by OECD (0.1%) and OPEC (-0.3%) in India's total imports respectively.

Growth Analysis of India's exports and imports to East Asian countries

The region of developing countries includes seven SAARC countries and seven other Asian developing countries. Out of these Asian countries, we have considered four major East Asian countries such as the People's Republic of China (PRC), Hong Kong, South Korea and Japan. For the whole study period (1991-92 to 2014-15), PRC recorded more than 30% export growth in India's exports whereas Japan recorded lowest growth i.e. less than 10%, Hong Kong and South Korea registered more than 15% growth rate in India's exports.

Table 10.1: Annual Average Growth rate of India's Export to Regions/Countries (percentage)

Regions/countries	1991-92 to 2014-15	1991-92 to 2000-01	2001-02 to 2010-11	2011-12 to 2014-15
(A) OECD	14.6	16.4	15.3	11.2
(B) OPEC	22.9	19.4	28.6	7.4
(C) Eastern Europe	8.4	6.7	6.3	9.9
(D) Developing Countries	21.4	21.3	23.2	12.1
(a) Asian Countries	20.6	20	22.3	10.3
(i) SAARC	19.4	19.2	19	25.5
1. Afghanistan	17.7	-	29.8	38.6
2. Bangladesh	15.6	18.9	11.7	29.4
3. Bhutan	27.2	12.3	24.3	27
4. Maldives	19.7	14.9	16.3	13.9
5. Nepal	24.2	15.1	24.9	28.6
6. Pakistan	24.9	23.2	35.2	15.9
7. Sri Lanka	19.4	20.1	16.8	25.4
(ii) Other Asian Developing Countries	20.9	20.1	23	7.2
(1) People's Republic of China	31.1	36.4	30.9	-3.3
2. Hong Kong	16.5	23.4	16.6	10.8
3. South Korea	20.1	17.3	28.2	10.6
4. Malaysia	19.7	19.6	21.7	21.2
5. Singapore	21.7	10.8	27.7	-8.3
6. Thailand	16.6	14.4	15.2	13.8
7. Japan	9.4	7.4	12.5	4.5
(E) Others/unspecified	19.9	2.5	34.9	-19.5
Total Exports	18	17.3	20.6	9.7

Source: Author's Calculations.

Table 10.2: Annual Average Growth rates of India's Imports from Regions/Countries (Percentage)

Regions/countries	1991-92 to 2014-15	1991-92 to 2000-01	2001-02 to 2010-11	2011-12 to 2014-15
(A) OECD	16.1	15.5	22	0.1
(B) OPEC	23.4	11.4	60.2	-0.3
(C) Eastern Europe	16.3	9.7	23.9	4.2
(D) Developing Countries	23.2	22.9	30	12.4
(a) Asian Countries	23.7	22.5	31.5	12.2
(i) SAARC	19.3	23.8	17.6	12.2
1. Afghanistan	23.5	-	29.3	43.1
2. Bangladesh	22.1	41.6	26.7	7.8
3. Bhutan	26.8	49.9	25.8	-0.8
4. Maldives	23.2	3	53	-35
5. Nepal	18.9	40	6.3	13.8
6. Pakistan	14.5	6.6	27.2	14.1
7. Sri Lanka	25.1	23	21.2	10.8
(ii) Other Asian developing	23.8	22.4	32	12.2
1. People's Republic of China	38.6	55.4	42.4	9.6
2. Hong Kong	25.1	31	29	-11.2
3. South Korea	22.3	23.3	26.2	8.9
4. Malaysia	20.1	30.3	22.6	12.4
5. Singapore	16.8	18.6	23.8	1.8
6. Thailand	27.8	34.4	31.3	11.3
7. Japan	13.2	12.6	18.7	0.2
(E) Others/ unspecified	56.7	98.7	28.9	95.7
Total Import	20.1	19.2	25.2	4.9

Source: Author's Calculations.

For the two decades of the study period i.e. 1991-92 to 2000-01 and 2001-02 to 2010-11, the growth rate of PRC, Hong Kong and South Korea remained more than 15% whereas Exports to Japan grew by less than 13% in India's exports. During 2011-12 to 2014-15, PRC recorded a negative growth rate while Hong Kong and South Korea recorded a growth rate of around 10% and Japan recorded less than 5% in India's exports.

In the case of Imports, the highest growth rate is registered by PRC i.e. more than 35% whereas Hong Kong and South Korea registered more than 20% growth rate and Japan recorded less than 20% for the whole of the study period and decade wise sub-periods. During 2011-12 to 2014-15, PRC and South Korea recorded more than 5% in India's imports while Hong Kong recorded a negative growth rate and Japan recorded negligible growth rate.

Structure and Concentration of India's Exports and Imports

(i) Region-Wise Structure (in percentage shares)

The country-wise analysis of India's Exports and Imports shows that there are some regions/east Asian countries which have high shares in Exports and Imports whereas others have least shares. Different regions whose share in India's exports/imports generally increased may be described as leading regions and whose share generally declined may be described as lagging regions of India's exports/imports. The regions with very low and almost constant shares for the whole of the study period may be described as low and negligible regions.

Table 10.3 provides an analysis of the structure of India's region-wise/East Asian country-wise exports and imports. It indicates that there are some regions which have a high share in India's exports like OECD, OPEC and Developing Countries. The OECD region registered double-digit shares in India's total exports for all the years of the study period (1991-92 to 2014-15). Over the period, it has registered declining shares although it remained more than 30%. The OPEC region recorded double-digit shares since 1997-98 and continued to increase for all years of the study period. The Eastern Europe Region showed single-digit shares in India's total exports and continued to decline with less than 2% share since 2005-06. Others/Unspecified region have recorded low and negligible share (i.e. less than 0.5%) for seven years of the study period.

The developing countries recorded double-digit shares for all years of the study period with more than 20% share in India's exports and it is more than double in 2014-15 as against the year 1991-92. During 1991-92, this region has experienced 20.08% share in India's Exports which is increased to 29.2% for the year 2000-01. The share of developing countries in India's Exports is continued to increase and recorded the share of 44.47% during 2014-15 as against the share of 38.29% for the year 2010-11. The increased share of this region in India's Exports is reflecting a revival of demand, recovery from East Asian crisis during 1999-2000, diversification of export market and less impact of global slowdown during 2007-08 (During 2007-08, its share in India's Exports is more than 40%).

The above analysis of shares shows that Developing countries are the most leading region followed by OPEC (1991-92 to 2014-15). The OECD region lagging due to more than 20% decline in share in 2014-15 as compared to 1991-92. Eastern Europe and Others/Unspecified regions are considered as low regions having low and constant shares in India's total exports.

India's imports (Table 10.3) from OECD registered double-digit shares in India's total imports for all the years of the study period (1991-92 to 2014-15). The share shows a declining trend but remained more than 30% except for few years 2011-12 to 2014-15.

OPEC has recorded double-digit shares since 1991-92 and continued to increase for the whole of the study period except for few years (2000-01 to 2005-06) and remained more than 30% for rest of the study period (2006-07 to 2014-15). The least share (2000-01 to 2005-06) may suggest a change in the sourcing of oil imports away from the OPEC region, given the relative stabilisation of crude oil prices (as OECD recorded 39.89% share during 2000-01) (Economic Survey, 2000-01).

Table 10.3: Percentage of shares of Regions and Asian countries in India's Total Exports and Total Imports

Regions/ Countries	1991-92		1995-96		2000-01		2005-06		2006-07		2007-08		2008-09	
	Export	Import	Export	Import	Export	Import	Export	Import	Export	Import	Export	Import	Export	Import
(A) OECD	57.86	54.21	55.69	52.38	52.68	39.89	44.46	34.72	41.99	35.23	39.45	35.42	37.45	32.25
(B) OPEC	8.74	19.69	9.68	20.84	10.88	5.32	14.79	7.49	16.58	30.35	16.57	30.75	21.27	32.62
(C) Eastern Europe	10.93	5.11	4.21	4.56	2.96	1.68	1.92	2.54	1.23	2.11	1.13	1.52	1.1	2.21
(D) Developing Countries	20.08	20.99	28.93	22.21	29.2	22.08	38.55	25.4	39.9	31.87	42.46	31.52	37.5	32.41
(a) Asian Countries	16.88	14.8	22.98	17.52	22.53	16.74	30.05	20.41	29.77	25.5	31.6	25.51	28.04	26.33
(i) SAARC	3.48	0.68	5.41	0.7	4.33	0.92	5.38	0.95	5.12	0.81	5.9	0.84	4.62	0.6
1. Afghanistan	–	–	–	–	–	–	0.14	0.04	0.14	0.02	0.15	0.04	0.22	0.04
2. Bangladesh	1.81	0.03	3.3	0.23	2.1	0.16	1.61	0.09	1.29	0.12	1.79	0.1	1.35	0.1
3. Bhutan	0.01	0	0.05	0.09	0	0.04	0.1	0.06	0.05	0.08	0.05	0.08	0.06	0.05
4. Maldives	0.03	0	0.05	0	0.06	0	0.07	0	0.05	0	0.05	0	0.07	0
5. Nepal	0.43	0.15	0.5	0.13	0.32	0.5	0.83	0.25	0.73	0.16	0.92	0.25	0.85	0.16
6. Pakistan	0.22	0.44	0.24	0.12	0.42	0.13	0.67	0.12	1.07	0.17	1.19	0.11	0.78	0.12
7. Sri Lanka	0.97	0.06	1.26	0.11	1.44	0.09	1.96	0.39	1.79	0.25	1.73	0.25	1.3	0.12

Cont.

Table 10.3: (*Cont.*)

(ii) Other Asian Developing	13.4	14.12	17.57	16.82	18.2	15.82	24.67	19.47	24.65	24.69	25.7	24.67	23.42	25.73
1. People's Republic of China	0.27	0.11	1.05	2.21	1.87	2.97	6.56	7.29	6.56	9.4	6.65	10.78	5.07	10.74
2. Hong Kong	3.44	0.55	5.73	1.06	5.93	1.69	4.34	1.48	3.7	1.34	3.87	1.07	3.61	2.16
3. South Korea	1.34	1.65	1.41	2.25	1.01	1.77	1.77	3.06	1.99	2.59	1.75	2.4	2.18	2.89
4. Malaysia	1.13	2.03	1.24	2.46	1.36	2.33	1.13	1.62	1.03	2.85	1.58	2.39	1.88	2.37
5. Singapore	2.18	3.58	2.84	2.98	1.97	2.9	5.26	2.25	4.8	2.96	4.52	3.23	4.49	2.51
6. Japan	9.24	7.05	6.97	6.73	4.03	3.65	2.41	2.72	2.27	2.47	2.37	2.51	1.64	2.61
7. Thailand	1.11	0.25	1.49	0.46	1.19	0.67	1.04	0.81	1.14	0.94	1.11	0.92	1.04	0.9
(E) Others/ unspecific	2.39	0.01	1.49	0.01	4.28	31.03	0.29	29.84	0.3	0.44	0.39	0.8	2.69	0.5

Source: Author's Calculations.

Table 10.4: Percentage of shares of Regions and Asian countries in India's Total Exports and Total Imports

Regions/ Countries	2009-10		2010-11		2011-12		2012-13		2013-14		2014-15	
	Export	Import	Export	Import	Export	Import	Export	Import	Export	Import	Export	Import
(A) OECD	35.99	32.75	33.23	30.63	33.82	29.66	34.18	27.84	34.79	25.76	35.64	26.92
(B) OPEC	21.12	32.13	21.33	33.58	19.03	35.43	20.91	38.6	17.79	36.34	18.36	31.12
(C) Eastern Europe	1.01	2.14	1.12	1.55	1.06	1.75	1.31	1.79	1.13	1.73	1.12	1.75
(D) Developing Countries	39.33	32.6	38.29	33.05	40.74	32.25	41.54	31.34	42.99	35.49	44.47	39.74
(a) Asian Countries	29.87	25.72	27.93	27.09	29.6	25.84	28.53	24.18	30.53	28.19	30.59	31.29
(i) SAARC	4.69	0.57	4.64	0.59	4.3	0.51	4.91	0.53	5.61	0.55	6.68	0.68
1. Afghanistan	0.26	0.04	0.17	0.04	0.17	0.02	0.16	0.02	0.15	0.05	0.14	0.06
2. Bangladesh	1.36	0.09	1.29	0.12	1.25	0.12	1.70	0.13	1.97	0.11	2.10	0.14
3. Bhutan	0.07	0.05	0.07	0.05	0.07	0.04	0.07	0.03	0.11	0.03	0.11	0.03
4. Maldives	0.04	0.00	0.04	0.01	0.04	0.00	0.04	0.00	0.03	0.00	0.05	0.00
5. Nepal	0.86	0.16	0.86	0.14	0.83	0.09	1.01	0.11	1.15	0.12	1.49	0.15
6. Pakistan	0.88	0.10	0.81	0.09	0.51	0.09	0.61	0.10	0.73	0.10	0.61	0.11
7. Sri Lanka	1.22	0.14	1.40	0.14	1.43	0.15	1.32	0.13	1.46	0.15	2.19	0.17

Cont.

Table 10.4: (*Cont.*)

(ii) Other Asian Developing	25.19	25.15	23.29	26.51	25.31	25.34	23.62	23.65	24.92	27.64	23.91	30.63
1. China	6.47	10.71	6.16	11.77	5.93	11.77	4.49	11.06	4.79	11.42	3.90	13.75
2. Hong Kong	4.41	1.64	4.12	2.54	4.24	2.17	4.09	1.64	4.08	1.63	4.43	1.27
3. South Korea	1.91	2.97	1.48	2.83	1.42	2.68	1.46	2.74	1.34	2.78	1.50	3.08
4. Malaysia	1.60	1.80	1.55	1.77	1.31	1.95	1.48	2.13	1.34	2.07	1.90	2.53
5. Singapore	4.25	2.25	3.91	1.93	5.49	1.73	4.52	1.57	3.96	1.52	3.19	1.62
6. Japan	2.03	2.34	2.03	2.34	2.09	2.50	2.09	2.55	2.18	2.11	1.75	2.31
7. Thailand	0.97	1.02	0.91	1.16	0.97	1.11	1.24	1.12	1.18	1.20	1.13	1.33
(E) Others/ unspecified	2.55	0.37	6.04	1.20	5.35	0.91	2.06	0.44	3.29	0.67	1.53	1.74

Source: Author's Calculations.

Imports from Eastern Europe has recorded single-digit share and declining trend throughout the study period. The share of Eastern Europe is remained less than 2% for the period 2001-02 to 2002-03, 2007-08 and 2010-11 to 2014-15. The region others/unspecified has experienced low and negligible shares in India's Imports (i.e. less than 0.5%) for most of the years of the study period.

Imports from Developing countries have registered double-digit shares for all the years of the study period. The share of Developing Countries fluctuated between 20% and 30% in India's Imports for the period 1991-92 to 2000-01, except for the few years (1992-93 to 1993-94). The share of the region in India's Imports has experienced the decline of 32.25% during 2011-12 which is increased to the highest level of 39.74% during 2014-15 and the lowest share is recorded for the year 1993-94 (i.e. 19.03%).

The above analysis of shares of India's imports in different regions shows that developing countries emerged as the leading region followed by OPEC. The OECD region lagging due to the sharp decline from around 50% share in 1991-92 to around 27% share in 2014-15. Eastern Europe and Others/unspecified regions are considered as negligible regions due to low and constant shares in India's imports.

(ii) Structure and Trade Balance Analysis of East Asian Countries in India's Total Exports and Total Imports

East Asian countries Such as People's Republic of China (PRC), Hong Kong, South Korea and Japan have shown fluctuating trend of its share in India's total exports and total imports. For the year 1991-92 to 2000-01, the share of Japan has declined from 9.24% to 4.03% in India's exports. After this, the share of Japan is remained constant around 2% up to the year 2010-11. During the 2011-12 to 2014-15, the share of Japan declined from 2.09% to 1.75% in India's exports. [Table 10.3]

The share of PRC has shown a fluctuating trend throughout the study period. Its share in India's export was 0.27% which is increased to 1.87% in 2000-01. After this, the share of PRC has increased continuously up to the year 2010-11, except for minor fluctuations. During 2011-12 its share was 5.9% which is declined to 3.9% in the year 2014-15. The share of Hong Kong is recorded as 3.4% in 1991-92 which is increased to 4.4% in 2014-15 in India's exports, except minor fluctuation. During 2001-02 to 2010-11, Hong Kong recorded a declining share and its share has remained constant at around 4% for most of the years. For the last four years of the study period, its share has remained constant around 4% in India's exports.

The share of South Korea has remained constant around one percent in India's exports for the whole of the study period except for a few years. The country registered less than 1% share in India's exports during 1992-93 to 1993-94 and 1998-99 whereas it has recorded the highest share in the year 2008-09 (2.18%).

In the case of India's imports, the share of PRC is remained constant around 2% for the years 1991-92 to 2000-01, except during 1991-92 to 1993-94 and 1996-97. During 2001-02 to 2010-11, the share of PRC starts increasing and reached to 11.77% in India's import. For the last four years of the study period, its share has increased from 11.77% to 13.75% in India's imports. The share of Hong Kong remained constant around 1% in India's imports, except for a few years such as 1991-92 to 1993-94, 1996-97 to 1997-98, 2008-09 and 2010-11. During 2011-12 to 2014-15, its share declined from 2.5% to 1.2% in India's imports. South Korea has shown a share fluctuating between 1% and 3% in India's imports for the years 1991-92 to 2000-01. During the last four years of the study period, its share has increased marginally from 2.68% to 3.08% in India's imports.

The share of Japan has declined from 7.05% in 1991-92 to 3.65% in 2000-01 in India's imports. During 2001-02 to 2014-15, its share remained constant around 2%, except for the two years 2001-02 (4.17%) and 2003-04 (3.41%) respectively.

Here, the trade Balance of India is estimated with its East Asian partner countries. Table 10.5 provides information about India's trade deficit and a trade surplus with its Asian Partners for the different years of the study period. It is observed that India has a trade deficit with

Japan for most of the study period except for the years from 1991-92 to 1993-94 and 2002-03. This is due to reduced demand for raw material from India by China (bulk of exports to China include Iron Ore and Iron Sand) because of existence of slow pace of growth, overcapacity in iron and steel sector and tight policy in the real estate sector in the Chinese economy (Singh and Satpal, 2014). India has a trade surplus with Hong Kong for the whole of the study period (1991-92 to 2014-15). The trade surplus is increasing throughout the study period, except for minor fluctuations. India has a trade deficit with South Korea for the whole of the study period.

The Concentration of India's Exports and Imports (Regions)

With the help of measures of concentration, the country/region concentration of India's exports and imports are calculated for the study period of 1991-92 to 2014-15. Table (10.6) shows the concentration figures for India's Exports and Imports for regions and table (10.7) shows the region wise frequency of India's Exports and Imports in CR (4).

For calculating region concentration, CR (4) is used and regions considered for concentration measure are OECD, OPEC, Eastern Europe, Developing countries and others/unspecified for the study period of 1991-92 to 2014-2015. The concentration Ratio (4) measures the sum of shares of the top four regions in India's Exports and Imports. As per table (10.6), the concentration figures are higher than 0.97 for all the years of the study period 1991-92 to 2014-2015. As per CR(4), OECD, OPEC, developing countries and Eastern Europe have listed on top four positions in India's Exports which experienced marginal fluctuation from 0.97 to 0.99 for the years 1991-92 to 2014-15.

Table 10.6 depicts that the import concentration figures are higher than 0.97 for all the years of the study period. For the year 1992-93 and 1999-00, the import concentration is turned to be 1 which shows perfect concentration and zero diversification. OECD, OPEC and Developing Countries have listed on the top four positions in India's imports for all the years of the study period.

Table 10.5 : Trade balance between India and Asian countries in 1991-92 to 2014-15 (Rupees Billion)

Countries	1991-92	1995-96	2000-01	2005-06	2006-07	2007-08	2008-09	2009-10	2010-11	2011-12	2012-13	2013-14	2014-15
1. Afghanistan	–	–	–	3.73	6.66	5.62	12.31	16.13	12.59	18.07	19.45	15.91	9.68
2. Bangladesh	7.85	32.22	39.05	68.06	63.32	107.09	99.00	102.96	127.21	155.94	244.42	345.08	356.46
3. Bhutan	0.02	-0.58	-0.91	0.46	-3.80	-4.34	-1.79	-1.62	-1.16	1.30	2.66	12.36	11.36
4. Maldives	0.12	0.52	1.11	2.90	2.97	3.44	5.72	3.61	3.10	5.06	6.26	6.19	9.07
5. Nepal	1.20	3.71	-5.22	21.26	28.17	35.36	48.98	51.05	75.32	104.91	136.11	185.66	239.43
6. Pakistan	-1.13	1.06	5.61	22.57	46.44	66.69	48.64	61.56	77.41	55.31	72.07	112.26	83.12
7. Sri Lanka	4.01	12.05	27.19	64.06	80.77	88.33	92.70	84.40	136.84	175.16	180.39	235.8	363.95
8. China (PRC)	0.68	-16.03	-30.65	-181.92	-414.79	-655.19	-1049.44	-913.35	-1276.65	-1883.29	-2220.37	-2184.16	-2963.96
9. Hong Kong	12.52	47.95	81.72	100.25	99.40	145.18	6.58	149.84	42.13	111.59	229.62	331.34	490.3
10. South Korea	-1.99	-12.60	-20.24	-121.16	-103.68	-128.26	-213.05	-244.24	-307.48	-421.22	-493.55	-498.08	-546.28
11. Malaysia	-4.73	-17.05	-25.98	-55.51	-180.57	-138.39	-168.11	-109.90	-120.69	-266.83	-326.84	-304.88	-323.04
12. Singapore	-7.54	-6.36	-26.81	91.71	26.22	-30.20	31.96	53.25	121.86	396.31	318.40	339.06	163.03
13. Thailand	3.70	10.14	8.78	-6.03	-13.63	-19.85	-36.29	-56.61	-91.14	-115.34	-96.01	-99.49	-146.53
14. Japan	6.95	-8.43	-2.18	-69.95	-78.41	-99.42	-220.25	-147.51	-161.26	-276.23	-339.35	-159.56	-291.52

Source: Author's Calculations.

Frequency of regions in CR (4)

According to table 10.7 the regions OECD, OPEC and Developing Countries have remained in the listed top four export destinations and import sources of India for all the 24 years of the study period. Eastern Europe is in the top four export destination list for 15 years and others/ Unspecified region has emerged as the top export destination under CR (4) for 9 years only. In the case of imports, Eastern Europe has remained in the list of top four import sources of India for 18 years whereas Others/unspecified is in the list for 6 years only.

Asian Country Concentration in India's Exports and Imports

Concentration ratio for Exports: CR(4) and CR(8) are calculated under concentration ratio (CR) measure for destination-wise exports and imports of Asian Countries for the whole of the study period. The table (10.8) reveals that the discrete concentration measures i.e. CR(4) gives exports concentration figure fluctuating between 0.14 to 0.19 for the years 1991-92 to 2014-15. On the contrary, the CR(8) concentration measure recorded more than 0.20 country-wise export concentration figure for the years 1991-92 to 2014-15 (Table 10.8).

On the whole, the CR(8) gives higher values of concentration than the CR(4) which indicates that 20% to 25% exports are dominated by top eight trading countries and CR(4) indicates that 13% to 19% exports are controlled by top four countries.

Concentration ratio for Imports: [Table (10.9)] The CR(4) measure for country-wise import concentration recorded between 0.12 to 0.21 for the whole of the study period. The CR(8) gives a higher value than CR(4) for destination-wise India's imports. The CR(8) import concentration figures are 0.15 or more than 0.15 for most of the years of the study period. The CR(8) import concentration figures are more than 0.20 for the years 1998-99 to 1999-00, 2003-04, and 2006-07 to 2014-15. For the rest of the years, the CR(8) import concentration fluctuated between 0.15 and 0.26 respectively.

Table 10.6: CR(4) of Regions in India's Total Exports and Total Imports

Years	CR(4) Exports	CR(4) Imports
1991-92	0.98	0.99
1992-93	1	1.00
1993-94	0.98	0.99
1994-95	0.98	0.99
1995-96	0.98	0.99
1996-97	0.98	0.99
1997-98	0.99	0.99
1998-99	0.99	0.99
1999-2000	0.99	1
2000-01	0.97	0.98
2001-02	0.97	0.98
2002-03	0.99	0.98
2003-04	0.99	0.98
2004-05	0.99	0.98
2005-06	1.00	0.97
2006-07	1.00	0.99
2007-08	0.99	0.99
2008-09	0.99	0.99
2009-10	0.99	0.99
2010-11	0.99	0.98
2011-12	0.99	0.99
2012-13	0.98	0.99
2013-14	0.99	0.99
2014-15	0.99	0.98

Source: Author's Calculations.

Table 10.7: Frequency of Regions In India's Total Exports/Total Imports under CR(4) and CR(8)

Regions	CR(4) years Exports	CR(4) years Imports
OECD	24	24
OPEC	24	24
Eastern Europe	15	18
Developing Countries	24	24
Others/Unspecified	9	6

Source: Author's Calculations.

The concentration ratio(8) reveals that 15% to 26% of imports controlled by the top eight partner countries of India and CR(4) reveals that 12% to 21% of imports are dominated by top four partner countries of India for different years of the study period.

Frequency of Asian Countries under CR (4) and CR(8) in India's Total Exports and Total imports.

Table 10.8: CR(4) and CR(8) of Asian countries in India's Total Exports

Years	CR(4) Exports	CR(8) Exports
1991-92	0.17	0.21
1992-93	0.17	0.22
1993-94	0.19	0.24
1994-95	0.19	0.24
1995-96	0.19	0.24
1996-97	0.17	0.23
1997-98	0.15	0.22
1998-99	0.15	0.20
1999-00	0.15	0.20
2000-01	0.14	0.20
2001-02	0.13	0.20
2002-03	0.15	0.22
2003-04	0.16	0.23
2004-05	0.18	0.24
2005-06	0.19	0.25
2006-07	0.17	0.24
2007-08	0.17	0.24
2008-09	0.15	0.22
2009-10	0.17	0.23
2010-11	0.16	0.22
2011-12	0.18	0.23
2012-13	0.15	0.21
2013-14	0.15	0.21
2014-15	0.14	0.21

Source: Author's Calculations.

Table 10.10 shows the destination wise frequency of India's exports under CR(4) and CR(8). The Asian countries Bangladesh, Hong Kong, People's Republic of China, Singapore and Japan are found to be listed on top four positions for export destinations of India for the different years of the study period (1991-92 to 2014-15). The countries which are listed on top eight positions for export destinations are found to be

Table 10.9: CR(4) and CR(8) of Asian countries in India's Total Imports

Years	CR(4) Imports	CR(8) Imports
1991-92	0.14	0.16
1992-93	0.13	0.15
1993-94	0.13	0.15
1994-95	0.15	0.19
1995-96	0.14	0.18
1996-97	0.13	0.17
1997-98	0.13	0.18
1998-99	0.16	0.21
1999-00	0.15	0.20
2000-01	0.12	0.16
2001-02	0.13	0.18
2002-03	0.12	0.17
2003-04	0.14	0.21
2004-05	0.14	0.19
2005-06	0.14	0.19
2006-07	0.18	0.23
2007-08	0.19	0.24
2008-09	0.19	0.24
2009-10	0.18	0.23
2010-11	0.19	0.24
2011-12	0.19	0.24
2012-13	0.18	0.23
2013-14	0.18	0.23
2014-15	0.21	0.26

Bangladesh, Sri Lanka Hong Kong, Singapore, and People's Republic of China, Japan, South Korea, Malaysia and Thailand for different years of the study period (1991-92 to 2014-15).

CR(4) which reflects the top four export destinations of India, includes Hong Kong and Japan for 24 years and 21 years of the study period respectively. The export shares of People's Republic of China (PRC) are in the top four countries for 13 years of the study period. The export shares of South Korea are in the top four lists for only one year.

As per CR (8), the exports concentrated on East Asian countries such as Hong Kong and Japan for 24 years of the study period. The countries PRC and South Korea have maintained their position in the top eight destinations of India for 20 years and 18 years respectively.

Table 10.11 shows the Asian countries frequency in India's total imports under CR (4) and CR(8).

For the study period (1991-92 to 2014-15), the Asian countries PRC, South Korea, Malaysia, Singapore and Japan are listed on the top four importers for India. Similarly, the top eight importer countries are listed as Nepal, Pakistan, Sri Lanka, PRC, Hong Kong, South Korea, Malaysia, Singapore, Thailand and Japan for different years of the study period. As per CR(4), Japan appeared in top four lists for 24 years of the study period (1991-92 to 2014-15). Both PRC and South Korea have maintained its position for 17 years of the study period Whereas Hong Kong appeared in CR (4) for one year only.

As per CR (8), Among Asian Countries, Hong Kong, Japan and South Korea appeared in the top eight importers of India for the whole of the study period (i.e. 24 years). PRC appeared in the CR(8) for 23 years of the study period.

CR (4) of Asian countries in India's Exports/Imports to Developing countries

The concentration Ratio (4) measures the sum of shares of the top four Asian countries in India's Exports and Imports for Developing Countries. As per table (10.12), the concentration figures for India's exports to Developing countries are higher than 0.71 for the initial

Table 10.10: Frequency of Asian countries In India's Total Exports under CR(4) and CR(8)

Countries	CR(4) Exports	CR(8) Exports
1. Afghanistan	–	–
2. Bangladesh	12	24
3. Bhutan	–	–
4. Maldives	–	–
5. Nepal	–	–
6. Pakistan	–	–
7. Sri Lanka	1	24
8. People's Republic of China	13	20
9. Hong Kong	24	24
10. South Korea	1	18
11. Malaysia	–	21
12. Singapore	24	24
13. Thailand	–	12
14. Japan	21	24

Source: Author's Calculations.

Table 10.11: Frequency of Asian countries In India's Total Imports under CR(4) and CR(8)

Countries	CR(4) Imports	CR(8) Imports
1. Afghanistan	–	–
2. Bangladesh	–	–
3. Bhutan	–	–
4. Maldives	–	–
5. Nepal	–	12
6. Pakistan	–	4
7. Sri Lanka	–	8
8. People's Republic of China	17	23
9. Hong Kong	1	24
10. South Korea	17	24
11. Malaysia	14	24
12. Singapore	24	24
13. Thailand	–	24
14. Japan	24	24

Source: Author's Calculations.

four years of the study period. As per CR(4), Asian countries listed in the top four positions have experienced a decline in concentration from the year 1995-96 to 2014-15. The import concentration figures are higher than 0.50 for all the years of the study period except for one year (2002-03).

Table 10.12: CR(4) of Asian Countries in India's Total Exports/Total imports to Developing countries

Year	CR(4) Exports	CR(4) Imports
1991-92	0.73	0.68
1992-93	0.74	0.66
1993-94	0.72	0.67
1994-95	0.71	0.63
1995-96	0.65	0.65
1996-97	0.57	0.62
1997-98	0.56	0.58
1998-99	0.55	0.58
1999-00	0.52	0.51
2000-01	0.48	0.53
2001-02	0.43	0.52
2002-03	0.44	0.48
2003-04	0.44	0.53
2004-05	0.49	0.57
2005-06	0.48	0.60
2006-07	0.43	0.55
2007-08	0.41	0.60
2008-09	0.41	0.58
2009-10	0.43	0.58
2010-11	0.43	0.59
2011-12	0.44	0.62
2012-13	0.36	0.61
2013-14	0.35	0.55
2014-15	0.31	0.57

Source: Author's Calculations.

Analysis of Product Concentrated among East Asian Countries

The analysis of Product exports and imports for India through East Asian countries such as Hong Kong, PRC, Japan and South Korea for the specific period such as 1996-97, 2005-06 and 2014-15 has been done (Table 10.13 and Table 10.14).

The top five commodities exports to Hong Kong are registered as Natural or cultured Pearls, Precious & Semi-precious Stones etc. (71), Cotton (52), Raw hides and skins (41), Electrical Machinery and

Table 10.13: Top Five Exports of India (HS Codes)

Countries (Exports)	1996-97	2005-06	2014-15
People's Republic of China	23	26	74
	26	72	27
	3	52	25
	72	28	29
	52 **(78.84%)**	29 **(76.83%)**	3 **(59.71%)**
Hong Kong	71	71	71
	52	52	52
	41	41	41
	85	85	85
	29 **(83.51%)**	27 **(88.34%)**	3 **(95.69%)**
Japan	3	3	3
	71	71	71
	26	26	27
	52	23	29
	72 **(70.73%)**	27 **(59.57%)**	72 (58.53%)
South Korea	52	52	52
	23	23	27
	26	26	76
	29	29	27
	72 **(69.70%)**	27 **(68.07%)**	76 (63.33%)

Source: Author's Calculations.

Note: Combined Shares of Top Five commodities for each country are given in brackets.

equipment (85) and Organic Chemicals (29) which jointly contribute 83.51% share in exports to Hong Kong by India for the year 1996-97. During 2005-06, all the above five exports (1996-97) are directed towards Hong Kong except organic chemicals (29) which are replaced by mineral fuels (27). All these top five export commodities jointly contributed 88.34% share in exports to Hong Kong by India for the year 2005-06. During 2014-15, all the above five exports (1996-97) are directed towards Hong Kong except Organic Chemicals (29) which is replaced by

Table 10.14: Top Five Imports of India (HS Codes)

Countries (Imports)	1996-97	2005-06	2014-15
People's Republic of China	29	29	29
	27	27	31
	50	50	72
	85	85	85
	84 **(61.12%)**	84 **(67.7%)**	84 **(64.7%)**
Hong Kong	71	71	71
	85	85	85
	84	84	84
	29	52	85
	91 **(74.95%)**	89 **(84.25%)**	91 **(90.72%)**
Japan	84	84	84
	87	90	87
	98	89	98
	85	85	85
	72 **(63.84%)**	72 **(66.64%)**	72 **(62.96%)**
South korea	84	84	84
	39	39	39
	29	72	29
	85	85	85
	87 **(69.63%)**	87 **(75.85%)**	72 **(61.27%)**

Source: Author's Calculations.

Note: Combined Shares of Top Five commodities for each country are given in brackets.

Fish and Crustaceans (3). All these top five export commodities jointly contributed 95.69% share in exports to Hong Kong by India for the year 2014-15.

In case of imports, the top five imports from Hong Kong consists of natural or cultured pearls (71), electrical machinery and equipment (85), nuclear reactors, (84), organic chemicals (29) and clocks and watches and parts thereof (91) which jointly contribute 74.95% share in Imports of India for the year 1996-97. During 2005-06, organic chemicals (29) and clocks (91) replaced by cotton (52) and ships, boats and floating structures (89) and rest of the composition remain the same. Its joint contribution to imports of India from Hong Kong is equal to 84.25%. During 2014-15, all the above commodities are imported from Hong Kong remained the same but cotton (52) and ships, boats and floating structures (89) are replaced by special woven fabrics (58) clocks and watches and parts thereof (91) which jointly contributed 90.72% share in India's imports from Hong Kong.

For the Year 1996-97, the top five exports to China consist of residues and waste from the food industries (23), ores, slag and ash (26), fish and crustaceans (03),iron and steel (72) and cotton (52) which jointly have 78.84% share in India's total exports to China. For the year 2005-06, the top five exports from China remained the same as in 1996-97, but residues and waste from the food industries (23), and fish and crustaceans (03) replaced by Organic Chemicals (29) and Inorganic Chemicals (28) and joint share has decreased to 76.83% in India's total exports to China. For the year 2014-15, all the top five exports remained the same as in 1996-97 except ores, slag and ash (26), iron and steel (72) and inorganic chemicals (28) which is replaced by copper and articles thereof (74), mineral fuel (27) and salt (25) All these top exports jointly contribute 59.71% share in total exports of India to China.

For the Year 1996-97, the top five imports from China consist of Organic chemicals (29), Mineral fuels (27), Silk (50), Electrical Machinery and equipment (85) and nuclear Reactors (84) which jointly have 61.12% share in India's total imports from China. For the year 2005-06, the top five imports from China remained the same as in

1996-97, but their joint share has increased to 67.7% in India's total imports from China. For the year 2014-15, all the top five imports remained the same as in 1996-97 except Mineral fuels (27) and Silk (50) which is replaced by Fertilisers (31) and Iron and steel(72). All these top five imports jointly contribute 64.7% share in total imports of India from China.

For the Year 1996-97, the top five exports to Japan consists of fish and crustaceans (03) natural or cultured pearls (71), ores, slag and ash (26), cotton (52) and iron and steel (72) which jointly have 70.73% share in India's total imports from Japan. For the year 2005-06, the top five imports from Japan remained the same as in 1996-97, but cotton (52) and iron and steel (72) replaced by residues (23) and mineral fuels (27), their joint share has decreased to 59.57% in India's total exports to Japan. For the year 2014-15, the entire top five imports remained the same as in 1996-97 except ores, slag and as (26), cotton (52) which is replaced by mineral fuels (27) and Organic Chemicals (29). All these top five exports jointly contribute 58.53% share in total exports of India to Japan.

For the Year 1996-97, the top five imports from Japan consists of Nuclear Reactors (84), Vehicles other than Railway (87), Project goods (98) Electrical Machinery and equipment (85) and Iron and Steel(72) which jointly have 63.84% share in India's total imports from Japan. For the year 2005-06, the top five imports from Japan remained the same as in 1996-97, but Project goods(98) and vehicles(87) replaced by Optical (90) and ships (89),their joint share has increased to 66.64% in India's total imports from Japan. For the year 2014-15, the entire top five imports remained the same as in 1996-97 except Optical (90) which is replaced by vehicles (87). All these top five imports jointly contribute 62.96% share in total imports of India from Japan.

For the Year 1996-97, the top five exports to South Korea consists of cotton (52), residues (23),ores, slag and ash (26), Organic Chemicals (29) and iron and steel (72) which jointly have 69.70% share in India's total exports to South Korea. For the year 2005-06, the top five exports to South Korea remained the same as in 1996-97, but iron and steel (72) is replaced by mineral fuels (27), their joint share is 68.07% in India's total exports to South Korea. For the year 2014-15, the entire top five imports remained the same as in 1996-97 except residues (23), ores, slag and ash (26) which is replaced by mineral fuels (27) and Aluminum and articles (76). All these top five exports jointly contribute 63.33% share in total exports of India to South Korea.

For the Year 1996-97, the top five imports from South Korea consists of Nuclear Reactors (84), Plastic and Articles (39), Organic Chemical (29), Electrical Machinery and equipment (85) and vehicles other than railway (87) which jointly have 69.63% share in India's total imports from South Korea. For the year 2005-06, the top five imports from South Korea remained the same as in 1996-97, but Organic Chemical (29) replaced by Iron and Steel (72), their joint share has increased to 75.85% in India's total imports from Japan. For the year 2014-15, the entire top five imports remained the same as in 1996-97 except vehicles other than railway (87) which is replaced by iron and steel. All these top five imports jointly contribute 61.27% share in total imports of India from South Korea.

Conclusion

- The comparison of the growth of Indian exports to Asian Countries with East Asian Countries gives an idea that India's exports to South Korea recorded equal growth whereas India's exports to China recorded higher growth than Asian export growth for the whole study period.
- The growth of India's imports from China and Hong Kong is more than the growth of India's imports from Asian countries for the given study period.
- In terms of growth, China has recorded a maximum growth rate of more than 30% (imports as well as exports) but appeared only for 13 and 17 years (Exports and Imports respectively) in top four countries lists for India. Further, the growth rate for imports from China is higher than export to China, which confirms about maximum coverage of the Indian Market by China and that is too specifically 2002-03 year onwards. The joint share of the top five products

exports to China is declining with some changes in Commodity composition.

- Hong Kong recorded higher growth than Japan but less growth than Asian countries. The joint share of the top five exports to and imports from Hong Kong shows an increasing trend with almost the same commodity composition over the considered years of the study period. In the case of Japan, the combined share of top five exports is declining while the joint share of the top five imports from Japan is increased over the considered period, with almost the same commodity composition.
- Also, import concentration is higher than export concentration under CR(4) and CR(8) of Asian countries in India's total exports and total imports whereas export concentration is higher than import concentration under CR(4) of Asian countries in India's total exports/total imports to Developing countries for selected years only.
- It is observed that India experienced an increasing trade deficit with China, South Korea and Japan with minor fluctuations whereas India has trade surplus even during crisis years (and increasing since 2011-12) with Hong Kong.
- The major exports to East Asian countries include the almost same composition of the products such as Natural or Cultured pearls (Hong Kong and Japan), Cotton (China, Hong Kong, Japan and South Korea) and Ores, slag and ash (Japan, South Korea and China).
- In case of Imports, Electrical, Machinery and Equipment (Hong Kong, Japan, China and South Korea), Iron and Steel (China, Japan and South Korea) and Nuclear Reactors (Hong Kong, China, Japan and South Korea) appeared as major imports.
- The analysis of the combined share of exports and imports of East Asian countries reveals that India's trade is more concentrated towards Hong Kong (trade surplus with more than 80% share covered by top five products exported and imported) while India's trade is less concentrated towards China, Japan and South Korea

(trade deficit with less than 75% share covered by top five products exported and imported).

Policy Implications

- India faces a huge trade deficit with China so there is need to explore possibilities to boost the demand for top five exports to China and it is important to create possibilities to generate FTA specifically for the products in which India and China are trading.
- The India-ASEAN FTA can be strengthened by following Regional Comprehensive Partnership Agreement (RCEP) among ASEAN members and its six FTA partners (Australia, China, India, Japan, South Korea and New Zealand). This Agreement is not finalised yet and can be viewed as an alternative to Trans-Pacific partnership Agreement signed on 5th October 2015 which includes twelve nations but excludes China, India and South Korea. The biggest challenge in RCEP negotiations is to seek markets for global majors in such a way that it doesn't promote shifting the manufacturing base to develop India into a manufacturing hub which further help in boosting the economy and support to create more jobs (Business Today, November, 2018).
- India's huge and increasing trade deficit with China is due to discrimination from China itself. For Example, India's Exports of Cashew to China faces 10% import duty but Vietnam exports of Cashew enjoy nil duty from China. (Prasad et al. 2014). Hence, India needs to explore the markets where import duty is at its lowest level and discrimination is less on various products in demand.
- Initially, India was importing mineral fuels (HS Code 27) from China for the years 1996-97 and 2005-06, whereas this product shifted to top five exports of India to China. So, there is a need to explore the possibility of increasing exports by focusing on China as market for this product (i.e. 27).
- India should focus more on exports of Natural or cultured pearls (HS Code 71) and Electrical Machinery and Equipment (HS Code 85)

to Hong Kong as these items have a prominent position in India's top five exports to Hong Kong.

- There is strong need to explore the Possibilities of Intra Industry Trade in case of Natural or cultured pearls (71) and electrical machinery and equipment (85) as these items are present in both India's exports to China and imports from China.
- As per Ease of doing business report 2019, India's rank for starting a new business is recorded at the lower level as compared to East Asian Countries (i.e. China, Japan, Hong Kong and South Korea). Trading Across border Rank of India showed an improvement (from 146 to 80) but it is again lower than considered East Asian countries. Hence, there is a need to remove difficulties by reducing the time and cost of exports and imports in terms of documentary and border compliance.

References

Asher, M., & Sen, R. (2005). India-East Asia Integration: A Win-Win for Asia. *Economic and Political Weekly*, *40*(36), 3932-3940. Retrieved September 23, 2020, from http://www.jstor.org/stable/4417108

Asian Development Bank. (2007). *Asian Development Outlook 2007: Growth amid change.*

Barthwal, R. (2011). *Industrial Economics: An Introductory Textbook.* New Age Third Revised Edition. (Bank, 2007)

Bhatia, S. K., Bhardwaj, M., & Kaur, P. (2018). An Empirical Analysis of India-UK Bilateral Trade.

CARE Ratings. (2013). "India's Foreign Trade: A study on Direction & Composition of Trade".

Chakraborty 1, A., & Chakraborty 2, D. (2017). Economic and Political Cooperation between India and East Asia: The Emerging Perspective. MPRA Paper No. 78676. Retrieved September 23, 2020, from, https://mpra.ub.uni-muenchen.de/id/eprint/78676

Economic Survey. Government of India (Various issues).

Haraguchi, N., & Rezonja, G. (2009). Structural Change and Sectoral Growth in Selected East Asian Countries. *Research and statistics branch, UNIDO.*

Kaur, N., & Gopal, K. (2016). Growth, Composition and Direction of Exports: A Case Study of India. *International Journal in Management and Social Science, 04* (09), 263-271.

Malhotra, N., & Meenu. (2012). Measuring Structural Changes and Concentration of India's Imports. (S. Ahmed, & S. Ashraf, Eds.). *International Trade in Emerging Economies*, 248-268.

McDonald, S., Robinson, S., & Thierfelder, K. (2008). Asian growth and trade poles: India, China, and East and Southeast Asia. World Development, 36(2), 210-234.

Michaely, M. (1958). Concentration of Exports and Imports: An International Comparison. *The Economic Journal, 68*(272), 722-736. doi: 10.2307/2227283

Murshed, M.S. (2001). Patterns of East Asian trade and Intra-industry trade in manufactures *Journal of the Asia Pacific Economy* 6(1) 2001: 99–123. doi: 10.1080/13547860020024558

Nayak, D., & Kumra, A. (2010). India's Exports: An Analysis of Export Growth and Instability in the Post-reform Period. *Foreign Trade Review, 45* (1), 3-31.

Prasad, H.A.C., Sathish, R. & Singh, S.S. (2014) *India's Merchandise Exports: Some Important Issues and Policy Suggestions*, Working Paper No. 3, Department of Economic Affairs Ministry of Finance, Government of India.

RBI Bulletin, Government of India. (Various Issues)

Salvatore. (2013). *International Economics* (11th Edition). Wiley.

Sahni, P. (2014). Trends in India's Exports: A Comparative Study of Pre and Post Reform Period. *IOSR Journal of Economics and Finance, 3* (2), 08-18.

Seshadri, V.S. (2009). The changing face of India's External Trade. *Economic and Political Weekly, 44* (35), 43-49.

Singh, J., & Santpal. (2014). A Comparative Study of India-China Bilateral Trade. *International Journal of Commerce, Business and Management, 3* (2), 269-279.

Veeramani, C. (2012). Anatomy of India's Merchandise Export Growth, 1993-94 to 2010-11. *Economic and Political Weekly, 47* (1), 94-104.

Webliography

www.rbi.org.in

https://mpra.ub.uni-muenchen.de/78676/

https://www.businesstoday.in/opinion/perspective/rcep-is-good-for-regions-but-not-for-india-at-least-not-in-present-form/story/291375.html

https://www.orfonline.org/research/india-japan-economic-partnership-agreement-gains-and-future-prospects/

https://www.ibtimes.com/india-japan-free-trade-agreement-win-win-deal-267457

https://economictimes.indiatimes.com/news/economy/foreign-trade/india-south-korea-sign-agreements-on-trade-and-commerce/articleshow/64914925.cms

Appendix 2

Table 10.15: Commodity Description With HS Codes

S. No.	Hs codes	Commodity description
1	3	Fish and crustaceans, molluscs and other aquatic invertebrates.
2	23	Residues and waste from the food industries; prepared animal fodder.
3	25	Salt; sulphur; earths and stone; plastering materials,
4	26	Ores, slag and ash.
5	27	Mineral fuels, mineral oils and products of their distillation; bituminous substances; mineral waxes.
6	28	Inorganic chemicals; organic or inorganic compounds of precious metals, of rare-earth metals, or radi. Elem. Or of isotopes.
7	29	Organic chemicals
8	39	Plastic and articles thereof.
9	41	Raw hides and skins (other than furskins) and leather
10	50	Silk
11	52	Cotton.
12	71	Natural or cultured pearls, precious or semiprecious stones, pre.metals, clad with pre.metal and articles thereof; imit jewellery; coin
13	72	Iron and steel
14	76	Aluminum and articles thereof.
15	84	Nuclear reactors, boilers, machinery and mechanical appliances; parts thereof.
16	85	Electrical machinery and equipment and parts thereof; sound recorders and reproducers, television image and sound recorders and reproducers, and parts.

17	86	Railway or tramway locomotives, rolling-stock and parts thereof; railway or tramway track fixtures and fittings and parts thereof; mechanical
18	87	Vehicles other than railway or tramway rolling stock, and parts and accessories thereof.
19	89	Ships, boats and floating structures.
20	90	Optical, photographic cinematographic measuring, checking precision, medical or surgical inst. And apparatus parts and accessories thereof;
21	91	Clocks and watches and parts thereof.
22	98	Project goods; some special uses.
23	99	Miscellaneous goods.

Source: DGFT, EXIM Databank.

11

Export Diversification and Economic Growth

A Case Study of Some Selected Emerging Economies

Vishal Sarin & Naveen Sood

Introduction

Many developing countries which are commodity dependent or a limited export basket affected from the problem of export instability. The reason for the same is inelastic and unstable global demand. To alleviatc these constraints, export diversification has been advocated by various economists. Countries export need to be competitive vis a vis global markets, if they want to succeed in export diversification (www.worldbank.org). The underlying question is that export diversification plays a role in the growth of the economy? What are the theoretical arguments which advocate diversification of export for economic growth? As per structural models of development, countries need to diversify its primary export into manufactured export to achieve the goal of sustainable growth. (Chenery, 1979; Syrquin, 1989). Export instability is another reason for the advantages of export diversification because commodity products of subjects to price volatility so those countries that are dependent on few products are bound to suffer from export instability. The investment by risk-averse firms is discouraged due to export instability which further leads to macroeconomic uncertainty and proves to be detrimental to the long-run economic growth. Export diversification proves to be helpful to stabilise export earnings in the long run (Ghosh and Ostry, 1994; Bleaney and Greenway, 2001). Learning by doing in the manufacturing sector for sustained growth assumes utmost importance in the endogenous growth models (Matsuyama, 1992). Knowledge spillovers from new management, marketing practices and new techniques of production could be the benefits which are associated with export diversification (Amin Gutierrez de Pineres and Ferrantino, 2000). The dynamic effect of export diversification on higher per capita income growth can be seen in the form of producing an expanding set of export products. In this context, Agosin (2007) develops a model of export diversification and growth where countries below the technological frontiers broaden their comparative advantage and limitating existing products. Moreover, diversity of exports products by the innovating North and imitators South and exports the products to economies with cheap labour. Economies was obtained in the product cycle literature (Vernon, 1966; Krugman, 1979; Grossman and Helpman, 1991).

Within countries studies, Amin Gutierrez de Pineres and Ferrantino (1997) and Herzer and Nowak-Lehmann D. (2006) verify the modesty of export diversification as a good driver of economic growth of the Chilean economy and they in the long run, Chile export diversification has improved relative to what it would have been with a concentrated export basket over the period from 1960 to 1990. By adding various measures of export concentration to the basic growth regression of conventional cross-sectional country data from 1961 to 1981 for 91 countries, Al-Marhubi (2000) find that economic growth is promoted by export diversification. Further Agosin (2007) finds that per capita income growth is strongly affected by export diversification especially when a country's exports grow faster than alone. In a dynamic cross-country panel model, some evidence of the diversification-led growth was also found by Lederman and Maloney (2007). Naude and Rosouw

(2008) examined the relationship between economic growth and export diversification in South Africa with the help of time series data from 1962 to 2000 and analyse that export diversification granger cause growth in GDP per capita. Haseeb et al. (2014) by using time series data from 1971-2013 and the VAR technique, empirically prove that exports and foreign direct investment have a positive impact on economic growth in Malaysia. Sanjay (2011) by applying Vector Error Correction Modeling and the Johansen co-integration analysis finds an negative relationship between export concentration and economic growth. The study was for Mauritius from 1980-2008. Yokoyama and Alemu (2009) by using panel data of 41 countries over the period 1965 to 2000 give a detailed analysis of export diversification in East Asia and Sub-Saharan Africa (SSA). Empirical results show that export diversification is an important factor to enhance economic growth. Kaur (2010) discussed about Complementarities in Production and Trade between ASEAN and India. Many of the ASEAN countries are dependent on health care equipments and imported drugs. Therefore India could also cooperate with ASEAN in the pharmaceutical and health care service sectors. Kim (2012) evaluates the effect of export diversification on economic growth in the Korean economy. Developing a theoretical framework, he finds that from the last five decades Korea has made a large economic growth due to trade openness and export diversification. Dennis and Shepherd (2011) argue that diversification is directly related with a country's growth prospects. They advocate that the policy of trade facilitation can be highly effective in promoting export diversification in developing countries. Nicet-Chenaf and Rougier (2008), concluded that excessive export diversification may prove to be detrimental to the growth of the economy. The researchers used GMM and focused on Egypt, Morocco, Tunisia, Jordan, Israel and Algeria. Aditya and Roy (2009) by using GMM and studying 68 countries reached the same conclusion regarding the effect of export diversification on economic growth. In view of this, the objective of the paper is to study the statistical significance of association and causality between export diversification and economic growth of selected emerging economies.

Data Methodology

- ***Data and Variables Description*:** The data used in this study are annual data for the period 1995 to 2017. The data set is compiled from secondary sources such as UNCTAD and International Financial Statistics of the IMF. Six selected emerging economies for the study are India, China, Korea, Mexico, Turkey and Argentina because IMF has identified these economies as emerging economies (based on the GDP, share in the global trade, ease of doing business and inflation rate). In this paper, the variables are the gross domestic product (at constant prices, 2010) and export diversification/concentration index (HHI). The related measures used by UNCTAD is the concentration index or Hirschman index which is calculated using the shares of all three-digit products in a country's exports. HHI takes a value between 0 to 1. An index closer to 0 reflects exports/imports are diversified among a series of products and on the other hand an index closer to 1 indicates a country's exports/imports are highly concentrated on a few products.
- ***Empirical Framework*:** The paper uses time series techniques of cointegration and Granger causality tests to examine the long-run relationship and dynamic interaction between the variables of interest. For proper model specification, we have conducted the unit root and cointegration tests. Augmented Dickey-Fuller (ADF) unit root test has been applied for determining the order of the variables of integration. Furthermore, to test for cointegration we employ a vector autoregressive (VAR) based on Johansen cointegration test. Having implemented unit root and cointegration tests we proceed to specification and the estimation of Granger causality. If the variables are non-stationary and are not cointegrated then the use of Granger causality of VAR model in first difference is advocated.

Results and Discussion

a) Trends and Descriptive Statistics of Export Diversification and Economic Growth

The following graph gives an overview of export diversification (HHI) and economic growth (GDP) of six selected emerging economies:

Figure 11.1: Export Diversification (HHI)

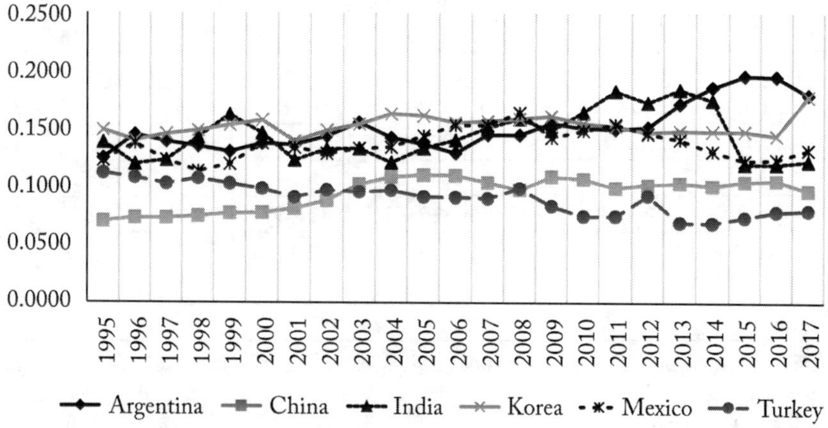

Table 11.1: Descriptive Statistics of Export Diversification (HHI)

	Argentina	China	India	Korea	Mexico	Turkey
Mean	0.151064	0.094252	0.143888	0.212119	0.136214	0.089999
Median	0.144585	0.100596	0.140052	0.186737	0.133797	0.090995
Maximum	0.195842	0.109997	0.183936	0.392023	0.163676	0.111406
Minimum	0.124355	0.070015	0.119262	0.097602	0.113271	0.068582
Std. Dev.	0.020683	0.014052	0.021345	0.105219	0.012872	0.012738
Skewness	1.011708	-0.588157	0.494396	0.479057	0.248206	-0.196899
Kurtosis	2.939910	1.728084	1.998765	1.627037	2.336922	1.949375
Jarque-Bera	3.927082	2.876425	1.897672	2.686216	0.657510	1.206436
Probability	0.140361	0.237352	0.387192	0.261033	0.719820	0.547048
Sum	3.474478	2.167806	3.309430	4.878743	3.132925	2.069971
Sum Sq. Dev.	0.009411	0.004344	0.010024	0.243563	0.003645	0.003570
Observations	23	23	23	23	23	23

Source: Authors' calculations are based on World Development Indicators, The World Bank & United Nations Conference on Trade and Development (UNCTAD) database.

Table 11.2: Descriptive Statistics of GDP (US $ Million)

	Argentina	China	India	Korea	Mexico	Turkey
Mean	366337.3	4748709	1350227	13547.73	1006092	719990.9
Median	362898.7	4002049	1209759	13879.59	1006297	704896.8
Maximum	460982.0	10161164	2608305	15127.18	1287994	1205763
Minimum	260025.5	1473518	596572.8	11626.80	707431.2	426265.0
Std. Dev.	73038.01	2787782	628719.8	968.7438	157704.6	236724.4
Skewness	0.038254	0.525365	0.558999	-0.429734	0.015571	0.597487
Kurtosis	1.377821	1.936380	2.054534	2.284437	2.241508	2.142173
Jarque-Bera	2.527429	2.142181	2.054499	1.198603	0.552269	2.073672
Probability	0.282602	0.342635	0.357990	0.549195	0.758711	0.354575
Sum	8425758.	1.09E+08	31055219	311597.8	23140110	16559790
Sum Sq. Dev.	1.17E+11	1.71E+14	8.70E+12	20646218	5.47E+11	1.23E+12
Observations	23	23	23	23	23	23

Source: Authors' calculations are based on the data extracted from the World Development Indicators, The World Bank & United Nations Conference on Trade and Development (UNCTAD) database.

b) Significance of Association between GDP and Export Diversification

Many empirical studies have been conducted on the effect of export diversification on economic growth. Most of the studies have shown the positive effect of export diversification on economic growth; although some have shown a negative effect but with little evidence to support the fact. For the present study, analysis has been done regarding the statistical significance of the association between GDP and Export Diversification. The results of the study report that the association between GDP and Export Diversification for all the countries under study is statistically significant.

c) Causality between Export Diversification and Economic Growth

After studying the statistical significance of the association between GDP and Export Diversification the paper attempts to study the causality between the variables under study. The causality between

Table 11.3: Association between GDP and Export Diversification

Country	Null Hypothesis	Variables	Correlation	Prob	Statistical Association
Argentina	The association between GDP and Export diversification is statistically insignificant.	GDP and Export Diversification	0.72	0.0013*	Significant
China	The association between GDP and Export diversification is statistically insignificant.	GDP and Export Diversification	0.63	0.0187*	Significant
India	The association between GDP and Export diversification is statistically insignificant.	GDP and Export Diversification	0.23	0.0034*	Significant
Korea	The association between GDP and Export diversification is statistically insignificant.	GDP and Export Diversification	0.68	0.0312*	Significant
Mexico	The association between GDP and Export diversification is statistically insignificant.	GDP and Export Diversification	0.26	0.0011*	Significant
Turkey	The association between GDP and Export diversification is statistically insignificant.	GDP and Export Diversification	-0.83	0.0198*	Significant
* Rejection of null hypothesis at 0.05 level of significance					

Source: Authors' calculations are based on World Development Indicators, The World Bank & United Nations Conference on Trade and Development (UNCTAD) database.

export diversification and economic growth of selected emerging economies has been established with the help of econometric tool vector error correction model and the findings of the study are as follows:

Unit Root Tests

For better and robust results of the time series, the stationarity assumption must hold good that is its mean and variance should remain constant over time. For forecasting purposes, therefore, nonstationary time series will be of little practical value. Hence, to test for stationarity, the Augmented Dickey-Fuller (ADF) test is performed based on the model with constant and no trend. Results of the study report unit root tests statistics that examine the presence of unit roots (non-stationary) *at the level* for GDP and HHI in each six selected emerging economies. GDP and HHI series of all the economies are made stationary after *first differencing*.

Cointegration Tests

In order to study the dynamic relationship between the observed variables, their cointegration relationship was tested through Johansen Cointegration test which allows us to draw conclusion about the number of cointegrating relationship among the observed variables. Since the data series in the present model were integrated processes of order one or I (1), the linear combination of cointegrating vectors of one or more of these series may exhibit long run relationship.

The trace test and the maximum eigenvalue test were employed to establish the number of cointegrating vectors. Results of the study report that as per trace test at 0.05 level, there are two cointegrating equations for Argentina, India, Korea, Turkey and Mexico but there is only one cointegrating equation for China.

Granger Causality Tests

Results of the study exhibit cointegration between the variables under study therefore it becomes imperative to study the direction of the causality. Results of the study report that in case of Argentina, India, Mexico, Korea and Turkey we cannot reject both of the null hypothesis. Therefore, Null Hypothesis is accepted and it may be concluded that GDP does not Granger cause export diversification and export diversification does not Granger cause GDP. Thus, Granger causality results show that statistically insignificant causality effects between GDP and export diversification for Argentina, India, Mexico, Korea and Turkey. In other words, we can say that both GDP and export diversification are independent. However, in the case of China, the results show that GDP Granger cause HHI and HHI Granger cause GDP at 5% level of significance. So, there exists bidirectional causality from GDP to export diversification and from export diversification to GDP. In other words, Granger causality results show that, for China, statistically significant causality effects between GDP and export diversification.

Table 11.4: Results of Granger Causality Tests

Granger Causality of Argentina		**Granger Causality of Mexico**	
Null Hypothesis	Prob.	Null Hypothesis	Prob.
GDP does not Granger cause HHI	0.8335	GDP does not Granger cause HHI	0.1306
HHI does not Granger cause GDP	0.2846	HHI does not Granger cause GDP	0.880
Granger Causality of China		**Granger Causality of Korea**	
Null Hypothesis	Prob.	Null Hypothesis	Prob.
GDP does not Granger cause HHI	0.0157	GDP does not Granger cause HHI	0.4763
HHI does not Granger cause GDP	0.0025	HHI does not Granger cause GDP	0.3924
Granger Causality of India		**Granger Causality of Turkey**	
Null Hypothesis	Prob.	Null Hypothesis	Prob.
GDP does not Granger cause HHI	0.7754	GDP does not Granger cause HHI	0.2726
HHI does not Granger cause GDP	0.4358	HHI does not Granger cause GDP	0.7212

Source: Authors' calculations are based on World Development Indicators, The World Bank & United Nations Conference on Trade and Development (UNCTAD) database.

Conclusion

There is no denying fact that more diversified countries tend to have faster and inclusive economic growth and this fact has been empirically proved. Seminal works by Herzer and Lehmann (2006), Agosin (2007) have given robust evidences about the positive association between export diversification and economic growth in emerging economies. However, some empirical studies Damuri (2006), Athukorala and Menon (2010), Chia (2010), Affendy, Sim and Bakri (2010) have also shown that over the years East Asian economies have concentrated trade in manufacturing products. Furthermore, greater economic integration in East Asian economies has led to export diversification (www.ijssh.org). India has been diversifying its export while on the other side its export is matching with UK's export. (Kaur et al 2018). The present paper attempted to study the causal relationship between export diversification and economic growth of selected emerging economies. The results show statistically insignificant causality effects between economic growth and export diversification for Argentina, India, Mexico, Korea and Turkey.

In other words, we can say that both economic growth and export diversification are independent. However, in the case of China, the results show that economic growth because export diversification and export diversification cause economic growth. So, there exists bidirectional causality from GDP to export diversification and from export diversification to GDP and this bidirectional causality is statistically significant.

References

Amin Guitierrez de Pineres, S., M. J. Ferrantino. (2000). Export Dynamics and Economic Growth in Latin America. Burlington, Vermont: Ashgate Publishing Ltd.

Agosin, M. R. (2007). Export Diversification and Growth in Emerging Economies. Working Paper No. 233. Departamento de Economía, Universidad de Chile.

Al-Marhubi, F. (2000). Export Diversification and Growth: An Empirical Investigation. Applied Economics Letters, 7, 559–62.

Bleaney, M., & Greenaway, D. (2001). The impact of terms of trade and real exchange rate volatility on investment and growth in sub-Saharan Africa. *Journal of Development Economics*, 65(2), 491-500.

Bhatia, S. K., Bhardwaj, M., & Kaur, P. (2018). An Empirical Analysis of India-UK Bilateral Trade.

Chenery, H. (1979). Structural Change and Development Policy. New York: Oxford University Press.

Hesse, H. (2009). Export diversification and economic growth. Breaking into new markets: emerging lessons for export diversification, 55-80.

Herzer, D., and F. Nowak-Lehmann D. (2006). What Does Export Diversification Do for Growth? *An Econometric Analysis. Applied Economics,* 38, 1825–38.

Grossman, G., and E. Helpman. (1991). Innovation and Growth in the Global Economy. Cambridge, MA: MIT Press.

Ghosh, A. R., & Ostry, J. D. (1994). Export instability and the external balance in developing countries. Staff Papers, 41(2), 214-235.

Krugman, P. (1979). A model of innovation, technology transfer, and the world distribution of income. Journal of political economy, 87(2), 253-266.

Kaur, S. (2010). Complementarities in Production and Trade between ASEAN Countries and India. *Journal of Global Economy*, *6*(5), 363-386.

Lederman, D., and Maloney, W.F. (2007). Trade Structure and Growth. In Natural Resources: Neither Curse Nor Destiny, D. Lederman and W.F. Maloney, eds. Palo Alto: Stanford University Press.

Matsuyama, K. (1992). Agricultural productivity, comparative advantage, and economic growth. Journal of economic theory, 58(2), 317-334.

Naude, W., Rossouw, R. (2008). Export Diversification and Specialization in South Africa: Extent and Impact. Research paper 93/2008, UNU-WIDER, United Nations University.

Nicet-Chenaf, D., & Rougier, E. (2008). FDI, diversification and growth: An empirical assessment for MENA countries. IMF staff papers, 40, 151-172.

Nadeem, M. M., Azam, M., & Islam, R. (2012). An Investigation of the Various Factors Influence on Exports. Global Journal of Management and Business Research, 12(19).

Sanjay Provide initials (2011). "Export Diversification and Economic Growth", Case of Developing Country, Mauritius. 371.

Saviotti PP, Frenken K (2008). Export Variety and the Economic Ssemogerere N, Kaskende L (1994). "Constraint to Development and Diversification of Non–Traditional Exports in Uganda".

Vernon, R. (1992). International investment and international trade in the product cycle. In International economic policies and their theoretical foundations (pp. 415-435). Academic Press.

Syrquin, M. (1989). Patterns of Structural Change. In Handbook of Economic Development, H. Chenery and T. N. Srinavasan, eds. Amsterdam: *Elsevier Science Publishers*.

Appendix

Unit Root Test Results:

Unit Root Test Results: Argentina (Ho: Unit Root)

Series	Augmented Dickey-Fuller (ADF)	
	Level	First Difference
GDP t-statistic Prob.	-0.876383 0.7762	-3.515941 0.0179*
HHI t-statistic Prob.	-1.112792 0.6917	-3.954017 0.0078*

Unit Root Test Results: China (Ho: Unit Root)

Series	Augmented Dickey-Fuller (ADF)	
	Level	First Difference
GDP t-statistic Prob.	-0.865513 0.7787	-4.2527207 0.0038*
HHI t-statistic Prob.	-1.809605 0.3663	-3.265174 0.0301*

Unit Root Test Results: India (Ho: Unit Root)

Series	Augmented Dickey-Fuller (ADF)	
	Level	First Difference
GDP t-statistic Prob.	0.941507 0.9941	-3.551391 0.0166*
HHI t-statistic Prob.	-1.869352 0.3395	-4.089064 0.0067*

Unit Root Test Results: Mexico (Ho: Unit Root)

Series	Augmented Dickey-Fuller (ADF)	
	Level	First Difference
GDP t-statistic Prob.	-1.886531 0.3320	-3.924684 0.0074*
HHI t-statistic Prob.	-2.010919 0.2803	-4.941614 0.0008*

Unit Root Test Results: Korea (Ho: Unit Root)

Series	Augmented Dickey-Fuller (ADF)	
	Level	First Difference
GDP t-statistic Prob.	-0.205628 0.9242	-3.882587 0.0082*
HHI t-statistic Prob.	-2.099815 0.2465	-5.898852 0.0001*

Unit Root Test Results: Turkey (Ho: Unit Root)

Series	Augmented Dickey-Fuller (ADF)	
	Level	First Difference
GDP t-statistic Prob.	0.453911 0.9807	-4.192791 0.0041*
HHI t-statistic Prob.	-1.072274 0.7042	-5.945234 0.0001*

* denotes rejection of null hypothesis at the 0.05 level.

Source: Authors' calculations are based on World Development Indicators, The World Bank &United Nations Conference on Trade and Development (UNCTAD) database.

Results of Johansen Cointegration Test

Johansen Cointegration Test: Argentina

Null Hypothesis	Eigen Value	Trace Statistic	5% Critical Value	Prob
None	0.596618	22.18169	15.49471	0.0042*
At the Most 1	0.228553	4.930264	3.841466	0.0264*
Trace test indicates two integrating equations at 0.05 level				

Johansen Cointegration Test: China

Null Hypothesis	Eigen Value	Trace Statistic	5% Critical Value	Prob
None	0.602830	18.81371	15.49471	0.0152*
At the Most 1	0.114688	2.192675	3.841466	0.1387
Trace test indicates one integrating equation at 0.05 level				

Johansen Cointegration Test: India

Null Hypothesis	Eigen Value	Trace Statistic	5% Critical Value	Prob
None	0.526115	19.28837	15.49471	0.0127*
At the Most 1	0.277318	5.846146	3.841466	0.0156*
Trace test indicates two integrating equation at 0.05 level				

Johansen Cointegration Test: Mexico

Null Hypothesis	Eigen Value	Trace Statistic	5% Critical Value	Prob
None	0.693763	30.59482	15.49471	0.0001*
At the Most 1	0.347444	8.110297	3.841466	0.0044*
Trace test indicates two integrating equation at 0.05 level				

Johansen Cointegration Test: Korea

Null Hypothesis	Eigen Value	Trace Statistic	5% Critical Value	Prob
None	0.686187	36.51009	15.49471	0.0000*
At the Most 1	0.533560	14.48990	3.841466	0.0001*
Trace test indicates two integrating equation at 0.05 level				

Johansen Cointegration Test: Turkey

Null Hypothesis	Eigen Value	Trace Statistic	5% Critical Value	Prob
None	0.690919	29.16117	15.49471	0.0003*
At the Most 1	0.302774	6.852262	3.841466	0.0089*
Trace test indicates two integrating equation at 0.05 level				

Source: Authors' calculations are based on World Development Indicators, The World Bank & United Nations Conference on Trade and Development (UNCTAD) database.

12

India and ASEAN Trade Relations

An Empirical Analysis

Kuldeep Singh & Jaskiran Kaur

Introduction

Times have passed when regional co-operations were regarded as stumbling block to multilateral trade. Nowadays these regional co-operations are considered complementary while stimulating global trade liberalisation. Improved bilateral relations among nations is a key component of any foreign policy commensuration with national interest and security. The Indian economy has established its fruitful relations with different nations of the world. The first chief architect of India's foreign policy Jawahar Lal Nehru served as foreign minister. In lieu of globalisation and increased economic interdependence among Asia, both India and ASEAN are chasing free trade agreements among their trading partners. China entered into WTO and has emerged itself as a trade powerhouse expanding the investment and in turn increasing the competitiveness in exports and foreign direct investment. India is trading with almost all the nations including free trade agreements with Thailand, Sri Lanka, Nepal and Singapore. Apart from China, South Korea and Japan, ASEAN is also trading partner of India.

India become full dialogue partner of ASEAN at 5th ASEAN summit in Bangkok in 1955. India later on joined ASEAN Regional Forum (ARF) in 1996 to strengthen the trade partnership with ASEAN both economically as well as politically. Economic reforms and Liberalisation policy of India in 1990's complemented with India's initiative of "Look East Policy" further strengthen the India-ASEAN trade partnership. In 2014 Look East policy transformed to Act East policy with the aim to enhance more economic cooperation among partner nations along with developing a strategic relationship with countries by continuously engaging the Asia Pacific region at all bilateral, regional and multilateral levels. India being the foremost strong economy of the region should play an important role in creating negotiations and commitments below the South Asian Association for Regional Cooperation (SAARC) Agreement on Trade in Services (SATIS), particularly in competitive (Kaur et al 2020).

This "Look East Policy" was later on renovated as "Act East Policy" in year 2014 with intention of further strengthening trade relations. During the 11th East ASEAN Summit (2016) India's prime minister quoted" ASEAN is central to India's Act East Policy" (Daily Pioneer news Dec, 2016). Over the time period ASEAN become an imperative trade destination for India with ASEAN as the fourth largest trade partner of India) in World.

India trade with ASEAN in trade, investment, tourism, science and technology. In November 2002, first ASEAN-India summit was hosted in Phnom Penh, Cambodia which confluxes with certain outcomes as stated below:

1. Indian leader's desired to fortify their trade relations with ASEAN on basis of bilateral visits by Indian leaders to ASEAN economies.
2. ASEAN leaders also showed their keen interest to engage with India actively in order to develop a strong and balanced kinship with all major Asian economies.
3. A vast literature reveals that India's service sector is complementary ASEAN light manufacturers thus leading to mutual gain. (Gaur 2003)

India signed Free Trade Agreements with Thailand on October 2003 where India can import 84 items from Thailand at 50 per cent import duty in India which was to be effective from April 2004. Apart from this India is also in negotiation with Singapore to form a comprehensive Economic Cooperation Agreement. Success of regional trade agreements depends on the complementary trade structure as its imperative for all the partner nations to have such type of structure instead of having same trade structure. Nations or trading partners which have similar trade structures often struggle for improving their trade share expect substantial intra industry trade. (Alam, 2015). However with free trade agreement only the member nations are benefitted as it had trade creation effect among its member nations only. Moreover geographical distance also prevents the trade more strongly in lieu free trade agreements. (Kien, 2009).

Literature Review

Sen et al (2004) in their paper tried to study the trade kinship between AEAN and India. The secondary collected from CMIE, Foreign Trade and Balance of Payments, Centre for Monitoring India was analysed for computing the future prospects related to bilateral trade between given economies. The study concluded that though the trade relations among India and ASEAN are good but to achieve its goal of 'Vision 2020' the Indian economy needs to attract more partnership from ASEAN by diversifying its growth engines and by enhanced integration among member nations.

Hong (2007) inculcated the changes in India's relation with ASEAN from viewpoint of China. The study based on ASEAN Secretariat-ASEAN FDI Database revealed that ASEAN is trading with both India as well as china where the Indian economy lost its geo political economic status comparative to previous time due to advent of trade with Chinese economy. The study further recommended that the Indian economy must come forward and need to readjust its foreign trade policies to make its economy a hub for trade.

Joseph (2009) analysed the impact of India's trade with ASEAN on plantation sector of Kerala. The results based on the simple statistical analysis stated that reduction in tariff rates will reduce the protection thus resulting in price crash due to increased imports. The study further revealed that imports apart from tariff reduction also depends on productivity differences and exchange rates. The findings from the study implies that protection along with research and innovations are central under Free Trade Agreements.

Pal et al (2009) in their work evaluated the Indian tariff schedule and its impact on ASEAN-India trade relation. The study concluded that Indian agriculture sector will be negatively affected by this especially the plantation sector including tea, spices, coffee and rubber. Moreover the competition will increase among Marine and textile due to ASEAN-India free trade agreement. The study further implied that government should redistribute the increased wealth to looser from gainer in order to ensure increased total welfare.

Chandran et al (2012) studied the impact of Free Trade Agreement among India and ASEAN for the fisheries sector. The study is based on secondary data collected from Ministry of Commerce and Industry, Government of India. The results based on the simple revealed comparative advantage indices stated that such FTA via reduction in tariff rate will lead to trade creation effects and enhanced welfare. India is one of the major fish exporters in the world but share of fish import's in total imports of India is very small due to more consumption if fishes in Indian economy.

Varma (2015) in his paper analysed the structural transformation in trade i.e. exports and imports after the formation of free trade agreement between India and ASEAN. Study based on secondary data collected from export import data bank unveiled that there is minimal change in exports but on the contrary imports have grown at a faster rate especially during the year 2000-2014. The study further implied that government must provide adequate market facilities to domestic producers along with subsidies so that the Indian economy can also compete with their counterparts in ASEAN countries who have comparatively higher production levels.

Objectives

The aim of the given study is to estimate the India's total trade with ASEAN economies from the past 50 years along with growth rate of member nations of ASEAN. The study further makes an attempt to analyse the policies related to Free Trade Agreement between the nations.

Data Source and Methodology

The study is based on secondary data collected from various sources like Import- Export data Bank, Ministry of Commerce and Industry and UN COMTRADE. The data is collected on the aggregate amount of trade with ASEAN economies from past 50 years along with aggregate data on export and import trade balance from year 2010-2011 to 2017-2018. The given data is analysed using the pie charts and graphs.

Emergence of ASEAN

On 8th August, 1967 Association of Southeast Asian Nation was established with the signing of Bangkok declaration or ASEAN declaration in Bangkok, Thailand. The founder member of ASEAN were Indonesia, Malaysia, Philippines, Singapore and Thailand also named as ASEAN 5. From time to time certain other members joined ASEAN and become its trading partner. On January 7, 1984 Brunei Darussalam joined ASEAN where Vietnam joined ASEAN on 28 July, 1995. Later on Lao People's Democratic Republic (Lao PDR) and Myanmar become the member of ASEAN on July 23, 1997, and Cambodia joined ASEAN on April 30, 1999, thus in turn forming the ten member states of ASEAN. ASEAN has performed very well both economically and socially since its formation by narrowing down the developmental gap both across and within the ASEAN members.

International Trade and ASEAN

ASEAN has increased both the volume and amount of international trade withholding its position as the 4th leading trading region in the world after European Union, USA and China. Out of world's total trade ASEAN accounts for 7.1 per cent of total trade. The overall trade of ASEAN has increased from US$1.6 trillion to US$2.3 trillion from the year 2007 to 2016 respectively. Inflows of foreign direct investment has been more than double during the past few years thus showing an upward trend in the FDI inflows from US$ 41.9 billion in year 2005 to US$ 96.7 in the year 2016 respectively thus growing at a CAGR of 11.4 percent.

The total amount of FDI arose from US$ 3.0 billion in 1984 to US$ 96.7 in 2016. Resurgent Indian economy is the World's seventh largest economy based on nominal GDP and is third largest economy of the world on basis of purchasing power parity in 2016.India ASEAN celebrated its 25 year of dialog partnership and 15 year of summit level partnership in year 2017. On 8th October, 2003 India signed agreement named Comprehensive Economic Cooperation (CECA) with ASEAN in Bali Indonesia to institutionalise a basis for future economic cooperation. It is notable here that India's trade with ASEAN has moderated from past five years thus making India the 11th largest trading partner of ASEAN in 2016. India trade with ASEAN has decreased from US$ 75 billion in 2012 to US $ 64.6 in year 2016. Data reveals that there is decline in both exports and imports where the exports has decreased from US$ 32.3 billion in 2012 to US$ 26.4 billion in 2016 respectively. Imports has also moderated from US$ 42.7 billion in 2012 to US$ 38.2 billion in 2016.

ASEAN is the major hot spot of economic growth nowadays thus extending more investment and business opportunities. Time to time various modifications has been done to promote the investment opportunities where now ASEAN is implementing AIA (ASEAN Investment Area) and AIG (ASEAN Investment Guarantee) scheme to improve the India- ASEAN investment environment.

ASEAN Economy over past 50 Years:

There has been tremendous growth in ASEAN economy during past five years after the membership of ASEAN-10 where the total GDP has increased to US $ 2.55 trillion in 2016. As per the data, ASEAN as a single economy is the sixth largest economy in the world in terms of combined GDP and is the third largest in the Asia. Due to rapid economic growth the standard of living of people has improved as nominal GDP per capita is around US $4,021 in ASEAN-10 during 2016 as compared to ASEAN-5 where it was around US $ 122 in 1967.

Table 12.1: ASEAN over past 50 years

Indicators	1967	1984	1995	1997	1999	2005	2010	2016
GDP at current prices (US$)	0.02	0.22	0.65	0.72	0.58	0.94	1.93	2.55
GDP Growth rate (%)	4.3	4.4	8.1	4.5	3.4	5.8	7.5	4.8
% Share of ASEAN in world GDP (% based on US$ at PPP)	3.3	3.6	5.1	5.3	4.8	5.2	5.6	6.2
GDP per capita (US$ at current price)	122	765	1556	1462	1135	1701	3268	4021

Source: ASEAN Secretariat.

Findings from the table 12.1 depicts that growth rate has increased from 4.3 to 4.4 at the time when Brunei become the sixth member nation of ASEAN. Later on Vietnam joined the ASEAN as its seventh member on 28 July, 1995 when the growth rate was 8.1 which was almost doubled compared to 1984. Laos and Myanmar joined ASEAN on 23 July, 1997 whereas Cambodia become the member of ASEAN on 30 April, 1999. Leaders from eighteen countries held the meeting annually and participated in East Asia Summit where the first summit related to same was held on 14 December, 2005 in Kuala Lumpur. Though there was upward shift in the growth rate from 3.4 to 5.8 percent. On 11 May 2010, ASEAN Defense Industry Collaboration was proposed at fourth ASEAN Defense Ministers' meeting in Hanoi. GDP per capita has increased from year 1967 to 2016 with a moderation in year 1999.

ASEAN and International Trade

Looking at International trade, ASEAN total trade has increased to US$ 2.3 trillion in 2016 from US$ 1.6 trillion in 2007. Though it is notable here that there was decrease in international trade during 2009 due to global financial crisis thus following the same trend in 2015 with moderating global trade. Overall trade balance has moderated overtime but recorded a surplus in account.

Table 12.2: Evolution of ASEAN International trade

Indicators	1967	1984	1995	1997	1999	2005	2010	2016
% Share of ASEAN in the world exports	2.0	3.9	5.8	6.3	6.2	6.2	6.9	7.2
% Share of ASEAN in world imports	2.3	3.6	6.1	6.4	5.0	5.3	6.2	6.6
Trade to GDP ratio (%)	43.1	69.3	96.7	100.4	112.5	130.8	104.3	87

Source: ASEAN Secretariat.

The data collected from UN com trade for the period 2010-11 to 2017-18 shows that India trade with ASEAN nations. As it is evident from the table 12.1 the growth rate of exports has decreased during the year 2011-12 and showed a little improvement during the next period but again declined in year 2014-15 and 2015-16 respectively. For the last two years the trade relations have again shown an improvement whereas the imports have increased for the first three given periods and declined during the year 2013-14 and 2015-16.

Data Interpretations and Results

As already discussed above the imports are more and exports are less thus showing an decline in overall trade balance which clearly states that the Indian economy need to explore itself more and attract more trade from ASEAN economies on export side also because ASEAN is also trading with other nations like South Korea and China under Free Trade Agreement which further poses much more challenges for Indian economy.

Initially there were only five members among ASEAN named Indonesia, Malaysia, Philippines, Singapore, and Thailand. Remaining 5 members joined the ASEAN later on. As per the data provided by IMF, 2017 the Singapore is the economy among ASEAN with higher PCY with PPP (Purchasing power parity)amounting to US$ 90724

Table 12.3: India's trade with ASEAN from past 8 years

India's trade with ASEAN	2010-11	2011-12	2012-13	2013-14	2014-15	2015-16	2016-17	2017-18
Export (Bn. USD)	25.63	36.74	33.01	33.13	31.81	25.15	30.96	34.2
% Growth	41.48	43.38	-10.17	0.38	-3.99	-20.8	23.09	10.46
Import (Bn. USD)	30.61	42.16	42.87	41.28	44.71	39.91	40.61	47.13
% Growth	18.64	37.74	1.68	-3.71	8.33	-10.9	0.88	16.04
Total (Bn. USD)	56.24	78.9	75.87	74.41	76.53	65.06	71.57	81.33
Trade Balance (Bn. USD)	-4.98	-5.41	-9.86	-8.14	-12.9	-14.75	-9.65	-12.93

Source: GoI, Ministry of Commerce and Industry, Department of Commerce.

Figure 12.1: India's total trade with ASEAN from past 8 years

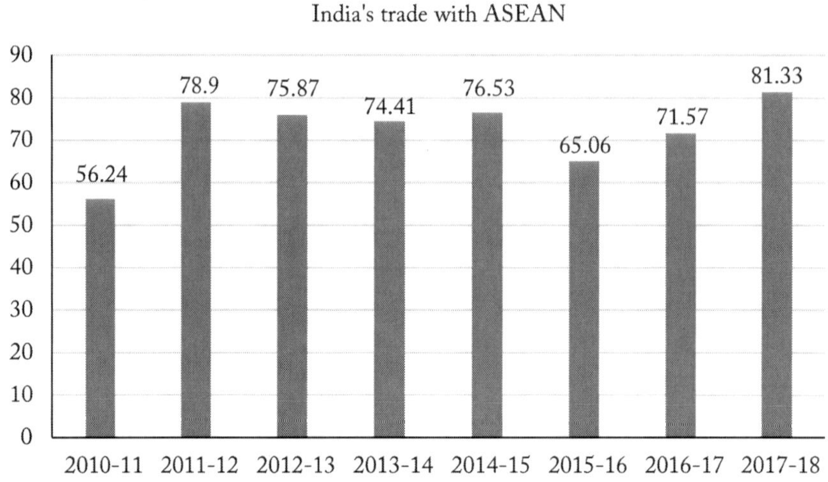

Source: Authors own calculations.

where the highest GDP is in Indonesia amounting to US$ 3,257,123 with Indonesia population of 26, 6794,980 making Indonesia the fourth highest populous country of the world. Cambodia has the low per capita GDP amounting to US$4022. Though it is notable here that during year 1997-98 the growth trade of the ASEAN economy was declining which also resulted in financial crisis.

Conclusion

India's population is almost twice to that of ASEAN population as a whole of over one billion persons. Apart from that the most populous nation of ASEAN i.e. Indonesia is having 1/5th of India's total population but higher per capita income of ASEAN which is 2.5 times more than the Indian economy.

India has benefit to trade with ASEAN in terms of transport cost. So, India should examine increasing sea transport connections to push trade, tourism and other economic activities (Kaur, 2010). Indian economy is an agrarian economy where the majority of people are still dependent on agriculture for occupation. India has increased its market access for semi processed and processed agricultural products which in turn decreases the demand of local agricultural products leading to decreased price of local crops and negatively affecting Indian agriculture. The MSME's are also negatively affected with these Free Trade Agreements as MNC's deep their integration across the regions. There are no market access benefits for Indian producers as the average percentage tariff drop in Malaysia, Indonesia and Thailand is lower than in India. India will also face increased difficulties in trading because ASEAN has trade relations with China and South Korea also. Recommended at the Commemorative Summit of 2012 about the ASEAN India Centre (AIC), the same has been implemented in 2013 to promote strategic partnership between India and ASEAN to strengthen the networking activities between the organisations and to establish a better think tank for policy research and advocacy. So India need to explore its areas more and the complementarity between the given two economies namely ASEAN and India via Free Trade Agreement can only be realised when the ideological and informational bunches are further lifted.

References

Alam, M. I. (2015). Indo-Asian Trade relation: An Analysis. *Journal of International Economics (0976-0792)*, *6*(1).

Chandran, B. S., & Sudarsan, P. K. (2012). India-ASEAN Free Trade Agreement: Implications for Fisheries. *Economic and Political Weekly*, 65-70.

Gaur, S. (2003). Framework agreement on comprehensive economic co-operation between India and ASEAN: First step towards economic integration. *ASEAN Economic Bulletin*, *20*(3), 283-291.

Hong, Z. (2007). India and China: Rivals or Partners in South East Asia?. *Contemporary South East Asia*, 29 (1), 121-142.

Kaur, S., Khorana, S., & Kaur, M. (2020). Is There Any Potential in Service Trade of South Asia?. *Foreign Trade Review*, *55*(3), 402-417.

Kaur, S. (2010). Complementarities in Production and Trade between ASEAN Countries and India. *Journal of Global Economy*, *6*(5), 363-386.

Joseph, K. (2009). ASEAN – India pact and plantation: Realities of Myth. *Economic and Political Weekly*, 44(44).

Kien, N.T. (2009). An empirical Application with implication for the ASEAN Free trade area. *ASEAN Economic Bulletin,* 26 (3), 266-77.

Pal, P. and M. Dasgupta (2009). The ASEAN- India free trade agreement: An assessment. *Economic and Political Weekly,* 44(38), 11-15.

Sen, R. and M.G. Asher (2004). ASEAN- India Economic relations: current status and future prospectus. *Economic and Political Weekly,* 1-36.

Varma, A. (2015). ASEAN- India free trade agreement: an assessment of merchandise exports and imports.1-20.

PART IV

Building Economic Relations in India-East Asia

13

Knowledge Economy, Institutions and Public Policy

The Case of East Asia and South Asian Economies

Baldev Singh Shergill

Introduction

Since second half of the twentieth century, supranational organisations played a notable role to develop economic ties between developing economies and developed ones for accelerating the development process in modern ways. These economic ties started through trade regimes, foreign aids, monetary supports, collaborations, cooperation and competition between the economies. Likewise, developing economies have been expanding their economic base with the support of developed economies to initiate the process of rejuvenation of socioeconomic processes after Second World War and decolonisation. And this free as well as subordinate political and economic environment provided space for new ties between the economies across the globe. This was the time when there were enormous divergences in terms of economic levels across the economies. To attain the position on the world map, the poor economies perpetuated economic, social, political and cultural processes by developing institutional set up to cater the needs of their population through centralised planning systems and inter-sectoral institutional developments. By this developing economies altered their production process and production activities and developed economies also influenced their production activities through trade of commodities, manufacturing goods, services and technology.

While understanding the economic positions of the countries, it was India and China, where the share of manufacturing trade share was higher than the other countries in the world during last decades of the 19th century and early years of 20th century. During the period of colonialism, the share of these countries declined sharply as compared to other countries where the industrial revolution took place. After the Second World War and decolonisation era, the developing world developed itself through some macro-policy mix but they were behind the developed economies except few Asian countries tried to catch up. Few economies from Asia successfully contested with the developed world. Japan did it in the first half of the last century. The "gang of four"- Hong Kong, Republic of Korea, Singapore and Taiwan did it in the second half of the last century. Three of what are called sometimes the next-tier Asian New Industrialised Countries- Indonesia, Malaysia and Thailand- also make it (Dahlman, 2007). During the 1980s onwards, the macroeconomic performance in the case of GDP growth rates, the Asian countries took a lead with high growth rates. The issue is to scrutinise the modern world economic order started with the sole agenda of 'how to increase the growth rate of the economies'. And with the path which adopted by developed economies and dictated by mainstream development thinking, developing economies have been facing serious socioeconomic problems: low income, unemployment, high inflation, and high inequalities in health, education and even social opportunity. In this case, economists who criticised macroeconomic policy with a neo-classical framework advocated the new perspective of development which is commonly known as national innovation systems.

The concept of knowledge economy is based on the view that knowledge and information are at the centre of economic growth and development (Kurtic and Donlagic, 2012). Fagerberg (2006). Similarly, Blomstrom et al. (2002) found two important reasons why successful modern economies are often referred to as 'Knowledge Economy'. One, economies may experience positive long run growth instead of the neo-classical steady growth. Second, competitiveness is based on both Human capital and institutional, organisation capacity.

We have witnessed global technological transformations which took place at the global level. Thus in recent times the development process moved to knowledge based economies which heralded to show the path of the development process to the developing world. Over the period of time after mid of twentieth century, some developing countries emerged as industrial and knowledge based economies and entered in the categories of middle income countries. In this case policies have focused on rent seeking rather than emphasis on consensus and an egalitarian distribution of the benefits and profits. "Developing countries identified by Western countries as embodiments of their endevours towards shifting themselves from low income countries to high income countries" (Ahmed and Krishnaswamy, 2013).

Across the world, it is not witnessing a generalised convergence of socio-economic process, of pattern of growth or of levels of wellbeing with heterogeneity and asymmetry due to different levels of development from factor driven stage of development to knowledge driven stage of development. There has been always a division between industrial societies called *centres* and agrarian societies called *peripheries.* Arocena and Sutz (2002) argued in a different way by calling learning divide between centres and peripheral economies that are growing in the 19th century as the fundamental studies of Paul Bairoch show the gap across the productive capabilities of the centres as well as the peripheries.

The Context

It is evident that the transitional shift from resource based competition to innovation based competitiveness; a new challenge arises to develop for the low income group economies. By developing a viewpoint from the above discussion, it is important to understand the development process of East Asian and South Asian economies in recent times in the context of the knowledge economy perspective. However, it is important to continue to raise questions about the influence of knowledge economy on public policies and processes. The inspiration and task of this work is to understand the direction of the transition to knowledge based economy of the South-East- Asian economies over last two decades of 20th century and one and half decade of 21st century. Second, to examine macroeconomic indicators which contribute to economic development of the countries? And third, it examines the distribution of the fruits of economic development in the context of inclusive growth. All selected economies have been in transforming their economies belong to low medium income group except Singapore having high income group status. Before analysis of macroeconomic indicators and knowledge economy, it attempts to analyse the relative position of selected economies in the context of global competitive index and technology index in recent times.

While analysing the position of South Asia and East Asian economies, the data revealed that Singapore is ranked the seventh most competitive economy and second is the most technologically developed country in the world and Pakistan and Bangladesh scored at the lower end from sample economies as well as with respect to 140 countries. And Thailand, Vietnam, India and Philippines are in the middle of their ranks relative to the others. The simple proposition can be worked out that we have a mixture of economies in South Asia and East Asian economies which are otherwise an interesting case for analysis the status of these economies in the background of knowledge economy perspective.

In order to comprehend these objectives, this paper is divided into six sections including the introduction and the context section which examines the global competitiveness index and technology index that vindicates the ground for analysis. Section two briefs the research methodology. Section third deals with theoretical as well as empirical literature to comprehend the relationship between knowledge economy and economic growth issue. Section fourth examines the broad macroeconomic indicators of East Asian and South Asian economies in a comparative mode. Section fifth examines the knowledge economy indicators. Section sixth deals with broad conclusions and public policy suggestions.

Table 13.1: Global Competitiveness Index and Technology Index of the Sample Economies

C.C.	Income Group	Global competitiveness index (Rank from 140 countries)			Technology index		
South Asian Economies		Rank	Rank	Score	Rank	Rank	Score
BGD	LM	114	9	23.72	107	8	3.76
IND	LM	60	4	35.47	55	5	4.31
PAK	LM	113	8	23.80	126	9	3.45
LKA	LM	90	7	29.85	68	7	4.21
East Asian Economies							
IDN	LM	87	6	30.10	37	3	4.52
MYS							
PHL	LM	73	5	32.48	47	4	4.39
SGP	HI	7	1	58.69	2	1	5.68
THA	UM	51	3	37.57	32	2	4.64
VNM	LM	47	2	38.44	56	6	4.30

Source: Global Competitiveness Report and World Economic Forum.

Research Methodology and data regarding macroeconomic and knowledge economy indicator

This paper is based on secondary data sources to examine the structural changes, knowledge economy of East Asia and south Asian economies and the idea of inclusiveness during the period 1980-2014. For the analysis, we used standard methodology developed by the World Bank famously known as KAM Methodology for ten economies. Except this, we tried to analysis the indicators on technological ranking of the countries and global competitiveness ranking which illustrate the position of selected economies in a comparative mode. Four pillars of knowledge economy were taken into consideration: education attainment pillar, innovation pillar, information pillar and regulatory environment pillar. Knowledge Economy Index was calculated of selected economies at five points of time: 1980, 1990, 2000, 2010 and 2014 to analyse the changing position of the respective economy which reflect the policies adopted by the concerned economy. However, some macroeconomic indicators and indices were used to analyse the macroeconomic picture of inclusiveness among sample economies. Among the South Asian economies, Bangladesh, India, Pakistan and Sri Lanka were preferred and as of the East Asian economies, Indonesia, Malaysia, Philippines, Singapore, Thailand and Vietnam were chosen for analysis. The selection of the economies from particular region is based on the basis of relative percentage share of GDP of each economy.

Theoretical Developments and Empirical Literature

The notion and nature of competition among economies, industries, firms, and regions has been changing from mercantilist era to neo-liberal transnational financial world economic order which is commonly known as techno-globalism era. Porter differentiate four stages in the competition into nations i.e. factor driven competition, investment driven competition, innovation-led competition and wealth-driven competition. So "Knowledge based economy concept is linked to innovation led competition and also the role of application of knowledge to identify and pursue chances for innovation that are likely to improve competitive advantage" (Sum and Jessop, 2013). In this way, Complexity and multifaceted is present into Knowledge economy which has continues to attract the attention of researchers (Vinnychuk et al 2014, Skrashchuk and Vinnychuk, 2014). To begin with, Lundvall (1994) established the term the new economy at a very centre of the OECD-discourse shifting from one techno-economic paradigm to another techno-economic paradigm which challenged old macroeconomic understanding regarding long term growth termed as the end of history applied to macroeconomics. Definitions and leading policy discourses of knowledge economy are linked to different economic imaginaries since 1996 with OECD document titled 'The knowledge-based economy'. According to Sum and Jessop (2013), knowledge economy is directly linked with information, learning and creative economy and information society. Policy experts, politicians and business corporate of both the developing as well as developed economies have a challenge for transition to an innovation-driven economy and knowledge economy by adopting different policy frameworks even they have some commitments with other partner countries and with the other world. In this context, these organisations recommend policies of 'Knowledge for Development' as route to economic progress in developing economies.

Evidently, knowledge has always been a part of discourse regarding trade competitiveness, higher productivity enhancement and growth effects. Contrary to this, Fagerberg (1994) argued that theoretical work tended to ignore the role of knowledge in development for a long time. However, the idea that knowledge plays an important role in the economy is not new. "Economic development concept is knowledge based but the importance of knowledge to economic processes has basically changed in the last few years" (Arvanitidis and Petrokos, 2011).

Empirical literature on knowledge economy which draws insinuation from theoretical foundations around knowledge economy perspectives and policy agenda for the development of economies has been increasing during the recent period. The present part of the section attempts to review few studies on knowledge economy perspective.

Sheehan (1999) analysed "the importance of knowledge in modern economies. China faces an daunting task in moving through the transition from plan to market while the global economy grapples with the rise of the knowledge economy."

Piech (2002) focused on the knowledge economy of Central and East European Countries like Poland by analysing that still lagging are the CEE countries as compared to all the OECD economies are moving towards the knowledge- based economy while European Union as a whole tries to catch up. The author argued that Poland as well as other Central and East European countries should first solve old problems with first transition: from socialism to market economy, however in the same time preparing for the next one from market economy to the knowledge-based one.

Shapira et al. (2006) analysed levels of knowledge content through a survey of over 1800 Malaysian firms in 18 manufacturing and service industries. They found positive associations between technological innovations and at least one knowledge content except four industries and study also confirmed that knowledge based innovation is modest in the economy.

Karagiannis (2007) analysed the effects of knowledge based economy on the growth process of European Union. Author revealed that "the R&D investments originating from abroad robustly enhance growth performance. And knowledge-based policies are not only dependent on increasing R&D spending and tertiary education level, but are more a matter of the existing framework, conditions and the flanking policies. Specific group estimations indicated that only high income countries are able to benefit from foreign R&D spillovers while in relatively poorer member-states."

A fresh perspective in the context of knowledge economy explored by Kaur and Singh (2015) which raised some important questions on the role of knowledge in the developing countries. By analyzing the relationship between knowledge economy index and economic growth of forty developing economies, the research study stated that knowledge accumulation leads to the enhancement of economic growth but after that points its impact on economic growth begins to decline. It provided grounds for breaking the common understanding that economies always grow at an increasing rate of growth in the providing policy framework. Shergill (2015) focused on position of south Asian economies in the context of knowledge economy and inclusive growth. The author found that the position of India has been found better than other south Asian economies which it has very low value of knowledge economy index during the study period.

Empirical Evidence

The empirical part is divided into three main parts: first, deals with the macroeconomic indicators which describes the position of sample countries, second, deals with knowledge economy indicators which show the position of South Asian and East Asian economies and third focuses on some important distributional indicators which deals with the socioeconomic headway of the economies in question.

Part First-Analysing Macroeconomic Indicators

Protagonists of knowledge economy or learning economy proposed the thesis of knowledge economy by arguing that economies would seek their development process on the basis of knowledge economy indicators includes only macroeconomic environment by ignoring macroeconomic policy framework. It can be argued that macroeconomic stability is an important yardstick to enhance economic development. When we look at macroeconomic stability, macroeconomic indicators have an importance for any economy whether it is developing or developed. For making a point, it is necessary to understand macro- economy of the South Asian and East Asian economies.

Table 13.2: Gross Domestic Product Growth (Annual %)

CN	CC	1960-1970	1970-1980	1980-90	1990-2000	2000-10	2010-2014
Europe & Central Asia (all income levels)	ECS	5.33	3.70	2.37	1.89	1.97	1.29
Latin America & Caribbean (all income levels)	LCN	5.71	6.03	1.99	3.05	3.21	3.45
North America	NAC	4.25	3.07	3.00	3.25	1.91	2.24
Middle East & North Africa (developing only)	MNA	7.86	5.94	2.82	4.33	4.53	1.66
East Asia & Pacific (all income levels)	EAS	7.99	4.62	5.11	3.59	4.15	4.63
South Asia	SAS	4.28	3.30	5.57	5.32	6.73	6.85
Sub-Saharan Africa (all income levels)	SSF	4.63	4.05	1.72	2.02	5.10	4.42
World	WLD	5.29	3.84	3.06	2.83	2.75	2.80

Source: World Development Indicators, Various Issues.

During the period of 1960-1970, GDP annual growth rate of East Asia and Pacific recorded highest followed by Middle East and North America, Latin America and Europe & Central Asia which was above the world average. The rest group of economies was behind the world average. During the next ten years, 1970-1980, all the groups except Latin America and Caribbean economies recorded low growth rate as compared to previous period. During 1980-90, East Asia & Pacific and South Asia recorded highest growth rates and other groups were on the fall sharply. During 1990-2000, some groups picked up marginally and others noted lower than the previous periods. In the two phases, 2000-10 and 2010-14, South Asia & Pacific and South Asia noted highest GDP growth rates as compared to other groups. Two broad findings can be primed from the above analysis. First, there has been no consistent pattern of GDP growth rates among all the groups across the globe which resulted into the structural transformation across all the developing and developed economies. Second, East Asia & Pacific recorded GDP growth rate above the world average since 1960 and South Asia region has noted this trend since 1980 onwards.

Among the East Asian economies in 1960, the share of Indonesian economy was highest followed by Philippines, Malaysia and Singapore. This trend remained the same till 1990. From 2000 onwards, the share of Indonesian economy was highest followed by Thailand, Malaysia, Singapore and Philippines. Two broad finding are: Indonesian economies remained on the top throughout the period of analysis and Thailand and Singapore emerged among the East Asian economies from 1980 onwards.

In the case of South Asian economies, the percentage share of GDP of the total GDP of South Asia, India had the highest share with 77.10 per cent in 1960 which increased to 82.34 per cent in 2014 followed by 7.80 per cent in 2014 with marginal increase overtime. Contrary, the share of Bangladesh, Sri Lanka and other economies of the South Asia declined during the whole period. Taking the case of East Asian economies, Indonesian economy had on first position with share of

Table 13.3: Share of GDP between the East Asian Economies

	1960	R	1970	R	1980	R	1990	R	2000	R	2010	R	2014	R
Indonesia	45.41	1	33.22	1	33.77	1	34.45	1	31.72	1	32.20	1	33.20	1
Vietnam	0.00	6	0.00	6	0.00	6	0.00	6	0.00	6	0.14	6	0.15	6
Malaysia	14.41	3	13.22	4	13.39	4	13.16	4	15.92	3	15.23	3	15.52	3
Philippines	32.73	2	25.90	2	21.94	2	14.26	3	11.51	5	11.18	5	11.62	5
Singapore	7.45	4	8.82	5	10.01	5	11.58	5	14.03	4	15.04	4	14.66	4
Thailand	0.00	5	18.85	3	17.44	3	20.41	2	19.22	2	17.90	2	16.33	2

Source: World Development Indicators.

Table 13.4: Share of GDP within the South Asian Economies

C.C.	1960	1970	1980	1990	2000	2010	2014
BGD	10.85	10.57	8.52	7.41	6.99	6.12	6.12
IND	77.10	75.08	75.10	75.67	77.68	81.66	82.34
PAK	7.50	9.93	11.67	12.60	11.06	8.50	7.80
LKA	2.50	2.58	2.95	2.61	2.59	2.18	2.27
Others	2.05	1.84	1.75	1.71	1.68	1.53	1.48

Source: World Development Indicators.

45.41 per cent in 1960 which declined to 33.20 per cent but remained on the same position. Malaysia, Philippines, Singapore and Thailand had increased their shares.

As we tried to examine the stage of economic development by economic activities as percentage share of GDP, the table clearly indicates the structural changes in all South Asian economies. During 1960, agricultural economic activities contributed more than fifty percent share in GDP and by approaching to 2014, over a period of more than half century more than fifty percent share contributed by the service sector except Bhutan in South Asian region of the world. The data reveals the fact that all the economies shifted their economic activities from agriculture to manufacturing and service sector.

Composition of Gross Domestic Product

The share of economic activities in GDP has been changing across all the south Asian countries since 1960. Two broad findings can be traced from the data: One, the share of agriculture declined sharply over the period of time, share of service sector increased sharply as compared to industrial sector and after 2000, the share of service sector touched to more than fifty percent of Bangladesh, India, Pakistan and Sri Lanka except Bhutan and Nepal in South Asian economies.

Table 13.5: Changing Pattern of Economic Activities among South Asian Economies (% share of GDP)

Country Code		BGD	BTN	IND	NPL	PAK	LKA	SAS
Series Name								
1960	Agriculture	57.47	NA	42.56	NA	46.22	31.66	43.68
	Industry	6.97	NA	19.30	NA	15.60	20.40	18.12
	Services	35.55	NA	38.14	NA	38.18	47.95	**38.68**
1970	Agriculture	54.56	NA	41.95	67.29	36.83	28.30	42.09
	Industry	8.73	NA	20.48	11.53	22.32	23.79	19.93
	Services	**36.71**	**NA**	**37.57**	**21.18**	**40.85**	**47.91**	**37.98**
1980	Agriculture	31.55	43.64	35.39	61.77	29.52	27.55	34.54
	Industry	20.63	11.75	24.29	11.92	24.92	29.64	24.14
	Services	**47.81**	**44.62**	**40.32**	**26.31**	**45.56**	**42.81**	**41.32**
1990	Agriculture	32.75	35.28	29.02	51.63	25.98	26.32	29.05
	Industry	20.70	24.85	26.49	16.24	25.19	25.97	25.89
	Services	46.55	39.87	44.48	32.13	48.83	**47.71**	**45.06**
2000	Agriculture	23.77	27.39	23.02	40.82	25.93	19.90	23.44
	Industry	23.31	35.99	26.00	22.13	23.33	27.28	25.53
	Services	**52.91**	**36.62**	**50.98**	**37.05**	**50.74**	**52.82**	**51.03**
2010	Agriculture	17.81	17.49	18.21	36.53	24.29	12.81	18.89
	Industry	26.14	44.55	27.16	15.63	20.58	29.43	26.32
	Services	**56.05**	**37.96**	**54.64**	**47.84**	**55.13**	**57.76**	**54.79**
2014	Agriculture	15.89	17.12	16.96	34.35	25.12	9.86	17.77
	Industry	27.87	42.26	30.05	15.23	21.28	33.81	28.89
	Services	56.24	40.63	52.99	50.43	53.59	56.33	53.34

Source: World Development Indicators.

Structure of Demand in South Asia and East Asian Economies

Some key indicators are very useful to examine macroeconomic position and strength of the economies. Gross fixed capital formation and General government final consumption expenditure are important indicator which fundamentally have the capacity to change the structure of demand in the economy which ultimately lead to socio economic transformation of the economy. In the case of our analysis, the highest share of gross fixed capital formation share in GDP in 1980 was of Singapore and Sri Lanka and in 2013, Indonesia was on the top and Pakistan was on the lowest end in East Asia and South Asian region respectively. Taking the case of general government final consumption expenditure, it was highest share with 12.80 per cent share by Vietnam and lowest share with 4 per cent by Bangladesh in 1980 as well as in 2013. The data shows somehow declining trends as well as increasing trends on capital formation and government expenditure by the selected economies which can be reasoned as the different policy approaches executed by the economies overtime.

Gross domestic saving and gross saving of the economies are also vital indicators which plays a role into structural changes in the economies. The share of gross domestic savings and gross saving has increased intensely during the study period which shows the dynamic changes regarding production, employment and demand among the economies.

Part Two- Knowledge Economy Indicators

According to Lundvall and Johnson (1994) in the context of knowledge based economies or learning economies which results not only in the production and introduction of new knowledge but also learning by doing and learning by using by generating technological capabilities and absorptive capacity among the developing economies.

As we divide economies between developed and developing ones, the divide between those two types of the societies- the emergent learning societies and the rest can be partially gauged by means of different

Table 13.6: Changing Pattern of Capital Formation and Consumption Expenditure

	Gross fixed capital formation (% of GDP)					General government final consumption expenditure (% of GDP)				
C.C	1980	1990	2000	2010	2013	1980	1990	2000	2010	2013
BGD	14.44	16.46	23.81	26.25	28.39	6.14	4.05	4.97	5.08	5.12
IND	17.92	23.82	22.74	30.92	29.69	10.14	11.86	12.56	11.44	11.26
PAK	17.63	17.30	15.88	14.20	12.97	10.04	15.14	8.64	10.32	10.96
LKA	31.33	21.88	28.04	25.91	29.24	8.55	9.76	10.51	15.57	13.11
IDN	21.57	28.34	19.85	31.00	32.12	10.52	8.84	6.53	9.01	9.50
PHL	27.22	23.11	22.10	20.52	20.45	9.07	10.10	11.42	9.72	11.10
SGP	39.53	31.71	32.04	26.13	26.44	9.65	9.51	10.73	10.19	10.11
THA	27.77	40.38	21.97	24.73	26.73	12.29	9.40	11.33	12.96	13.81
VNM	18.22	21.28	25.62	32.64	23.82	12.8	12.34	5.95	5.99	6.16
WLD	25.21	23.98	23.16	21.54	21.80	16.36	16.40	16.13	18.02	17.59
HIC	25.37	24.20	23.00	19.87	20.12	17.07	17.04	16.59	18.93	18.33
MIC	24.47	23.03	24.01	29.79	30.17	12.86	13.35	13.98	13.56	13.97
LIC	16.90	17.50	18.45	23.48	24.29	14.10	13.90	12.84	12.81	12.69
EAP	28.20	26.99	30.85	40.35	41.26	14.18	13.17	14.05	12.41	13.00

Source: World Development Indicators.

Table 13.7: Changing Pattern of Gross Domestic Savings and Gross Savings

	Gross domestic savings (% of GDP)					Gross savings (% of GDP)				
C.C	1980	1990	2000	2010	2013	1980	1990	2000	2010	2013
BGD	2.05	9.31	19.18	20.49	21.17	5.44	16.49	26.95	38.77	38.84
IND	14.99	23.53	23.22	32.16	29.56	16.98	23.11	25.00	34.16	31.81
PAK	6.87	11.10	15.98	9.97	7.86	25.58	22.40	20.35	21.55	21.03
LKA	11.19	14.32	17.43	19.27	20.05	19.06	20.32	21.53	25.41	25.83
IDN	38.04	32.26	32.76	34.78	33.26	28.69	28.07	24.95	32.65	30.72
PHL	24.19	18.38	16.38	18.73	15.59	24.21	18.32	40.55	60.78	43.25
SGP	38.11	45.69	47.19	54.29	52.21	32.10	43.60	45.43	51.53	46.89
THA	22.89	33.84	31.47	33.37	32.53	22.72	32.83	30.38	30.96	28.52
VNM	3.13	3.33	24.13	27.48	28.83	21.87	24.83	27.95	30.47	30.16
WLD	25.01	24.74	24.18	22.34	22.29	23.99	23.64	23.92	22.22	22.59
HIC	24.94	24.40	23.75	20.55	20.72	24.46	22.99	23.54	20.13	20.95
MIC	25.63	26.67	26.49	31.41	30.32	25.63	26.88	25.91	32.63	30.91
LIC	4.53	5.88	8.65	8.09	8.35	9.56	11.29	13.46	15.85	14.60
EAP	33.50	35.70	35.44	45.88	45.46		36.00	34.74	47.03	45.33

Source: World Development Indicators.

indicators (Arocena and Sutz, 2002). In this section, we explored the position and changing pattern of South Asian and East Asian economics in a comparative mode with respect to some indicators of knowledge economy. After the descriptive analysis of knowledge economy indicators, we developed a composite index of knowledge economy of each economy at different points of time.

Education Attainment among South Asia, East Asia and the World

In modern economic development, education contributes a major role to accelerate the process of economic development and societal progress. From the viewpoint of modern growth theorists investment in humans in the case of education accelerate the level of earnings by shifting from basic economic activities to skill based economic activities.

The divide (discussed in induction part) between those two types of societies- the emergent "learning societies" and the rest- can be partly gauged by means of different indicators. For example, the simultaneous consideration of tertiary enrollment and the level of investment in R&D offers a good "proxy" to the notion "existing capabilities and opportunities for using them creatively" (Arocena and Sutz, 2002). And developing economies have the potential to grow and for convergence is conditional on the economy's level of human capital (Blomstrom, Kokko and Sjoholm, 2002).

To understand the position of South Asian and East Asian economies in the case of education attainments indicators: adult literacy rate, primary, secondary and tertiary enrollment rate of the selected countries between 1980 and 2014.

Taking adult literacy rate in consideration first, data has shown groundbreaking changes. In the case of East Asian economies, they all touched to more than ninety percent and Thailand secured highest position among East Asian as well as South Asian economies. Correspondingly, South Asian economies performed well and Sri Lanka secured top position with 91.18 per cent and Pakistan secures lowest position with 56.76 percent. Overall adult literacy rate of East Asian economies remained 94.92 per cent which is greater than adult literacy rate of south Asian economies and world average i.e. 85.20 percent. In the case of primary enrollment rate, South Asian economies got behind with 111.49 per cent as compared to East Asian economies with 116. 52 per cent and both the regions have higher percentage than the world average i.e. 107.99 percent. In case of secondary enrollment rate, the economies of both the regions have crossed more than fifty per cent and improved their positions overtime. Similarly, tertiary education share has been improved among all the economies overtime. The data reveals the fact that all the economics have been focusing on education attainment which is crucial pillar of knowledge economy and the South Asian economies have been lagging behind in comparison with the East Asian economies during the period of study.

Innovation performance in South Asia and East Asian Economies

R&D expenditure is considered the most important indicators of knowledge economy which determine the position of economies from resource- based stage of development to knowledge based stage of development where knowledge and knowledge base activities become the prime mover of the strength of the economy. In this part, the comparative analysis is based on the percentage share of GDP spent on R&D to increase productivity and competitiveness. The limitation of the analysis in this context is unavailability and missing data in the world development indicators report which is the sole source of data of some economies related to innovation indicators. Investment in knowledge (defined by the OECD as spending on education, software and R&D) now exceeds 10 per cent of GDP for the OECD countries as a whole (OECD, 1999).

In the case of R and D expenditure, all South Asian economies spent less than 1 per cent of their GDP and all the East Asian economies spent more than 1 per cent of their GDP over time from 1980 to recent times.

Table 13.8: Education Attainment among South Asia, East Asia and the World

	Literacy Rate, Adult Total					School Enrollment, Primary (% Gross)				
C. C.	1980	1990	2000	2010	2013	1980	1990	2000	2010	2013
BGD	29.23	35.32	47.49	59.72	59.72	69.79	80.56	95.79	104.46	114.20
IND	40.76	48.22	61.01	69.30	69.30	82.17	92.78	96.28	113.47	114.06
PAK	25.73	35.61	45.32	55.38	56.76	47.89	55.97	70.43	94.81	92.12
LKA	86.78	88.73	90.68	91.18	92.32	98.96	110.00	106.76	99.05	98.30
SAS	34.94	46.48	58.02	66.73	67.76	77.34	87.22	91.93	110.38	111.49
IDN	67.31	81.52	87.32	92.81	92.81	111.53	116.27	110.26	109.92	108.53
MYS	69.52	82.92	88.69	93.12	94.56	94.16	92.69	98.08	102.54	105.67
PHL	83.32	93.57	92.60	93.08	94.83	108.35	110.04	109.60	107.78	106.96
SGP	82.91	89.10	92.55	95.86	96.54					
THA	87.98	90.67	92.65	96.43	96.53	95.97	98.82	97.67	94.92	95.83
VNM			90.16			108.76	103.42	107.16	104.91	104.92
EAS		82.05	91.61	94.92	94.92	110.49	118.51	104.55	117.59	116.52
LIC		47.02	53.76	57.50		69.39	62.54	76.06	103.57	104.28
MIC		69.69	78.63	83.44		99.00	103.76	100.77	110.23	109.74
HIC			98.29	98.67		101.88	102.68	102.00	102.55	102.57
WLD		75.83	81.91	85.20		97.38	99.92	98.37	108.26	107.99

Source: World Development Indicators.

Table 13.9: Education Attainment among South Asia, East Asia and the World

	School Enrollment, Secondary (% gross)					School Enrollment, Tertiary (% gross)				
C. C.	1980	1990	2000	2010	2013	1980	1990	2000	2010	2013
BGD	18.63	20.24	47.80	49.89	53.65	3.12	4.13	5.43	13.15	13.23
IND	28.56	36.48	46.09	65.07	71.47	4.94	5.87	9.53	18.23	24.69
PAK	16.50	21.19	27.56	34.07	38.32	2.11	3.01	5.42	8.31	9.82
LKA	53.61	71.99	79.54	97.22	99.18	2.83	4.56	10.21	16.04	18.76
SAS	26.62	35.73	43.53	59.71	65.53	4.42	5.35	8.16	15.97	21.15
IDN	28.72	47.33	55.82	78.43	83.05	3.39	8.51	15.06	24.89	31.51
MYS	45.64	54.66	66.16	66.88	70.80	4.05	7.19	25.74	37.13	37.20
PHL	65.48	71.96	74.68	79.83	85.37	24.02	24.58	30.37	29.45	33.84
SGP										
THA	27.70	28.54	59.65	83.48	85.91	10.32	15.88	35.14	50.03	51.23
VNM	42.96	34.43				2.40	2.73	9.33	22.39	24.58
EAS	45.23	44.28	60.65	80.44	86.61	5.08	7.30	15.45	27.36	33.07
LIC	15.10	18.10	21.66	37.31	39.63	1.70	2.64	2.91	7.05	7.68
MIC	41.48	45.00	55.91	70.51	75.25	6.08	7.48	12.53	23.28	27.87
HIC	86.33	90.83	96.42	98.41	104.02	34.08	42.61	55.01	73.05	73.76
WLD	48.97	51.13	59.43	71.06	75.21	12.26	13.63	19.02	29.34	32.88

Source: World Development Indicators.

World average was also more than 2 per cent during the same period. The reason of increase in gross domestic product and other indicators which contribute to maintain the position of economy could be traced through spending on R & D. Second important indicator is to examine knowledge economy that how many researchers involved into research and innovation activities. These both indicators contribute to new innovations on one side and its acquisition, adaptation, dissemination and use of knowledge on the other side. East Asian countries have secured better position than South Asian economies. In the case of scientific and technical research articles, India remained on the top position among both the regions and followed by Singapore overtime. This indicator has shown increasing trend which can be recongnised as the increasing share of tertiary education attainment over the period of time. Likewise, East Asian economies have considerable share of high-technology exports in the manufacturing sector and the share has increased from 1990 to 2000 then the share declined. In the case of South Asian economies, only India got considerable position as compared to other economies which has less than one or slightly more than one percent share of high-technology goods in the manufacturing sector. South Asian economies except India in case of one indicator have been at the low ranking as compared to East Asian economies and South Asia is known as weak technological capabilities and skills.

Position of Information Infrastructure among South Asian and East Asian Economies

Information and Communication technologies are pillar of the knowledge economy and as an effective tool for promoting economic growth and sustainable developments in recent years. In the case of OECD countries, investment in information and communications technologies accounts for more than 6 per cent of GDP in OECD countries, and about 8 per cent in some of these countries (OECD, 1999). This section deals with the condition of infrastructural developments in the selected economies.

Table 13.10: Innovation performance in South Asian and East Asian Economies

	R&D (% of GDP)		Researchers in R&D (per million people)		Scientific and technical journal articles			High-technology exports (% of manufactured exports)		
C. C.	2000	2010	2000	2010	1990	2000	2010	1990	2000	2010
BGD	..	..	..	..	116	154.8	270.2	0.48	0.21	0.18
IND	0.74	0.8	111.24	159.93	9200	10276.4	20881.8	3.94	6.26	7.18
PAK	0.13	..	..	..	257	267.1	1109.6	0.07	0.39	1.69
LKA	0.14	0.16	134.61	103.09	106	97.8	131.2	0.6	3.09	1.03
IDN			215.3		104	181.6	247.1	1.59	16.37	9.78
MYS	0.47	1.07	274.24	1458.96	233	459.6	1607.7	38.21	59.57	44.52
PHL	..	..	..	..	157	184.6	221.7	..	72.63	55.26
SGP	1.85	2.05	4245.02	6306.51	572	2361	4377.3	39.89	62.79	49.91
THA	0.25	..	..	..	282	663.3	2106.4	20.87	33.36	24.02
VNM	..	..	..	..	60	146.8	389.6	..	11.07	8.61
SAS	0.65	0.77	111.65	158.99	9700.77	10844.1	22462.4	2.78	4.77	6.38
EAS	2.32	2.5	935.65	1422.97	62792.31	114375.4	198336.7	22.22	33.25	26.08
LIC	..	..	..	..	533.83	665.43	995.63	..	2.25	..
MIC	0.64	1.19	339.21	552.95	29635.24	57730.4	156515.2	..	20.58	18.52
HIC	2.34	2.41	3011.2	3553.07	451050.7	577290.1	..	18.82	25.28	17.31
WLD	2.1	2.11	1079.13	1277.31	479347.4	633299.1	806273.1	18.21	24.46	17.58

Source: World Development Indicators.

Table 13.11: Internet Users and Mobile + Landline Users (per 100 people)

Internet Users (per 100 people)				Mobile + Landline				
C. C.	2000	2010	2014	1980	1990	2000	2010	2014
BGD	0.07	3.7	9.6	0.12	0.2	0.58	45.79	76.61
IDN	0.93	10.92	17.14	0.26	0.61	4.94	104.8	137.9
PAK	0.1	8	13.8	0.38	0.76	2.34	60.79	75.98
LKA	0.65	12	25.8	0.36	0.71	6.35	100.86	115.65
MYS	21.38	56.3	67.5	2.86	9.18	41.63	136.05	163.44
PHL	1.98	25	39.69	0.89	0.98	12.25	92.55	114.31
SGP	36	71	82	22.22	36.66	119.78	184.7	193.65
THA	3.69	22.4	34.89	0.77	2.45	13.87	118.31	152.9
VNM	0.25	30.65	48.31	0.1	0.14	4.12	141.44	153.12

Source: World Development Indicators.

Table 13.12: ICT Exports and Imports Share of Selected Economies

	ICT goods exports (% of total goods exports)		ICT goods imports (% total goods imports)	
Country Code	2000	2010	2000	2010
BGD	0.07	0.05	2.67	4.05
IND	1.69	2	5.45	6.31
PAK	0.1	0.2	1.75	3.35
LKA	2.79	0.46	4.48	2.95
IDN	2.44	4.98	4.24	8.49
MYS	52.68	34.01	40.92	29.8
PHL	38.82	26.77	38.08	31.63
SGP	54.97	34.33	40.81	27.85
THA	28.69	18.93	23.56	14.18
VNM	5.42	7.91	4.4	8.4

Source: World Development Indicators.

In the case of internet and mobile users, all the economies have been seen on the progressive position and position has been going in an improving stage. But there have been wide difference within the south Asian economies and between both the regions. East Asian economies can be considered as advanced economies as compared to South Asian economies. The share of ICT exports and imports of South Asian economies has been extremely low during the study period. Contrary to this, the share of ICT exports and imports has been considerably high among East Asian economies overtime. The data reveals the fact that all South Asian economies stayed behind in terms of information infrastructural developments.

Status of Conducive Economic and Institutional arrangements among South Asian and East Asian Economies

In addition to a well functioning macroeconomic policy mix and innovation system, potential for gaining catch up and move forward also requires a congenial environment with regard to government effectiveness, political stability and absence of violence/terrorism, regulatory control and rule of law. Features of conducive economic and institutional arrangements include an effective, accountable and corrupt-free government and a legal system that support and enforces the basic rules of commerce and protects property rights (Chen and Dahlman, 2005). These are new institutional arrangements which contribute to accelerate economic progress by private business through multinational corporations.

While analysing data regarding political stability, except Malaysia and Singapore, all economies of the South Asia and East Asia were prone to political instability and occurrence of terrorism/violence were prevalent among both the regions. With regard to government efficiency, regulatory quality and rule of law indicators, South Asian economies were on the weak end as compared to East Asian economies overtime.

Table 13.13: Government Effectiveness

	1996		2000		2010		2014	
South Asia								
C. C.	Est.	S. E.	Est.	S. E.	Est.	S. E.	Est.	S. E.
BGD	-0.73	0.25	-0.56	0.17	-0.75	0.19	-0.77	0.20
IND	-0.08	0.23	-0.14	0.19	0.02	0.19	-0.20	0.19
PAK	-0.59	0.25	-0.58	0.18	-0.76	0.19	-0.75	0.20
LKA	-0.26	0.25	-0.35	0.17	-0.18	0.19	0.09	0.20
East Asia								
IDN	-0.42	0.23	-0.27	0.17	-0.20	0.19	-0.01	0.19
MYS	0.75	0.23	1.05	0.19	1.13	0.19	1.14	0.20
PHL	-0.18	0.23	-0.14	0.19	-0.02	0.19	0.19	0.19
SGP	2.10	0.23	2.17	0.21	2.26	0.21	2.19	0.22
THA	0.27	0.23	0.20	0.19	0.19	0.19	0.34	0.19
VNM	-0.47	0.24	-0.44	0.17	-0.26	0.19	-0.06	0.20

Source: World Development Indicators, Various Issues, Washington, World Bank.

Table 13.14: Political Stability and Absence of Violence/Terrorism

	1996		2000		2010		2014	
South Asia								
C. C.	Est.	S. E.	Est.	S. E.	Est.	S. E.	Est.	S. E.
BGD	-0.61	0.37	-0.77	0.33	-1.40	0.24	-0.88	0.20
IND	-0.91	0.37	-0.99	0.30	-1.23	0.24	-0.96	0.20
PAK	-1.21	0.37	-1.14	0.33	-2.67	0.24	-2.44	0.20
LKA	-1.80	0.37	-1.93	0.33	-0.92	0.24	-0.25	0.20
East Asia								
IDN	-1.18	0.37	-2.04	0.30	-0.85	0.24	-0.37	0.20
MYS	0.47	0.37	0.04	0.30	0.12	0.24	0.34	0.20
PHL	-0.48	0.37	-1.41	0.30	-1.63	0.24	-0.70	0.20
SGP	1.07	0.37	1.04	0.30	1.14	0.24	1.23	0.20
THA	0.40	0.37	0.38	0.30	-1.43	0.24	-0.91	0.20
VNM	0.41	0.37	0.31	0.33	0.11	0.24	0.00	0.20

Source: World Development Indicators, Various Issues, World Bank.

Table 13.15: Regulatory Quality

	1996		2000		2010		2014	
South Asia								
C. C.	Est.	S. E.	Est.	S. E.	Est.	S. E.	Est.	S. E.
BGD	-1.06	0.32	-0.87	0.24	-0.83	0.16	-0.94	0.18
IND	-0.44	0.27	-0.16	0.22	-0.37	0.17	-0.45	0.18
PAK	-0.45	0.32	-0.73	0.27	-0.58	0.16	-0.69	0.18
LKA	0.08	0.32	0.25	0.24	-0.20	0.16	-0.08	0.18
East Asia								
IDN	0.19	0.27	-0.18	0.22	-0.40	0.17	-0.10	0.18
MYS	0.69	0.27	0.52	0.22	0.59	0.17	0.84	0.19
PHL	0.26	0.27	0.16	0.22	-0.22	0.17	-0.01	0.18
SGP	2.25	0.27	2.12	0.23	1.80	0.20	2.23	0.21
THA	0.21	0.27	0.49	0.22	0.19	0.17	0.27	0.18
VNM	-0.53	0.29	-0.72	0.24	-0.61	0.16	-0.59	0.18

Source: World Development Indicators, Various Issues, World Bank.

Table 13.16: Rule of Law

	1996		2000		2010		2014	
South Asia								
C. C.	S. E.	Est.	S. E.	Est.	S. E.	Est.	Est.	S. E.
BGD	0.21	-0.96	0.16	-0.95	0.14	-0.79	-0.72	0.15
IND	0.19	0.26	0.16	0.28	0.14	-0.04	-0.09	0.15
PAK	0.21	-0.67	0.17	-0.95	0.14	-0.74	-0.78	0.15
LKA	0.21	0.17	0.16	0.17	0.15	-0.08	-0.15	0.15
East Asia								
IDN	0.19	-0.37	0.15	-0.75	0.14	-0.64	-0.35	0.15
MYS	0.19	0.61	0.16	0.31	0.14	0.53	0.64	0.15
PHL	0.19	-0.01	0.16	-0.44	0.14	-0.58	-0.33	0.15
SGP	0.19	1.28	0.16	1.27	0.16	1.68	1.89	0.16
THA	0.19	0.54	0.16	0.55	0.14	-0.20	-0.15	0.15
VNM	0.20	-0.40	0.16	-0.34	0.14	-0.53	0.15	-0.31

Source: World Development Indicators, Various Issues, World Bank.

Appraisal of Knowledge Economy Index

We developed two cases as regards to examine the knowledge economy index: KEI with Regulatory Environment Pillar and KEI without Regulatory Environment Pillar. Index is the simple average of the normalised country scores on the key variables. The variables are normalised on a scale from 0 to 10 relevant to comparison groups.

Table 13.17: Knowledge Economy Index with Regulatory Environment Pillar

C. C.	1980	1990	2000	2010	2013
South Asia					
BGD	0.77	1.27	1.33	1.50	2.24
IND	1.98	2.66	2.32	2.85	2.97
PAK	0.66	1.25	1.27	1.51	2.15
LKA	1.60	1.71	1.75	1.91	2.86
East Asia					
IDN	1.32	1.60	1.79	2.09	2.89
MYS	2.00	2.81	3.38	3.71	3.65
PHL	2.46	2.55	3.18	3.26	3.10
SGP	7.60	5.28	5.53	4.72	4.37
THA	1.69	2.08	2.65	3.55	3.32
VNM	0.46	1.07	1.26	1.86	2.72

Source: Author's Calculations.

The data regarding KEI, East Asian economies have on better position than South Asian except India over the period of time. At the disaggregated level, Singapore remained on the top position followed by Malaysia, Thailand, Philippines, Indonesia and Vietnam among East Asian region. Correspondingly, among the south Asian economies, India continued as the top performer during the period of study followed by Sri Lanka, Bangladesh and Pakistan. In the East Asian economies, Vietnam had lowest value of KEI throughout the study period. And Pakistan from South Asian region has recorded the lowest value of

KEI overtime. There have been little variations regarding the values of KEI While calculating KEI with or without Regulatory Environment Pillar.

Table 13.18: Knowledge Economy Index without Regulatory Environment Pillar

C. C.	1980	1990	2000	2010	2013
South Asia					
BGD	0.77	0.58	0.75	0.97	1.79
IND	1.98	2.53	2.05	2.76	2.21
PAK	0.66	0.56	0.66	0.98	1.65
LKA	1.60	1.17	1.29	1.50	2.71
East Asia					
IDN	1.32	1.11	1.35	1.74	2.78
MYS	2.00	2.72	3.46	3.91	3.88
PHL	2.46	2.39	3.20	3.30	3.10
SGP	7.60	6.01	6.22	5.14	4.86
THA	1.69	1.76	2.49	3.68	3.43
VNM	0.46	0.37	0.65	1.45	2.51

Source: Author's Calculations.

Part Three- Some Indicators regarding Inclusiveness

The journey to knowledge economy or learning economy (Lundvall, 2009) reveals the fact that economies would be more egalitarian in nature. After the Lisbon Agenda passed by the European economies in 2000, the entire world economic order has been put forward in the process of changing their macroeconomic environment. Our question is to put a serious concern by analysing some factors which describes the inclusive growth of the economies.

"Distribution of income has its relationship with poverty and is also intimately tied to the process of inclusive growth" (Shergill, 2014). "In recent decades it is often noted that increase in per capita GDP do not necessarily correlate with increased human welfare" (Sheehan, 1999).

Reduction of poverty through trickle-down effect is one of the important policy agenda of all economies across the globe. We focused on some of indicators which shed light upon the increasing inequalities between and within the economies over time: GINI index, Income share, life expectancy, mean years of schooling and Human Development Index (HDI).

Life expectancy and HDI are both the indicators on which developing economies has been improving a lot due to the implementation of health and education policies particularly in the public sector by the respective state governments of the economies. But in comparison with the developed countries and high income economies, registered high inequalities with respect to mean years of schooling and life expectancy. In the case of HDI rank across the world, only Singapore was on fifth rank and Afghanistan occupied 169th rank among the selected economies. Data indicates the high differences between the values of HDI and HDI rank of South Asia and East Asian economies.

In terms of rising inequality in terms of income and inequality of HDI and other indicators, the economies of South Asia and East Asia shares share this problem with most of the developing economies as well as developed economies. This a major challenge for the proponents of knowledge economy who advocates that global knowledge economy will reduce the gap between and within economies across the globe.

Data explores the approximately identical picture of each selected economy. Lowest twenty percent of the population had less than 10 per cent share of income. And all the selected economies have a rising trend in inequality since 1980. The diversity of trends observed across selected economies since 1980 shows that inequality dynamics are formed by a wide array of national, institutional and political context. Besides various factors responsible for increasing inequality, educational inequalities and asset ownership inequality play a fundamental role to increase inequality among economies

Female labour force describes the democratic process of the economies which they uphold the equality of gender. Over the period of time, it is the common consensus among all the economies across

Table 13.19: Human Development Index (HDI)

C. C.	1990	2000	2010	2015	HDI Rank (2015)	Rank (with in sample economies)
BGD	0.39	0.47	0.55	0.58	139	8
IND	0.43	0.49	0.58	0.62	131	7
PAK	0.40	0.45	0.53	0.55	147	9
LKA	0.63	0.69	0.75	0.77	73	3
IDN	0.53	0.60	0.66	0.69	113	5
MYS	0.64	0.73	0.77	0.79	59	2
PHL	0.59	0.62	0.67	0.68	116	6
SGP	0.72	0.82	0.91	0.93	5	1
THA	0.57	0.65	0.72	0.74	87	4
VNM	0.47	0.58	0.65	0.68	116	6

Source: World Development Indicators.

Table 13.20: Income Index of Selected Economies

C. C.	1980	1990	2000	2010	2013
BGD	0.35	0.36	0.40	0.48	0.50
IND	0.38	0.44	0.49	0.58	0.60
PAK	0.48	0.52	0.53	0.57	0.58
LKA	0.49	0.53	0.59	0.65	0.68
IDN	0.51	0.56	0.60	0.66	0.68
MLS	0.65	0.69	0.75	0.80	0.81
PHL	0.57	0.56	0.57	0.61	0.63
SGP	0.80	0.88	0.94	0.99	1.00
THA	0.55	0.63	0.68	0.73	0.74
VHHD*	0.82	0.85	0.88	0.90	0.91
HHD**	0.54	0.61	0.63	0.72	0.74
MHD$	0.46	0.49	0.53	0.60	0.62
LHD@	0.47	0.44	0.44	0.49	0.51

Source: World Development Indicators and *Very high human development, ** High Human Development, $ Medium Human Development, @ Low Human Development.

Table 13.21: Income Share held by different sections among South Asian and East Asian Economies

	Series	highest 10%	highest 20%	lowest 10%	lowest 20%			highest 10%	highest 20%	lowest 10%	lowest 20%
BGD	1980	21.87	35.84	4.13	9.72	IDN	1980	24.91	39.46	3.74	8.68
	1990	23.29	37.36	4.12	9.62		1990	24.68	38.89	4.17	9.39
	2000	27.58	42.37	3.77	8.72		2000	25.6	39.61	4.29	9.53
	2010	26.81	41.35	3.87	8.89		2010	28.18	43.65	3.36	7.63
IND	1980	25.72	40.14	3.77	8.69	MYS	1983	38.45	53.94	1.83	4.57
	1990	25.98	40.14	3.95	9.09		1990	37.02	53.13	1.89	4.66
	2000	28.26	42.35	3.75	8.63		2000	..	..	..	..
	2010	29.98	44.22	3.52	8.2		2010	..	..	..	..
NPL	1980	24.98	39.49	4.05	9.12	PHL	1980	32.73		2.77	6.44
	1990	30.24	45.12	3.40	7.83		1990	34.7		2.55	5.89
	2000	36.39	50.76	2.75	6.55		2000	36.27		2.2	5.38
	2010	26.32	41.42	3.51	8.34		2010	33.4		2.45	5.92
PAK	1980	27.62	42.17	3.48	8.32	THA	1980	35.51	51.4	2.29	5.42
	1990	27.06	41.77	3.37	8.08		1990	36.36	52.24	2.45	5.91
	2000	26.37	40.27	4.06	9.37		2000	33.69	49.74	2.56	6.16
	2010	25.62	39.52	4.21	9.59		2010	30.72	46.5	2.73	6.62
LKA	1980	26.42	41.12	3.59	8.29	SGP	1980				
	1990	27.49	41.69	3.72	8.74		1990				
	2000	33.02	48.41	2.9	6.86		2000				
	2010	31.8	46.49	3.04	7.27		2010				

Source: World Development Indicators, Various Issues, World Bank.

the globe initiated the process of being equal of all men and women. And they categorically improved their female labour force participation. At the aggregate level, female labour force was 39.55 per cent in 1990 and declined with 0.14 per cent in 2015. Data indicates that ongoing development process which leads economies to the knowledge oriented economies marginalised the female labour force overtime.

Table 13.22: Labour force, Female (% of Total Labour Force)

Country Code	1990	2000	2010	2014
BTN	36.24	38.29	41.30	39.87
PAK	12.71	15.22	21.57	21.91
IND	27.64	27.81	25.06	24.13
EAS	44.25	44.03	43.55	43.51
IDN	38.43	37.49	38.12	37.73
LIC	46.36	46.46	47.00	46.83
MYS	34.52	34.87	35.39	37.60
PHL	36.42	37.45	38.67	39.06
MIC	38.51	38.63	37.80	37.61
SGP	39.12	40.66	43.52	44.26
HIC	41.46	42.88	43.83	43.99
WLD	39.55	39.92	39.55	39.44

Source: World Development Indicators.

Conclusions

All the selected economies have observed the process of de-agrarianisation and deindustrialisation with prompt progress in the service sector due to increasing education attainment, ICT developments innovation developments and other institutional reforms. In many areas, the selected economies have been lagging behind due to laggards and latecomers and policy changes may simply put these economies on a par with global trends which were not identical with their stages of economic development. It is no doubt that there is a close relationship between innovation policies and knowledge economy perspective and a country's level of development. From industrial revolution to recent changes in the global economy by adopting innovation and knowledge economy, it is quite clear- the fruits of development went to those countries who generated the economic application of knowledge and then to those who could readily access and expand on this knowledge (Sheehan, 1999). In this context, the East Asian economies performed in a better ways as compared to South Asian economies. There are some areas which need to be focus in the public policy framework which contribute to accelerate innovations and knowledge economy indicators as well as lower the gaps between the economies and the people that is the purpose to develop public policy in a direction of innovation system approach rather than abstract macroeconomic policies which have single focus agenda of high economic growth trajectory. An increasing inequality in income share in selected economies by contrast, responsible will raise questions about the sustainability of such countries' social and welfare models. In the course of KEI, We have examined the strengths and Achilles' heel of the South Asian and East Asian economies with regard to build the transition to the knowledge economy by way of macroeconomic stability and schema of balanced socio-economic steps forward processes of the economy. Despite the weak knowledge economy indicators due to complete negligence of the state as well as the private sector, the Asian countries have also developed local knowledge systems and skills which can be used into innovation-led development process which turns into knowledge economy by creation of technology. South Asian economies need to upgrade its production, increase technological innovations and enhance creativity and entrepreneurship to secure economic position to compete both the East Asian economies in comparison in the region and the developed world. In the case of positive distributional effects as expected from economic and institutional developments many indicators like HDI, income inequality and female labour force participation which describe inequalities that rise overtime. It is the need to initiate the process through supranational organisations and local governments for greater policy space differentiated by level of the development of each economy on the globe.

References

Ahmed, E. M., Krishnasamy, G. (2013). Human capital investment to achieve knowledge-based economy in ASEAN5: DEA applications. *Journal of the Knowledge Economy*, *4*(4), 331-342.

Arvanitidis, P. A., Petrakos, G. (2011). Defining knowledge-driven economic dynamism in the world economy: a methodological perspective. In *Innovation, growth and competitiveness*. Springer, Berlin, Heidelberg, 15-39.

Arocena, R., & Sutz, J. (2002). Innovation systems and developing countries. DRUID (Danish Research Unit for Industrial Dynamics) Working Paper, 2(05).

Alvaredo, F., Chancel, L., Piketty, T., Saez, E., Zucman, G. (Eds.). (2018). *World inequality report 2018*. Belknap Press.

Blomström, M., Kokko, A., Sjöholm, F. (2002). Growth and innovation policies for a knowledge economy: Experiences from Finland, Sweden, and Singapore. *Background paper for the LAC Flagship Report. Washington, DC: World Bank.*

Chen, D. H., Dahlman, C. J. (2005). The knowledge economy, the KAM methodology and World Bank operations. *World Bank Institute Working Paper*, (37256).

Dahlman, C. (2007). Technology, globalization, and international competitiveness: Challenges for developing countries. *Industrial development for the 21st century: Sustainable development perspectives*, 29-83.

Fagerberg, J. (2006). Innovation, technology and the global knowledge economy: Challenges for future growth. In *Green Roads to GrowthProject and Conference, Copenhagen.*

Fernandes, A. M., M. Honorati and T. Mengistae (2010). Is Growth Constrained by Institutions? In Ejaz Ghani (ed.), The Poor Half Billion in South Asia: What is Holding Back Lagging Regions. London: Oxford University Press.

Formica, P., Varblane, U., & Mets, T. (2008). Knowledge Transfer Mechanisms from Universities and Other HEIs to the Sector. In Knowledge Matters (pp. 21-51). Palgrave Macmillan, London. DOI: 10.1057/9780230582262_2

Human Development Report (2016). Human Development for Everyone. UNDP, New York.

Karagiannis, S. (2007). The Knowledge-Based Economy, Convergence and Economic Growth: Evidence from the European Union. *Working Paper No. 91, Centre of Planning and Economic Research, Athens, Greece.*

Kaur, M. and L. Singh (2015). Knowledge in Economic Growth of Developing Economies, Discussion Paper No. 12, Centre for Development Economics and Innovation Studies (CDEIS), Punjabi University, Patiala.

Kurtić, A., & Đonlagić, S. (2012). Determining key factors for knowledge economy development in Bosnia and Hercegovina. Management, Knowledge and Learning, 116-127.

Lundvall, B. Å. (2009). Why the new economy is a learning economy. *Techno-economic Paradigms: Essays in Honour of Carlota Perez, 22138.*

Undvall, B. Ä., & Johnson, B. (1994). The learning economy. Journal of industry studies, 1(2), 23-42.

Organization for Economic Cooperation and Development. (1996). The Knowledge – Based Economy, Paris: OECD.

Organization for Economic Cooperation and Development. (1999). The Knowledge – Based Economy: A Set of Facts and Figures, Paris.

Perkins, S. (2002). The challenge ahead: transition to an innovation-driven high-income economy. *Business Review, 4*(1), 1-9.

Shapira, P., Youtie, J., Yogeesvaran, K., & Jaafar, Z. (2006). Knowledge economy measurement: Methods, results and insights from the Malaysian Knowledge Content Study. *Research Policy, 35*(10), 1522-1537.

Sheehan, P. (1999). The Global Knowledge Economy: Challenges for China's Development. *CSES Working Paper No. 15, Centre for Strategic Economic Studies, Victoria University of Technology, Malbourne, Australia.*

Shergill, B.S. (2014). Knowledge Economy, Inclusive Growth and Economic Security of South Asia: Towards an Alternative Strategy. In edited Kamaljeet Singh and Surjit Singh Puar (2014) Emerging Policy Regimes in Indian Higher Education: Ensuring Issues and Concerns. Twenty-first Century Publications, Patiala, India.

Singh L. (2006). Innovations, High-Tech Trade and Industrial Development: Theory, Evidence and Policy. UNU-WIDER Research Paper No. 2006/27. UNU-WIDER, Helsinki, Finland.

Smith, K. (2002). What is the 'Knowledge Economy'? Knowledge Intensity and Distributed Knowledge Bases. UNU/INTECH Discussion papers, UNU, Institute for New Technologies, Maastricht.

Sum, N. L., and Jessop, B. (2013). Competitiveness, the Knowledge-Based Economy and Higher Education. Journal of Knowledge Economy, No. 4.

Vinnychuk, O., Skrashchuk, L., Vinnychuk, I. (2014). Research of Economic Growth in the context of Knowledge Economy. *Intellectual Economics*, *8*(1), 116-127.

14

Capital Goods Industry in East Asia

A Study of Indian Firms

Swarnjeet Kaur & Swati Mehta

Introduction

In the recent globalisation era, most of the questions arise about the benefits and adverse consequences of East-Asian economies during the last three decades. The dazzling performance of these countries raised doubts about the replicability of development experiences which can be easily understood through the global financial crisis (Haddad, 2016). In the manufacturing sector demand for exports and imports declined due crisis of 2008. The fall in internal and external demand, lead to the closure of various factories in LDCs. However, the overall growth of LDCs decreased from 7.6 per cent to 3.5 per cent in 2007 and 2009, respectively. Though all countries were affected by the global financial crisis but the manufacturing sector of LDCs was fragile particularly due to the crisis of 2008. Indonesia and Thailand, being newly industrialised countries also get affected by these shocks (Report of South center, 2010). The share of manufacturing declined in East-Asia from 47.3 per cent to 43.3 percent. The imports were increased and exports declined in these countries (Athukorala & Kothpalboon, 2009). According to the report of IMF WEO (various issues) report China, Korea, Malaysia, Thailand, Singapore and Philippines observed the decline in real GDP growth due to the global financial crisis, except India and Indonesia.

To achieve a higher rate of growth, it is required to spend more on capital goods (Hall &Jones, 1999; Griliches &Mairesse, 1984). Krugman (1994) found less use of technology as the key factor responsible for low TFP growth of East-Asian economies. Trade through production networks works as an engine for economic growth which is an important prerequisite for the industrial development of nations.

In the case of India, the capital goods industry was a core sector since the second five-year plan under the Nehru-Mahalanobis model of growth (Mundle & Mukhopadhyay, 1992). Further, various reasons as the weak position of payments for oil because of hike in prices through the Gulf war compelled the Indian government to approach for funds from IMF. The loans by IMF arrived with certain conditions for which the government was compelled to have economic reforms. There were some other reasons as the high BOP deficit and growth reduction, the new policy of economic reforms in 1991 was adopted for economic stabilisation and structural adjustment. Most of the economists (Uppal 1993, Parameswaran 2004) were of the view that the crisis was triggered with the rise of oil prices sharply during August of 1990. The economic reforms of 1991 were also objected to increasing the productivity performance the Indian capital goods sector. The economic reforms include the increase of competition and free access in imports of foreign technology. The present paper tries to explore the impact of trade liberalisation and the global financial crisis (2008) on the productivity of Indian capital goods industries. The paper is based on the hypothesis that there is a positive link between trade liberalisation and the productivity of the capital goods sector. The paper is organised as section 2 explains the review of literature and section 3 described the methodology of the paper. In section 4, empirical estimation has been given and in the end, section 5 describes the conclusion of the study.

Review of Literature

There are various studies related to the capital goods sector and the impact of economic liberalisation (Bowonder & Mani 1991; Balakrishnan & Babu 2003; Chaudhuri, 1995; Malik 2012; Sharma 2010; Keshari

2012) that highlighted different issues and concerns related to Indian capital goods industries. Concerning the whole Indian manufacturing industries, Goldar (2004) & Unni et al. (2001) found that there is a decline in the trend rate of growth after economic reforms. But few economists (Balakrishnan & Babu, 2003; Rodrik & Subramanian 2004; Singh 2009; Pattanayak & Thangavelu, 2005 and Rodrik, 2013) found an increase in the trend rate of growth for the period of liberalisation. However, some studies analysed the structure and growth of capital goods industries in India, with the special influence of economic reforms of 1991. Since independence, the major industrial policies were subjected to import-substitution strategy for capital goods industries to protect domestic industries from excessive competition (Bhagwati & Srinivasan, 1975). These policies were formulated to achieve self-sufficiency in production or self-reliance. From the 1980s with the initial level introduction of liberalisation, there was number of reforms that took place related to domestic capital goods industries (Uppal 1993). These reforms provide the way for the abolition of licenses required for the establishment of capital goods industries and exports were also subjected to allow freely (Pattnayak & Thangavelu, 2004).

A number of studies examined growth trends for overall manufacturing industries along with industries of the Indian capital goods sector. The economists (Parameswaran, 2004; Malik, 2012 and Sharma, 2010) analysed separately the industries of the Indian capital goods sector with the impact of economic liberalisation. Parameswaran (2004) explored the growth trends and pattern of sub-sectors (electronics, electrical machinery, and non-electrical machinery and transport equipment industries) of capital goods industries. Mazumdar (2010) had noticed a sharp decline in growth trends for electronics industries during the period of post-liberalisation, from 34.1 per cent in 1985-90 to 9.9 per cent in 2000-04. Further, Keshari (2012) found the trend growth of non-electrical and electrical machinery industries were declined from 6.7 per cent to 6.5 per cent and 25.7 per cent to 18 per cent in the post-reform period. Suresh (2004) found a decline in the trend rate of growth for non-electrical machinery industry from 11.3 per cent in 1980 to 8.43 per cent in 1990. However, there is not any study found which particularly examines the growth and pattern in capital goods industries of India, in the recent past. So to fulfill the gap of literature, the present study is based on the following objectives:

- To find the effect of economic reforms on growth rates of the Indian capital goods sector.
- To find the extent of increase or decrease in total factor productivity of the Indian capital goods sector.

Data Methodology

The paper analysed 22 industries classified into three-digit industries, under the classification of National Industrial Classification (NIC) 2008. Further, these three-digit industries of the capital goods sector are classified between four sub-sectors- electronics industries, electrical machinery industries, non-electrical machinery industries and transport equipments industries. The study used the Annual Survey of Industries (ASI) database for the period 1980-81 to 2013-14. To examine the objective of economic reforms of 1991, the period 1980-81 to 2013-14 is divided between two sub-periods:- 1980-81 to 1990-91 and 1991-92 to 2013-14. For the construction of variables, the study used suitable deflators constructed from the Wholesale Price Index (WPI) of 2012. To examine the impact of reforms on imports and exports of the capital goods sector, the study used the PROWESS database from the period 1994-95 to 2015-16. To analyse the impact of liberalisation at the firm level, the study period 1994-95 to 2015-16 also has been classified into two sub-groups:- from 1994-95 to 2007-08 and from 2008-09 to 2015-16. The period chosen for analysis consisted of implementation and recommendation of liberalisation policy and the period after liberalisation selected to analyse the direction of change in productivity and growth rates of the capital goods sector. To analyse the structure of Indian capital goods sector, the paper used both industry-level ASI database and firm-level PROWESS database. It was required to examine the growth trends of imports and exports of capital goods sector to examine the impact of economic reform. So the data related to imports and exports was extracted from the PROWESS database. The semi-logarithmic method has been used to compute trend rates of growth for the period 1980-81 to 2013-14. On the other hand, kinked exponential method was used to compute growth rates of both sub-periods from 1980-81 to 1990-91 and from 1991-92 to 2013-14 while the growth accounting method has been used for estimation of TFP index. The estimation of partial productivities and capital intensity were also taken to capture the impacts of liberalisation on labor productivity, capital productivity and capital intensity. Labor productivity (V/L) was constructed from gross value-added divided by total persons engaged and for capital productivity, (V/K) gross value added was divided by gross fixed capital. Further, Capital intensity (K/L) was a ratio of gross fixed capital to the total person engaged.

To estimate industry-level productivity analysis, Goldar & Kumari (2003) two input and one output framework has been used for industries in the capital goods sector. The following equation has been used under the two-input framework of the Translog index method

$$\Delta lnTFP(t) = \Delta lnY(t) - \frac{[sl(t)+sl(t-1)}{2} * \Delta lnL(t)] - \frac{[sk(t)-sk(t-1)}{2} * \Delta lnK(t) \ldots(7)$$

In the equation Y, L and K are value-added, total persons engaged and capital respectively. *Sl*and *Sk* are averages of labor and capital shares equal to unity. Share of labor was constructed from gross emoluments which were deflated with CPI (consumer price index) 2004-05 prices. The following are given the variables used in the present paper:

Table 14.1: Construction of Variables and method for construction of variable

Variables	Construction method	Database
Import of capital goods	Import of capital goods divided by sales of firms	PROWESS
Exports	Exports of related industry divided by sales	PROWESS
Gross value added	Gross value added	ASI
Labour	Total persons engaged	ASI

Source: Author's estimation.

Empirical Estimation

The empirical estimation of the present paper was an attempt to present the growth trends and structural changes of industries in the Indian capital goods sector. In table 14.2, the trend growth rates of imports of capital and exports have been given for the overall period 1994-95 to 2015-16 and sub-periods 1994-95 to 2007-08 and 2008-09 to 2015-16.

Table 14.2: Growth Rates of Import and Exports of Indian Capital Goods Sector

Industries	From 1994-95 to 2007-08	From 2008-09 to 2015-16	From 1994-95 to 2015-16
	Import of capital goods		
Electronics	-14.86	-35.38	-7.57
Electrical machinery industry	-6.55	-5.37	-3.4
Non-electrical machinery industry	-25.66	-25.94	-13.55
Transport equipment industry	-5.05	-43.68	-0.53
Capital goods sector	-7.12	-21.15	-4.75
	Exports growth		
Electronics	0.21	-2.53	-1.95
Electrical machinery industry	0.98	-9.77	-3.16
Non-electrical machinery industry	4.02	-2.57	1.43
Transport equipment industry	2.77	-3.67	-1.12
Capital goods sector	2.21	-3.64	-0.67

Source: Author's calculations, based CMIE database.

In the above Table 14.2, growth trends of imports of capital goods found a negative growth rate at aggregate as well as at disaggregate level. The non-electrical machinery industries found the highest negative growth (-13.55 percent) for the period 1994-95 to 2015-16 while the transport equipment industries found the lower impact of -0.53 per cent during the same period. However, the transport equipment industries also found the highest decline with negative (from -5.05 per cent to -43.68 percent) growth trend in the second sub-period of 2008-09 to 2015-16. The same trend has also been followed by electronics industries and non-electrical machinery industries, from -14.86 per cent to -35.38 per cent and -25.66 per cent to -25.94 per cent respectively. However, the capital goods sector at the aggregate level observed -4.75 per cent for period 1994-95 to 2015-16 which declined from -7.12 per cent in 1994-95 to 2007-08 to -21.15 per cent during the period 2008-09 to 2015-16. In the next Table 14.3, TFP indices have been presented for period 1983-84 to 2013-14 for capital goods sector at the aggregate level and for electronics industries, electrical machinery industries, non-electrical machinery industries and transport equipment industries at a disaggregated level. The values of TFP indices have been shown to increase in values during the initial years of liberalisation but a decline in TFP in later years. This indicates the decline of productivity in the Indian capital goods sector after the crisis of 2008.

In Table 14.4, the total factor productivity growth rates of sub-sectors and the capital goods sector have been given. The paper used the semi-logarithm method to compute trend growth for period 1980-81 to 2013-14. The single kinked method has been used for growth rates of pre-reform (1980-81 to 1990-91) and post-reform (1991-92 to 2013-14) period.

The data found that TFP growth is negative for all sub sectors expect electronics industries. However, it found a slight increase in all sub sectors during 1992-92 to 2013-14. TFP growth shows the negative trend in all sub sectors from 1980-81 to 2013-14. This shows the negative trend of -1.01 per cent for period 1980-81 to 1990-91 and -0.28 per cent during 1991-92 to 2013-14.

In Table 14.5, growth rates of partial productivities and capital intensity has been presented for the period 1980-81 to 2013-14.

In Table 14.5, the greater values of growth rates for capital intensities and labour productivities in various sub-sectors of the Capital Goods Sector/are found during the study period as compared to their capital productivity However, the non-electrical machinery sector's capital productivity had negative -0.46 per cent growth. The lower values of

Table 14.3: TFP (Total Factor Productivity) Indices of Capital Goods Sector

Year	Electronics	Electrical Machinery	Non-Electrical Machinery	Transport Equipment	Capital Goods Sector
1983-84	79.54	96.48	89.97	85.53	89.67
1984-85	79.55	117.33	100.21	86.04	95.96
1985-86	71.27	72.70	79.35	83.39	79.06
1986-87	75.08	108.70	90.98	101.10	93.83
1987-88	78.42	120.66	93.16	82.86	94.04
1988-89	76.81	91.96	82.60	87.60	85.61
1989-90	79.86	117.54	100.97	97.48	100.84
1990-91	57.42	114.97	90.85	94.50	94.85
1991-92	90.16	92.50	88.30	77.63	84.51
1992-93	75.35	104.42	86.10	86.20	88.96
1993-94	64.34	94.80	102.47	93.18	93.24
1994-95	119.41	123.62	97.82	94.93	104.91
1995-96	59.57	107.17	114.72	123.01	106.84
1996-97	77.74	89.90	88.61	88.21	88.00
1997-98	85.08	121.20	83.27	80.93	90.12
1998-99	77.11	101.24	85.18	58.77	79.34
1999-2000	80.55	73.48	113.19	110.38	96.38
2000-01	74.39	100.61	90.43	64.71	83.13
2001-02	81.90	101.56	88.89	106.25	96.37
2002-03	77.56	99.32	85.21	105.56	94.30
2003-04	71.96	115.54	107.69	126.10	108.22
2004-05	70.68	118.24	101.22	112.94	104.27
2005-06	94.26	110.67	104.16	110.94	108.87
2006-07	120.49	154.19	103.89	79.59	104.67
2007-08	56.66	96.54	102.42	72.86	83.83
2008-09	68.73	88.67	106.29	68.91	85.46
2009-10	78.30	106.71	92.81	113.54	99.63
2010-11	99.41	101.52	86.46	148.40	111.79
2011-12	63.89	98.97	105.74	45.65	74.33
2012-13	74.90	97.93	92.83	95.65	92.12
2013-14	83.60	137.03	74.22	76.73	87.96

Note: Author's calculations based on ASI database.

Table 14.4: Total Factor Productivity Growth of Sub-sectors of Capital Goods Sector

Industries	From 1980-81 to 1990-91	From 1991-92 to 2013-14	From 1980-81 to 2013-14
Electronics industries	0.78	0.35	0.15
Electrical machinery industry	-0.09	-0.02	0.10
Non-electrical machinery industry	-0.91	-0.41	-0.14
Transport equipment industries	-1.39	-0.42	-0.07
Capital goods sector	-1.01	-0.28	-0.03

Source: Author's calculations based on ASI database.

Table 14.5: Growth Rates of Partial Productivities and Capital Intensity of Indian Capital Goods Sector and its Sub-Sectors. 1980-81-2013-14

Industries	Labor Productivity	Capital Productivity	Capital intensity
Electronics	4.22	1.96	4.29
Electrical machinery industries	2.41	0.39	3.05
Non-electrical machinery	3.05	-0.46	3.56
Transport equipment industries	4.49	0.32	4.08
Capital goods	3.46	0.12	3.84

Note: Author's calculations based on ASI database.

capital productivity signify the inefficient use of labor force or lack of skilled labor force in industries. The increase in capital intensity for the same period also becomes a reason for the relative decline in capital productivity.

In Table 14.6, partial productivities and capital intensity have been presented at the disaggregated level for industries in the capital goods sector. These productivities presented for two sub-periods from 1980-81 to 1990-91 and from 1991-92 to 2013-14. The capital productivity increased for electronics industries but labor productivity and capital intensity declined in the same industries during the period 1991-92 to 2013-14. The capital intensity turned negative from 10.61 per cent to -0.99 per cent for optical instruments and equipment (NIC 267) industry.

Table 14.6: Partial Productivities and Capital Intensity of Indian Capital Goods Sector

NIC 2008	Capital Productivity		Labor Productivity		Capital Intensity	
	From 1980-81 to 1990-91	From 1991-92 to 2013-14	From 1980-81 to 1990-91	From 1991-92 to 2013-14	From 1980-81 to 1990-91	From 1991-92 to 2013-14
Electronics industries						
261 (Electronic valves and tubes and other electronic components)	-0.67	1.31	6.62	2.48	7.34	1.21
262 (Computer and peripheral equipment)	-2.07	-0.58	6.72	3.31	8.97	3.91
263+264 (Consumer electronics+Measure, testing and navigating watches & clocks)	0.15	0.44	8.16	5.05	8.00	4.62
267 (Optical instruments and equipments)	-6.34	4.54	3.60	3.50	10.61	-0.99
Electrical machinery industries						
271 (Electric motors, generators, transformers and electricity distribution and control apparatus)	0.36	-0.18	5.02	-0.94	4.65	-0.76
272 (Batteries and accumulators)	-1.75	-0.92	5.01	2.76	6.89	3.71
273 (Wires and wiring devices)	-2.52	-0.43	4.30	1.16	6.99	1.59
274+275 (Domestic appliances + electric lighting equipment)	-1.43	2.09	5.83	4.78	7.36	2.63
279 (other lighting equipments)	1.24	-1.21	0.52	3.25	5.85	4.51

Non-electrical machinery industries						
281 (General purpose machinery)	-1.04	0.01	4.52	2.98	6.04	2.97
282+304 (Special purpose machinery, weapons and ammunition)	-0.42	0.04	4.88	3.32	5.32	3.28
Transport equipment industries						
291 (Motor vehicles)	-4.52	-0.76	4.96	4.35	6.51	5.15
292+293 (Bodies for motor vehicles, trailers, semi-trailers, parts & accessories)	-2.43	-0.38	3.33	3.57	5.93	3.96
301 (Building of ships and boats)	1.74	-1.35	3.67	6.98	7.45	8.45
302 (Railway locomotives & rolling stock)	3.21	-0.35	4.55	4.45	1.31	4.82
303 (Air, spacecraft & related machinery)	4.70	0.63	7.48	2.44	2.66	1.80
309 (Transport equipments n.e.c)	-1.18	2.36	7.48	5.81	8.52	3.37

Source: Author's calculations based on ASI database.

Under electrical machinery industries, capital productivity increased for domestic appliances (NIC 274+ 275) industries with a decline in labor productivity and capital intensity. The highest decline was noticed in industries for capital intensity and labor productivity. The similar trend has been followed by non-electrical machinery industries. There was an increase in capital productivity for the general-purpose industry (NIC 281) and special-purpose industry (NIC 282). In the transport equipment industries, building of ships and boats (NIC 301) labor productivity increased and capital intensity was also increased. There was found a close relation between capital intensity and capital productivity in industries of the capital goods sector. The increase of capital intensity also indicates an acceleration of value-added or investment during the period of post-liberalisation. The lack of a skilled labor force to use technological inputs may be the reason for low capital productivity. The decline in labor productivity caused by the labor-saving nature of newly developed technologies and the use of more capital resulted in high capital intensity.

Conclusion

Although, policymakers denied from effects of the global financial crisis on the Indian economy. But the present paper clearly shows the impact of the crisis on the Indian capital goods sector. The study used the capital goods sector to analyses the impact of economic liberalisation which is base on the growth of Indian manufacturing industries. The study used both the ASI industry level and PROWESS firm-level database for empirical estimations. Due to the decline in exports, the productivity growth of industries also declined in later years of reforms including global financial. Among East-Asian countries, close ties of trade existed in regional networks of production with a systematic separation into parts and components. The machinery and electrical goods export of India was concentrated within these markets so it caused a slight decline in the growth of industries. There is a need to remove the restrictions on the movement of people in East-Asian countries by improving the air, visa, and transport related facilities (Kaur et al 2020).

It is also becomes imperative to explain the limitation of the present paper. The study used the growth accounting method with firm-level data. However, this can be explained more clearly with the help of some advanced techniques. To overcome the problem of decline in TFP and export growth, the government should adopt policies to boost the exports and efficient use of inputs. At the initial level, firms should be provided with taxation support for exports. For investment in R&D and technology, the rate of interest should be minimizing as financial support to industries.

References

Athukorala, P. C. and Kohpaiboon, A. (2009). *East Asian Exports in the Global Economic Crisis: the Decoupling Fallacy and Post-crisis Policy Challenges*. Working Paper No. 2009/13, Working Papers in Trade and Development.

Balakrishnan, P. & Babu, M. S. (2003). Growth and distribution in Indian industry in the nineties. *Economic and Political Weekly*, 38(38), 3997-4005.

Bhagwati, J., N. & Srinivasan, T. N. (1975). Foreign trade regimes and economic development: India. *NBER*, New York, London: Columbia University Press.

Bowonder, B. and Mani, S. (1991). Government Policy and Industrial Development: Case of Indian Computer Manufacturing Industry. *Economic and Political Weekly*, 26(8), M7-M11.

Chaudhuri, D., D. (1995). Technological capability in Indian electronic industry under economic liberalisation. *Economic and Political Weekly*, 30(7/8), M13-M18.

Goldar, B & Kumari, A, (2003). Import liberalization and productivity growth in Indian manufacturing industries in the 1990s. *The Developing Economies*, 41(4), 436-460.

Griliches, Z & Mairesse, J. (1984). Productivity and R&D at firm level. NBER chapters, in *R&D, patents and productivity*, National Bureau of Economic Research, 339-374.

Haddad, M. (2016). Trade integration in East Asia: The role of China and production networks. World bank policy research working paper 4160.

Hall, R. E. & Jones, C. I. (1999). Why do some countries produce so much more output per worker than others? *The Quarterly Journal of Economics*, Oxford University Press, Vol. 114(1), 83-116.

IMF IFS (various issues). International Financial Statistics. Washington, DC.

Keshari, P. K. (2012). Indian non-electrical machinery industry. Munich Personal RePEc Archive, MPRA paper no. 43047, 1-34. Accessed fro: http://mpra.ub.uni-muenchen.de/43047 on March 20, 2019.

Krugman, P. & Venables, A. J. (1994). Globalization and the inequality of the nations. CEPR discussion papers 1015.

Kaur, S., Khorana, S., & Kaur, M. (2020). Is There Any Potential in Service Trade of South Asia? *Foreign Trade Review, 55*(3), 402-417.

Malik, S. K. (2012). Capital goods sector in India, 1990-91 to 2009-10. 8th international PhD school on innovation and development, GLOBELICS academy, Rio de Janeiro, Brazil 20-31.

Mazumdar, R. (2010). Indian electronics hardware industry: growth and productivity (1993-2004). Economic and political weekly, 45(14), 72-77.

Mundle, S. and Mukhopadhayay, H. (1992). Protection, growth and competitiveness: study of Indian capital goods industry. *Economic and Political Weekly*, 27(9), M2-M8.

Pattnayak, S. S. Thangavelu, S. M. (2004). Economic reform and productivity growth in Indian manufacturing industries: an interaction of technical change and scale economies. *Economic Modelling*, 22(4), 601-615.

Parameswaran, M. (2004). Economic reforms, technical change and efficiency change; firm level evidence from capital goods industries in India' Indian economic review, 39. Jan-Jun, 239-260.

Report of the South Centre (2010). The impact of global economic crisis on industrial development of least developed countries.

Rodrik, D and Subramanian, A. (2004). From Hindu Growth to productivity surge: the mystery of Indian growth transition. *International Monetary Fund,* WP/04/77.

Rodrik, D. (2013). Structural change, fundamentals and growth: An overview. *Institute for Advanced Studies*, Sep, 1-23.

Sharma, C. (2010). Does productivity differ in domestic and foreign firms? Evidence from Indian machinery industry. *Indian economic review*, 45(1), 87-110.

Singh, A. (2009). The past, present and future of industrial policy in India: Adapting to the changing domestic and international environment Centre for Business Research, no. 376. University of Cambridge.

Suresh, M. P. (2004). Strategic approach to strengthening the international competitiveness in knowledge based industries: non-electrical machinery industry. RIS discussion paper.

Uppal, J. S. (1993). India's new economic policy. *Journal of Economic Development*, 18(2), 33-61.

Unni, J., Lalitha, N and Rani, U. (2001), Oct). Economic reforms and productivity trends in Indian manufacturing. *Economic and Political Weekly*, 36(41), 3914-3922.

15

Relationship between FDI Outflows and Economic Growth

Evidence from Developing Asia

Vishal Sarin & Suresh Kumar

Introduction

There was a time when it was assumed that Foreign Direct Investment (FDI) flows only from the capital-rich countries to relatively capital scarce countries or from more industrialised countries to less industrialised countries. But in recent times, a new phenomenon called 'Reverse FDI' has appeared (Bano & Tabbada, 2015). If we study the trends in outward FDI during the last two decades, we will find that the phenomenon of reverse flow of FDI or Outward Foreign Direct Investment (OFDI) from developing economies have grown significantly and captured the rising attention of the researchers.

The governments of developing countries have moved gradually from hampering to supportive outward FDI, although some forms of restrictions remain there in some of the developing countries, especially lower-income countries (Prera & Stephenson, 2017). Many emerging economies like India are gradually liberalizing their economies. These developments created several opportunities for many firms in developing economies to participate in international markets. Over some time, the nature and type of participation of developing countries in international markets have significantly changed. In the early period of internationalisation, participation by developing economies was mainly in the form of exports. But with time, the firms from many developing economies have started to internationalise by the way of Outward FDI. Regardless of their size and level of development, many developing countries now engage in outward FDI. Firms from many developing and transition economies have been establishing their manufacturing units in other developing economies for more than a decade but now they have also started to establish their manufacturing plants even in advanced countries.

In this way, the world economy is experiencing a dramatic shift in the pattern and structure of Foreign Direct Investment as developing economies are becoming an important source of FDI. Transnational corporations from developing and transition economies are showing their assertiveness in global markets by making investments in other countries. With this increasing trend of FDI flows from the developing and transition economies, a new dimension has been attached to the idea of globalisation and the concept of global competitiveness has also been redefined. This surge in FDI flows is also fueled by the volatile export revenues from natural resources and manufactured goods. Even the hope of global economy to come out of recessionary trends lies in the development of emerging developing economies (Gill & Singh, 2012).

The inducements for the firms to invest their funds abroad come from their need to modernise their obsolete technologies and also from their desire of acquiring control over the scare and important resources located in the host countries. Also, there may be significant advantages to firms in internationalizing their operations like they can have easier access to global technologies and market opportunities. Moreover, due to bigger markets in the host countries, the transnational corporations can enjoy greater economies of scale, better access to effective professional practices, more chances of getting bigger assignments and higher earnings for managerial and technical personnel. Due to these inducements, the flow of FDI from these developing and transition economies have grown significantly (both in absolute and relative terms) during the last two decades. Total FDI flows in the world during the year 1970 were to the tune of US$ 14141 million, out of which FDI flows from developing economies were US$ 41 million, which accounted for only 0.3 per cent share in the world OFDI. On the other hand, FDI flows from developed economies were US$ 14100 million (99.71 per cent of the world OFDI) during the same period. Thus almost all FDI flows were sources from developed countries only. If the developing economies were participating in international markets then that participation was in the form of exports only. But table 15.1 elucidates that the situation has dramatically changed during the last two decades. In the year 2018, the FDI outflows from developing and transition economies were US$ 455728 million (44.93 per cent of the world OFDI) and FDI flows from developed economies during the same period were US$ 558445 million (55.06 per cent of the world OFDI). Thus the gap between the shares of developing economies and developed economies in the world outwards FDI is narrowing down. This trend is contributing significantly to expanding the competitive strength of the firms from developing economies that are trying to have access over the strategic assets, natural resources, skill and the markets of other countries.

Table 15.1: Global trends of Outward Foreign Direct Investment (1970-2018)

Year	FDI Outflows (US$ at current price in millions)		Percentage share in World OFDI	
	Developing & Transition Economies	**Developed Economies**	**Developing & Transition Economies**	**Developed Economies**
1970	41	14100	0.3	99.7
1975	431	28057	1.5	98.5
1980	2728	49357	5.2	94.8
1985	3726	58378	6.0	94.0
1990	13108	230767	5.3	94.7
1995	52145	303966	14.7	85.3
2000	91945	1071786	7.9	92.1
2005	128500	704489	15.4	84.6
2010	407347	965843	29.7	70.3
2015	439085	1243500	26.1	73.9
2017	500106	925332	34.9	65.1
2018	455728	558445	44.9	55.1

Source: Author's Compilation from UNCTAD database (http://unctad.org/en/Pages/statistics.aspx).

The Rising Role of Asian economies in Outward FDI

If the share of all the countries of the world outward FDI is region-wise studied, then we will find that the significance and share of Asian economies are rising very fast and that of European economies is falling.

Table 15.2: Region-Wise share of economies in world Outward FDI

Year	African Economies	American Economies	Asian Economies	European Economies	Transition Economies
2005	0.3	7.5	16.5	73.6	2.1
2006	0.6	25.1	16.0	56.5	2.0
2007	0.5	23.0	14.8	59.4	2.3
2008	0.6	25.0	21.2	49.6	3.5
2009	0.5	31.2	27.2	37.6	3.5
2010	0.7	26.7	25.9	42.9	3.7
2011	0.3	32.0	27.9	36.1	3.6
2012	0.8	32.4	33.7	30.4	2.6
2013	0.8	28.7	36.8	28.2	5.5
2014	0.8	32.1	42.1	19.3	5.6
2015	0.4	21.2	30.8	46.5	1.4
2016	0.6	23.9	36.4	37.4	1.6
2017	0.9	29.3	40.6	26.5	2.7
2018	1.0	-0.7	54.3	41.6	3.9

Source: Author's Compilation from UNCTAD database (http://unctad.org/en/Pages/statistics.aspx).

The above table 15.2 elucidates that during the initial years, a large part of FDI was coming from the European economies. In the year 2005, 73.6% contribution in world OFDI was coming from the economies of Europe like France, United Kingdom, Italy, Canada, Spain and Germany. But with time this share kept on falling and time also came when in 2014, the share of European economies fell to just 19.3 percent, and in 2018 the European economies contributed 41.6 per cent share in world FDI outflows. On the other hand, the share of Asian economies in world FDI outflows is continuously increasing. In 2005, Asian economies were contributing 16.5 per cent share in world FDI outflows that increased to 42.1 per cent in 2014 and 2018, 54.3 per cent FDI came from the economies of Asia. It means in the year 2018 more than half of the

FDI is contributed by the Asian economies. Even otherwise also, Asia is the fastest-growing economic region and this region is the largest continental economy in terms of Gross Domestic Product (nominal and PPP in the world). Currently, the leading economies of the Asian region are China, Japan, India, South Korea and Indonesia.

Not only in the field of outward FDI but other fields also Asian region is making significant progress. As per the views of Anoop Singh (2010) (Head, Asia and Pacific Department, IMF) in the past, Asia has also helped the world to come out of recession and this region is going to become growth engine in the coming future. In his address at the National Council of Applied Economic Research, Singh said that share of the Asian region in world growth will increase and it will become the economic powerhouse over the next few decades. Asian economy will be larger than the combined economies of the European Union and the USA. Moreover, as whole Asian economies (if continue to grow at the same speed) will become larger than the economy of G-7 (Group of Seven leading economies) and will be half of the size of the G-20 (Group of Twenty advanced and emerging economies) by 2030 (Singh, 2010). Another important point to note about the Asian region in this discussion is that the developing economies of the Asian region contribute the largest share of OFDI from developing economies. The total share of developing economies in the world OFDI was 41.19% in 2018. Out of this 39.58%, OFDI was coming from the developing economies of Asia (UNCTAD, 2019). It means about 96% of outward FDI of the developing economies is contributed by the developing economies of Asia.

If the trends in the world outward FDI are analysed both from the angle of region and nature of economy then we will find that developing economies of Asia are the largest contributing economies in terms of the contribution of developing economies in world OFDI and their share is continuously increasing. In the year 2005, the total share of developing economies in the world OFDI was 13.3 per cent and out of which developing economies of Asia were contributing 10.7 per cent share (i.e. about 80 per cent share of OFDI from developing economies was contributed by the developing economies of Asia). But the volume

Table 15.3: Region-Wise Share of Developed, Developing & Transition Economies

Year	Developing Economies of				Developed Economies of				Transition Economies
	Africa	America	Asia	Total	America	Asia	Europe	Total	
2005	0.3	2.3	10.7	13.3	5.2	5.8	73.6	84.6	2.1
2006	0.6	3.1	11.1	14.8	22.0	4.9	56.5	83.4	2.0
2007	0.5	1.2	11.0	12.7	21.8	3.8	59.4	85.0	2.3
2008	0.6	2.2	13.3	15.5	22.8	7.9	49.6	80.3	3.5
2009	0.5	1.4	20.3	21.7	29.8	6.9	37.6	74.3	3.5
2010	0.7	4.0	21.2	25.9	22.7	4.7	42.9	70.3	3.7
2011	0.3	3.4	20.5	24.2	28.6	7.4	36.1	72.1	3.6
2012	0.8	3.1	23.9	27.8	29.3	9.8	30.4	69.5	2.6
2013	0.8	2.5	26.4	29.7	26.2	10.4	28.2	64.8	5.5
2014	0.9	1.8	31.7	34.4	30.3	10.4	19.3	60.0	5.6
2015	0.4	1.5	22.1	24.0	19.7	8.7	46.5	74.9	1.4
2016	0.7	0.7	25.7	27.1	23.2	10.7	37.4	71.3	1.6
2017	0.9	2.6	28.9	32.4	26.7	11.7	26.5	64.9	2.7
2018	1.0	0.6	39.6	41.2	-1.3	14.7	41.6	55.0	3.7

Source: UNCTAD database.

and share of developing economies of Asia in world OFDI tend to continuously increase. In the year 2018, out of 41.2 per cent share of developing economies in the world OFDI, 39.6 per cent share replace it with- was from developing Asian countries (more than 96 per cent OFDI from developing economies).

On the other side, in the case of developed economies, the developed economies of Europe are the most significant contributors. In the year 2005, they were contributing 73.6 per cent to the world OFDI (87 per cent of the share of the entire developed region) and in the year 2018, the economies of developed Europe contributed 41.6 per cent to the world OFDI (75 per cent of the share of developing economies in the world OFDI).

The following graph reveals that whatever may be the nature of the economy (developed or developing) the role of Asian economies in the world FDI outflows is continuously increasing. Moreover, an important feature of FDI outflows from Asian economies is that the share of developing economies of Asia (39.6 percent) is more than the share of developed economies of Asia (14.7 percent) in the world OFDI.

Figure 15.1: Percentage Share of Developed and Developing Economies of Asia in World FDI outflows

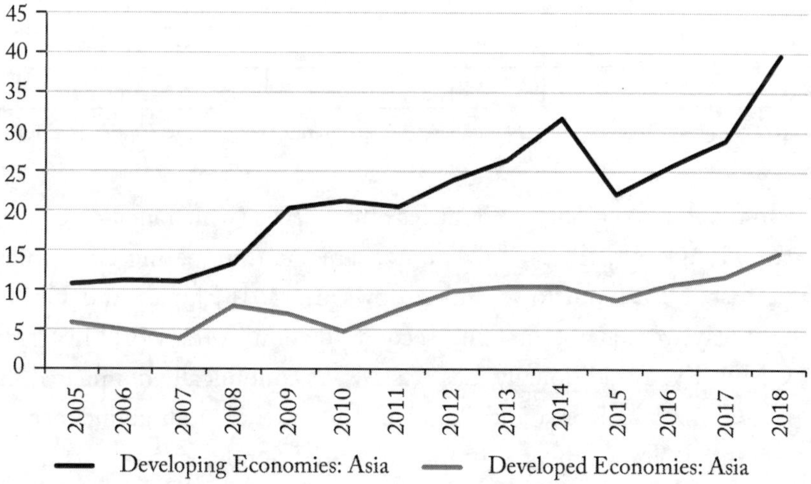

Source: Author's Compilation from UNCTAD database (http://unctad.org/en/Pages/statistics.aspx).

In Asia, there are a total of 39 economies. Out of which Japan and Israel are two developed economies and the rest are developing economies. It can be seen from the previous table 15.3 that much of the FDI from Asia is coming from developing economies and the share of developed economies of Asia is just 14.7 per cent against the 39.6 per cent share of developing economies of Asia. It means out of the total OFDI from Asia, 73 per cent is coming from developing economies of Asia and 23 per cent is contributed by the developed economies of Asia. Therefore, in our study relating to OFDI from Asian economies, developing economies of Asia are taken.

Table 15.4: Developing Asian Economics' share in World's Outward FDI (in%)

Year	East Asia	South Asia	South-East Asia	Western Asia	Total Asia
1980	-	-	-	-	2.28
1985	3.66	-	0.86	0.21	4.79
1990	3.95	0.02	0.95	-0.39	4.54
1995	9.48	0.03	3.40	-0.17	12.75
2000	5.71	0.04	0.77	0.25	6.79
2005	6.44	0.41	2.40	1.48	10.75
2010	14.16	1.18	4.60	1.29	21.24
2015	15.74	0.48	3.38	2.50	22.11
2017	19.49	1.81	3.84	2.62	28.9

Source: compiled from UNCTAD database (http://unctad.org/en/Pages/statistics.aspx).

In the Asian region, the countries of East Asia (which include China, Japan, Hongkong, Korea, Taiwan etc.) are the dominating economies in terms of FDI outflows and inflows. In 2018, Japan and China respectively were at the first and second position in the world in terms of OFDI. Even traditionally, East Asia was economically dominated by Japan, China and Korea and these economies traded an abundance of raw material and high-quality manufactured goods, exchange cultural ideas and practices. After the East Asian continent, the economies of South-East Asia, are the second-largest contributors in outward FDI from Asia. The major economies in this region are Vietnam, Indonesia, Philippines, Thailand, Malaysia, Singapore, Cambodia, Myanmar etc. As far as South Asia is concerned, it includes the countries like India, Pakistan, Bangladesh, Sri Lanka, Maldives and Afghanistan. In this region, India is the leading country whose share bin world OFDI is more than one percent in the year 2018. In Western Asia, countries like Saudi Arabia, the United Arab Emirates, Iran, Iraq, Israel, Turkey, Kuwait and Qatar are there. But Saudi Arabia and UAE are the two countries that are promoting FDI from their economies.

Impact of FDI Outflows on Source Economy: Theoretical Approaches

The OFDI can influence the source (home) economy in many ways. Whenever a firm goes for FDI in foreign countries, then it implies that it is substituting domestic production by foreign production and consequently domestic production will fall. But some studies show that this fall in domestic production will only be for a short period because there are some services and "capital which are specific to firm and produced only at the head office of the firm and then supplied to the plants abroad". In this manner, MNCs combine domestic production with foreign country's production lessen their cost of production and to increase the domestic product returns, which subsequently raise factor demand at home and also output at home (Desai et. al, 2005). In this way, the preliminary loss of finished goods can be more than counterbalanced by the increase in the production of intermediate goods and services to the affiliates (Kokko, 2006). Moreover, in the long run, horizontal foreign direct investment permits MNCs to increase their competitiveness by accessing new markets and all these things result in increased productivity at home market and hence more domestic output and hence to more growth (Herzer, 2010).

"Home country producers are get benefited by any domestic firm invest abroad and they also enjoy favorable effects of OFDI" (Blomstrom & Kokko, 1998). Other local firms can also copy technology which the foreign investing firm is using. In this way, their productivity will also improve. "Moreover, when firm use home input to produce in a foreign country then domestic suppliers start enjoying economies of scale. Therefore, OFDI via positive spillovers augment the growth of home economy".

But if there exist market imperfections in the home country, then the firms investing abroad will not be successful in compensating the fall in domestic production. Then, in such a case, the outward FDI would prove to be a substitute for the activities at home in short as well as in the long run.

If the other side of the story is examined, then it can be said that when a firm invests in different locations, then, it, is distributing its scarce resources in other countries and in this way outward FDI alternates foreign activities for domestic activities (Herzer, 2010). Thus domestic output and growth of the economy are adversely affected.

However, the effects of outward FDI on the economy of the investing country are theoretically ambiguous and thus need to be empirically tested. The study of the causal relationship between outward FDI and economic growth of source economy assumes more significance from the viewpoint of developing countries, where capital is relatively scarce and the rising levels of outward FDI have become an important feature of these economies.

Review of Literature

Many studies have attempted to measure the impact of foreign direct investments on home economies. These studies concluded that outward FDI tends to enhance employment (Navaretti et al., 2003; Federica et al., 2008; Masso et al., 2008), growth and output (Herzer, 2006 & 2010; Zulkifi, 2012; Barba et al., 2003), exports (Aizeman & Noy, 2006; Lie et al., 2015; Lipsey & Ramstetter, 2003; Kokko, 2006), Productivity and efficiency (Barba et al., 2003; Herzer, 2011), technical know-how (Almighini et al., 2010; Knoerich, 2014; Kokko, 2006), domestic investment (Dessai et al., 2005; Ameer et al., 2016). Outward

FDI is also considered as the best way through which developing countries can integrate with the world economy (Kevin, 1999). Herzer and Nunnenkamp, 2013 found the negative effect of FDI on income inequalities in home countries. There is also a strong unidirectional relationship between outward FDI and domestic investment running from OFDI to domestic investment. In the short run, domestic investment and outward FDI do not show Granger causality (Ameer et al., 2016).

Knoerich (2014) found that, whenever outward FDI is undertaken from of a country, then the investing firms generate various economies of scale in terms of financial, intangible capability and tangible capability returns.

Table 15.5: Impact of outward FDI on Home Economies: Evidence from the Literature

Source	Type of Outward FDI	Impact on Home economy
Kevin G. Cai (1999)	Chinese OFDI	OFDI is the best way through which China can integrate with the world economy
Chao-His Huang et al., (2001)	OFDI from East Asia and Latin America	International capital flows specially OFDI flows tend to be linked to more poverty in the source (home) country.
Giorgio Barba Navaretti & Castellani (2003)	Italian OFDI	OFDI increased employment, output & Total Factor Productivity of the firms.
Ari Kokko (2006)	OFDI from developed countries	Developed countries derive more benefits from outward FDI than developing countries. Effect of OFDI on employment and BOP is negative and on exports and domestic production.
Dessai, et al., (2005)	American Outward FDI	Greater Outward FDI is related to higher levels of domestic investment

Kokko, A. (2006)	Outward FDI from developed economies	Impact of outward FDI on exports and production is small but the impact on employment and Balance of Payment is mildly negative.
Pradhan J.P. (2006)	Indian service sector OFDI	Service sector OFDI can greatly help to reap the labour cost advantage to strengthen its presence in the world market.
Dierk Herzer (2007)	OFDI from 14 industrialised countries	Long-run causality between OFDI and domestic output is bi-directional
Stefano Federico, et. al., (2008)	OFDI from Italy	OFDI helps promote employment in home countries
Jaan Masso et al., (2008)	OFDI from Estonia	There is a strong home country employment effect of OFDI
Alessia Almighini et al., (2010)	OFDI from developing to developed economies	OFDI can help developing countries in technological catch-up.
Herzer (2010)	OFDI from the United States& 50 other countries	The association between OFDI & growth is highly positive and the causality is bidirectional.
Lee, C.G. (2010)	Japanese Outward FDI	In the long period, the changes in outward FDI per capita leads to changes in GDP per capita
Wong, K. (2010)	Malaysian outward FDI	Unidirectional relationship between outward FDI and economic growth, running from economic growth to outward FDI and Malaysian outward FDI do not precede the home country's economic growth.
Chen & Zulkifi (2012)	Outward FDI from Malaysia	Relationship between Outward FDI & economic growth is bidirectional
Chitra Singla et al., (2013)	Internationalisation of firms from India	Outward FDI intensity of firms has a significant negative impact on its performance
Jan Knoerich (2014)	OFDI from Chinese MNCs	OFDI has its impact in promoting development and catch-up in China

Jan Knoerich (2017)	OFDI from Less developed countries	OFDI complements in getting development benefits that many nations are already receiving through migration, trade & inward FDI
Ameer, et al., (2017)	China	Positive impact on domestic investment.

Note: This table lists only a selection of studies that find an effect of OFDI on the home economy.

Most of the literature on the home country impact of outward FDI is focused on the developed countries as a source of outward FDI and developing countries as the host countries for FDI (Navaretti et al., 2003; Herzer, 2007, 2010 & 2013; Alessia, 2010). However, the literature on the home country impact of outward FDI from developing countries is relatively less and it provides an oblique picture of whether and how outward FDI influence the home country's economic growth. But as developing, economies are now emerging as an important source of outward FDI; the research community should need to pay more attention to study the role of outward FDI in promoting the economic growth of these economies. If more knowledge is gathered regarding this aspect then it would help the government to frame suitable policies.

Data and Methodology

In this study, it has been attempted to analyse the causal relationship between outward FDI and GDP for the developing economies of Asia. All the developing economies of the Asian continent are divided into four regions (East Asia, South Asia, South-East Asia and Western Asia). Data regarding outward FDI and GDP for these economies has been collected from the online database of UNCTAD from 1991 to 2017. Both the variables are in terms of the constant US $ at 2010 prices. The OFDI data is taken as a flow measure because it is more comprehensive than the stock measure. After obtaining the data from the online source, it is transformed into natural logarithms to get stationarity invariance. The letter L preceding OFDI and GDP indicates a logarithmic form of the variables. The research methodology consists of various econometric tools. The techniques of Unit Root, Johanson's Co-integration test and Granger Causality tests have been used.

Results and Discussion

Unit Root Test

Before applying the procedure of causality, it is first required to check the stationarity of the series of OFDI and GDP. That is, whether both the series are having the problem of unit root or not. If the problem of unit root is present in the series (series are non- stationary) then it may lead to misleading results. That non-stationary series may be having high values of r^2 and t, that appears to be significant but that result will not be having any significant meaning (Enders, 2008). So, in the first stage, the order of integration of the data is investigated. To check the stationarity of the data, the Augmented Dickey-Fuller test is applied. Table 15.6 shows the results of the Augmented Dickey-Fuller unit root test on the natural logarithms on their levels, first and second difference for the two-time series viz. GDP and OFDI. The results show the rejection of the null hypothesis of the presence of unit root for the all-time series at their first difference. It means that both the variables (OFDI and GDP) are integrated of the same order i.e. I(1). Once the data becomes stationary, we can use it for further analysis.

Cointegration Results

After having checked the data for its stationarity, in the second stage, Johanson's maximum likelihood procedure is used to detect cointegrating relation in the context of VAR. This was done using two test statistics. The results of Johanson's cointegration tests are presented in table 15.7. We started the procedure with the null hypothesis of no cointegration among the variables (GDP and OFDI). The

Table 15.6: Results of the Augmented Dickey-Fuller Unit Root Test

Region	Variable with intercept	Level	First Difference	Second Difference
East Asia	LGDP	-1.621237 (0.4579)	-2.591841 (0.0174)**	-5.588048 (0.0001)**
	LOFDI	-1.663471 (0.4377)	-4.983944 (0.0005)**	-8.713927 (0.0000)**
South Asia	LGDP	1.684438 (0.9993)	-3.958351 (0.0056)**	-6.539291 (0.0000)**
	LOFDI	-0.530802 (0.8701)	-4.306362 (0.0024)**	-5.869921 (0.0001)**
South-East Asia	LGDP	-0.626578 (0.8486)	-3.964335 (0.0055)**	-5.562275 (0.0001)**
	LOFDI	-2.526763 (0.1206)	-3.508794 (0.0159)**	-5.13270 (0.0004)**
Western Asia	LGDP	0.139659 (0.9630)	-4.944088 (0.0005)**	-7.539252 (0.0000)**
	LOFDI	-0.186594 (0.9286)	-3.055921 (0.0428)**	-6.939098 (0.0000)**
Total Asia	LGDP	-0.366489 (0.9016)	-3.5392 (0.0149)**	-6.755269 (0.0000)**
	LOFDI	-1.798507 (0.3732)	-4.754523 (0.0008)**	-8.503221 (0.0000)**

Note: ** denotes the rejection of the null hypothesis of unit root at 5% level.

maxeigenvalue statistic and trace statistic both indicate that the null hypothesis of no cointegration between OFDI and GDP for the Asian region as a whole and different regions of Asia viz. East Asia, South Asia, South-East Asia & Western Asia is not rejected at 5% level of significance i.e. both trace statistic and eigen-value test show that there is no cointegration between OFDI and GDP, that proves no long-run relationship between outward FDI and GDP.

Table 15.7: Results of Johanson's Co-integration Test

Region	Hypothesized no. of CE(s)	Trace Statistics	Max. Eigen statistics	Interpretation of Trace test and Max-Eigen value test at the 0.05 level
East Asia	None	15.49471 (0.1578)	14.26460 (0.1679)	No cointegrating equation
	At most 1	3.841466 (0.2644)	3.841466 (0.2644)	
South Asia	None	15.49471 (0.7776)	14.26460 (0.8677)	No cointegrating equation
	At most 1	3.841466 (0.2423)	3.841466 (0.2423)	
South-East Asia	None	15.49471 (0.4340)	14.26460 (0.3684)	No cointegrating equation
	At most 1	3.841466 (0.6573)	3.841466 (0.6573)	
West Asia	None	15.49471 (0.6990)	14.26460 (0.6224)	No cointegrating equation
	At most 1	3.841466 (0.8383)	3.841466 (0.8383)	
Total Asia	None	15.49471 (0.2804)	14.26460 (0.2203)	No cointegrating equation.
	At most 1	3.841466 (0.7191)	3.841466 (0.7191)	

Results of the Granger Causality Test

In the third stage, the Granger Causality test is used to forecast one time series from the other. The co-integration test only explains the presence or absence of a long-run association between two variables. But, if we want to know the causal relationship between variables then the Granger Causality test is applied. The Granger causality test is based on the assumption that variable Y granger causes variable X, if X can be predicted in a better way using the histories of both Y and X then it can be predicted using the histories of X alone. This test is applied for establishing the direction of short causation between variables. In this paper, this test is applied to establish causality between outward FDI and GDP of developing economies of Asia.

If the causality runs from OFDI to GDP, then the equation is

$$\Delta LGDP=\sum_{i-1}^{n} a_{i}\Delta LGDP_{t-i}+\sum_{j=1}^{n} \beta_{j}\Delta LOFDI_{t-j}+\varepsilon_{1t}$$

If the causality runs from GDP to OFDI, then the equation is

$$\Delta LOFDI=\sum_{i=1}^{n} \gamma_{i}\Delta LOFDI_{t-i}+\sum_{j=1}^{n} \delta_{j}\Delta LGDP_{t-j}+\varepsilon_{2t}$$

Where OFDI and GDP represent outward FDI and Gross Domestic Product respectively, ε_{it} Is uncorrelated stationary random process, and the subscript 't' denotes the period. The letter 'L' preceding OFDI and GDP shows that the variables are in logarithmic form.

Table 15.8: Results of the Granger Causality Test between log GDP and log OFDI

Region	Null Hypothesis	F-statistics	Decision
Total Asia	LOFDI does not Granger cause LGDP	1.93726 (0.1690)	No causal relationship running from either side
	LGDP does not Granger cause LOFDI	2.80153 (0.0835)	
East Asia	LOFDI does not Granger cause LGDP	3.67727 (0.0427)**	Uni-directional relationship running from OFDI to GDP
	LGDP does not Granger cause LOFDI	3.13702 (0.0643)	
South Asia	LOFDI does not Granger cause LGDP	0.81309 (0.4570)	No causal relationship running from either side
	LGDP does not Granger cause LOFDI	0.26865 (0.7670)	
South-East Asia	LOFDI does not Granger cause LGDP	1.49530 (0.2471)	No causal relationship running from either side
	LGDP does not Granger cause LOFDI	0.52484 (0.5992)	
West Asia	LOFDI does not Granger cause LGDP	0.37207 (0.6938)	No causal relationship running from either side
	LGDP does not Granger cause LOFDI	1.00223 (0.3840)	

Note: ** denotes the rejection of the null hypothesis of no causal relationship.

Conclusion

In the present study, an attempt has been to investigate the relationship between GDP and outward FDI based on the economies of Asia by taking the data from 1991 to 2017. The test of causality has two parts (a) causality running from OFDI to GDP & (b) causality running from GDP to OFDI. The causality test shows that for all the regions of Asia, the two null hypotheses of no causal relationship running from GDP to OFDI and running from OFDI to GDP are accepted, which proves that there is no causal relationship between two variables from either side. Only for the East Asian region, there is a short-run causal relationship between these two variables running from OFDI to GDP. That means, in East Asia, higher OFDI leads to higher GDP. The East Asian region is the largest contributor in terms of OFDI from developing Asia. Out of the total 28.9 per cent share of developing Asia in world OFDI, 19.5 per cent came from the developing economies of East Asia (more than 67 percent). Thus the important implication that can be drawn from the above analyses is that neither the higher levels of OFDI are likely to be the cause of higher GDP nor the higher GDP is the guarantee of higher OFDI. But If the level of Outward FDI rises to a high level (as in the case of East Asia), only then it can positively affect GDP. Thus there is a critical minimum level of Outward FDI that must be achieved if it is to have a chance of increasing GDP through Outward FDI.

References

Alfaro, L., Chanda, A., Kalemli-Ozcan, S., and Sayek, S. (2004). FDI and economic growth: the role of local financial markets. *Journal of International Economics*, *64*(1), 89-112.

Ameer, W., Xu, H., and Alotaish, M. S. M. (2017). Outward foreign direct investment and domestic investment: Evidence from China. *Economic Research-Ekonomskaistraživanja*, *30*(1), 777-788.

Bano, S. and Tabbada, J., (2015). Foreign direct investment outflows: Asian developing countries. *Journal of Economic Integration*, 30(20), 359-398.

Barba Navaretti, G. and Castellani, D., (2004). *Investments abroad and performance at home: evidence from Italian multinationals* (No. 4284). CEPR discussion papers.

Bertrand, O., and Capron, L. (2015). Productivity enhancement at home via cross-border acquisitions: The roles of learning and contemporaneous domestic investments. *Strategic Management Journal, 36*(5), 640-658.

Bitzenis, A. P., and Vlachos, V. A. (2013). Greece's Outward FDI: A Window for Growth? In *Greece's Horizons* (pp. 249-259). Springer, Berlin, Heidelberg.

Blomström, M., & Kokko, A. (1998). Multinational corporations and spillovers. *Journal of Economic surveys, 12*(3), 247-277.

Branstetter, L. (2006). Is foreign direct investment a channel of knowledge spillovers? Evidence from Japan's FDI in the United States. *Journal of International economics, 68*(2), 325-344.

Chen, J. E., and Zulkifli, S. A. M. (2012). Malaysian outward FDI and economic growth. *Procedia-Social and Behavioral Sciences, 65*, 717-722.

Ciesielska, D., and Kołtuniak, M. (2017). Outward foreign direct investments and home country's economic growth. *Physica A: Statistical Mechanics and its Applications, 482*, 127-146.

Dritsaki, M., Dritsaki, C. and Adamopoulos, A., 2004. A causal relationship between trade, foreign direct investment and economic growth for Greece. *American Journal of applied sciences, 1*(3), 230-235.

Dunning, J.H., 1980. *Explaining outward direct investment of developing countries: in support of the eclectic theory of international production*. University of Reading, Department of Economics.

Forte, R. and Silva, V., 2017. Outward FDI and Home Country Exports: Theoretical Approaches and Empirical Evidence. *The International Trade Journal, 31*(3), 245-271.

Herzer, D. (2008). The long-run relationship between outward FDI and domestic output: evidence from panel data. *Economics Letters, 100*(1), 146-149.

Knoerich, J. (2014). Has outward foreign direct investment contributed to the development of the Chinese economy?. *Transnational Corporations, 23*(2), 1-48.

Knoerich, J. (2017). How does outward foreign direct investment contribute to economic development in less advanced home countries? *Oxford Development Studies, 45*(4), 443-459.

Kokko, A. (2006). *The home country effects of FDI in developed economies.* Working Paper Series, European Institute of Japanese Studies. Stockholm, 225, 1-37.

Kurtishi-Kastrati, S. (2013). Impact of FDI on economic growth: An overview of the main theories of FDI and empirical research. *European Scientific Journal, ESJ*, *9*(7).

Sandeep Kaur (2015). Migration and bilateral trade flows: evidence from India and OECD Countries. *Applied Econometrics and International Development, 15*(2), 179-196.

Lee, C. G. (2010). Outward foreign direct investment and economic growth: Evidence from Japan. *Global Economic Review, 39*(3), 317-326.

Lipsey, R.E., (2004). Home-and host-country effects of foreign direct investment. In *Challenges to globalization: Analyzing the economics* (pp. 333-382). University of Chicago Press.

Navaretti, G. B., and Castellani, D. (2004). Investments abroad and performance at home: Evidence from Italian multinationals. Development Working Papers 180, Centro Studi Luca d'Agliano, University of Milano.

Perea, J.R. and Stephenson, M., (2017). Outward FDI from Developing Countries. *Global Investment Competitiveness Report 2017/2018*, p. 101.

Retrieved from: https://www.monash.edu/__data/assets/pdf_file/0005/925466/

Singh, S. (2017). The Relationship between FDI outflows, Exports and GDP in India: An Application of the Autoregressive Distributed Lag Model. *Economic Affairs, 62*(3), 471-481.

UNCTAD (2007). http://stats.unctad.org/FDI.

UNCTAD (2018). Investor Nationality: Policy Challenges. Investment and New Industrial Policies, 2018. New York: United Nations

United Nations Conference on Trade and Development. (2006). *World investment report 2006: FDI from developing and transition economies: implications for development.* UN.

Vernon, R., (1992). International investment and international trade in the product cycle. In *International Economic Policies and their Theoretical Foundations (Second Edition), 80(2)*, (pp. 415-435).

Wong, K. (2010). Outward FDI and Home Country economic Growth: A Malaysian Case. Monash University Discussion Paper, 56, 1-11.